Rumors of Revolution

Writing the Early Americas

Anna Brickhouse and Kirsten Silva Gruesz, Editors

Rumors of Revolution
Song, Sentiment, and Sedition in Colonial Louisiana

Jennifer Tsien

University of Virginia Press
Charlottesville and London

University of Virginia Press
© 2023 by the Rector and Visitors of the University of Virginia
All rights reserved
Printed in the United States of America on acid-free paper

First published 2023

9 8 7 6 5 4 3 2 1

Library of Congress Cataloging-in-Publication Data

Names: Tsien, Jennifer, author.
Title: Rumors of revolution : song, sentiment, and sedition in colonial Louisiana / Jennifer Tsien.
Other titles: Writing the early Americas.
Description: Charlottesville : University of Virginia Press, 2023. | Series: Writing the early Americas | Includes bibliographical references and index.
Identifiers: LCCN 2022041060 (print) | LCCN 2022041061 (ebook) | ISBN 9780813949604 (hardcover) | ISBN 9780813949611 (paperback) | ISBN 9780813949628 (ebook)
Subjects: LCSH: Louisiana—History—To 1803. | France—Colonies—America—History—18th century. | France—Foreign relations—1715–1793. | France—Foreign relations—1792–1815. | France—History—18th century.
Classification: LCC F372 .T75 2023 (print) | LCC F372 (ebook) | DDC 976.3/02—dc23/eng/20220831
LC record available at https://lccn.loc.gov/2022041060
LC ebook record available at https://lccn.loc.gov/2022041061

The publication of this volume has been supported by *New Literary History.*

Cover art: Detail of portrait of Philippe d'Orléans, regent, by Bernard Picart, 1720. (Courtesy of British Museum Images, 01613583045)

Contents

	Acknowledgments	vii
	Introduction: Lousiana's Unsteady Foundations	1
1	The Regent's Seduction	21
2	Enlightenment Travelers: Scientific Description as a Critique of Monarchy	57
3	Louisiana Finds Its Voice: The Revolt of 1768	86
4	The Sentimental Aftermath of the Revolt	110
5	In the Age of Revolutions	136
	Conclusion: The Protest Tradition in New Orleans	163
	Notes	167
	Bibliography	219
	Index	231

Acknowledgments

My biggest thank-you goes to Gordon Sayre, who has been so generous with sources, connections, and his own expertise on colonial Louisiana. He presented me with a model for analyzing archival documents in a literary way that made sense to the community of Early Americanists. I am also profoundly grateful to Sophie Rosenfeld and Philippe Roger, who read drafts and offered all kinds of support not only for this project but throughout my whole career. In the years I have spent researching and writing this book, many more friends and colleagues have motivated me to complete it. Conferences organized by Florence Magnot-Ogilvy, Catherine Labio, Jenny Mander, and the Omohundro Institute gave me the opportunity to develop my ideas. Fayçal Falaky and Masano Yamashita invited me to give lectures that allowed me to take some of my chapters on test runs. Allison Bigelow gave me excellent suggestions that sent my research on a new track. Mike Bosia is the friend who first asked, "Why don't you write about New Orleans?" Russell Desmond, owner of Arcadian Books in the French Quarter of New Orleans and an expert on Louisiana history, gave me some initial ideas and resources. The University of Virginia granted me sabbatical leaves and travel funding that allowed me to do indispensable archival research in New Orleans, Paris, Aix-en-Provence, Madrid, and Seville. I am deeply thankful to Anna Brickhouse for helping me develop this manuscript into a book and leading me through the publishing process, as well as to Juliane Braun and Ralph Bauer for their excellent suggestions. On a personal level, I am grateful to my friends Njelle Hamilton, who has helped me achieve my writing goals over the last few years with almost daily nudges, and Omar Velázquez Mendoza, a dear friend who got me through the difficult times and who inspired me with his example of a dazzlingly productive scholar. Finally, I thank my family for their boundless support and for providing me a place to stay whenever I returned to New Orleans.

Rumors of Revolution

Introduction

Louisiana's Unsteady Foundations

When I was a child growing up in New Orleans, my family would occasionally drive past Lafreniere Park, Carondelet Street, De la Salle High School, Ursuline Academy, Napoleon House, or the riverboat *Natchez*. But I had no idea what these names referred to, since in the public schools I attended very little time was devoted to study of the state's history. Aside from having to memorize the names of parishes (the equivalent of counties) and a few facts about Cajun life, such as what a pirogue is (a type of canoe), I learned that the Louisiana Purchase had taken place and that Louisiana at the time stretched all the way to the Canadian border, but no one explained why or how it happened. I presumed that my classmates, with last names like Arceneaux and De la Houssaye, knew more about the state's history from their family lore. As an immigrant from El Salvador of Chinese descent (another story altogether), I had no roots there, so place names were simply puzzling and exotic to me.

Several decades later, as a specialist in eighteenth-century French literature living in another part of the United States, I began researching what was happening in Louisiana while Montesquieu and Voltaire were active in France. I was surprised at how little I had known about the state where I grew up and how little other Louisianians and outsiders knew. For example, many people do not know that the colony had been a Spanish colony for approximately forty years—though New Orleans hotels do tend to display the French, Spanish, American, and state flags. I also realized that some of the most explosive events of the colonial era, such as the Mississippi Bubble in 1720 and the New Orleans revolt of 1768, are familiar only to a tiny number of people, mostly academics who specialize in this field and a few local amateur historians. When I taught a seminar on New Orleans at the University of Virginia, a few students who were from New Orleans admitted that they had until then never known what exactly the word *Creole* meant—and some were Creoles themselves![1] Meanwhile, the non–New Orleanians began the semester with no knowledge about the area, just some familiarity with the Saints football team, some vague notion of "voodoo," and a tourist's version of Mardi Gras.

Had my public school education been lacking? I wondered. The students from New Orleans in my UVA seminars had attended elite private schools in New Orleans, where they also learned little about their own history. Or was the Louisiana educational system deliberately presenting the state as an American space, glossing over its Native American, French, African, and Spanish roots, not to mention later waves of immigration? Certainly, public schools all over the United States have blatantly ignored the country's Native American and African American past. In Louisiana, yet another erasure occurred at the state level. In public schools in the early twentieth century, Americanization was forced on residents of French descent through an egregious policy of punishments, sometimes physical, on Cajun and Creole schoolchildren to prevent them from speaking French.[2] Teachers inculcated the belief that the language students spoke at home was something inferior, shameful, and unintelligent. This policy effectively broke the linguistic chain of transmission that had previously connected one generation to the next. Only recently have activists started reviving bilingual schools, though so few locals know their grandparents' language that schools have hired teachers from other parts of the Francophone world, who will teach standard French rather than the local dialect. If the educational system shamed Louisianians of various backgrounds for not fitting into the dominant model of Anglo-American identity, their pre-American past was certainly not celebrated either.

In academia, Louisiana's colonial past has also been largely neglected, probably because it falls into the cracks between disciplines: people tend not to take the colony into consideration when they think about French colonial studies or early American studies, and people rarely mention it as part of the Spanish American empire. This academic marginalization reflects the fact that since its beginnings as a colony Louisiana has existed economically and politically on the margins of the successive empires that have ruled over it. The Spanish regime, for example, classified *Luisiana* not as its own administrative region but sometimes as part of the administration of Cuba, sometimes of Florida. However, Louisiana was not only France's largest colony in terms of surface area; it was also an important piece on the military chessboard of eighteenth-century global politics. It was one of the sites involved in the Atlantic slavery triangle, in the negotiations of the Seven Years' War, and in Napoleon's strategies in the Caribbean. It is only in recent years that scholars such as Sara E. Johnson and Cécile Vidal have studied this part of the Atlantic triangle transcolonially, as a region of ever-shifting imperial influence whose residents of various origins—Bambara,

Tunica, Wolof, French, Choctaw, Spanish, French Canadian—traded commercial goods and shared their intimate everyday lives with one another.

Also, only a small number of specialists link events in Louisiana's history to revolutionary movements that were occurring all over the world in the late eighteenth century. My book, *Rumors of Revolution,* brings attention to this part of North America and treats it as one of the places that played a part in the Age of Revolutions. It is not typically thought of as one of the great sites of revolution in that age because we understand the "success" of a revolution in narrow terms. Raúl Coronado, however, convincingly argues in *A World Not to Come* that in the colonial world of the eighteenth century seditious ideas found in "books, pamphlets, broadsheets, and manuscripts launched a *discursive* war against Spanish imperial rule" (emphasis added) and allowed readers to imagine a new, post-monarchical regime.[3] Like the Spanish American writings he focuses on, texts about and from Louisiana stirred up revolutionary sentiments and ideas that did not lead to winning independence, but texts of this kind "enable us to see no less than different visions of imagining communities that did not necessarily have to lead to nationalism, of conceptions of rights and subjectivity."[4] David Armitage and Sanjay Subrahmanyam, in their work that widens the geographical scope of the Age of Revolutions, define revolutions much as Coronado does. It is not the successful foundation of a new nation that makes them include examples from Bengal or Java, but "the *imagining* and construction of a type of *notionally* 'acephalous', non-monarchical polity" (emphasis added).[5] They also mention, as part of the traditional definition of revolution, "natural rights language."[6] I would add that this element remains an important part of revolutions of this period: verbal discourse, whether printed in philosophy books or discussed furtively among neighbors. It was thus in the realm of words, feelings, and imagination that revolutions began. How they ended depended on many factors. Some clearly succeeded and others did not, but even those movements that were suppressed had an influence on imperial history. For instance, the mere threat of revolution in Louisiana would determine the strategies of European powers in the New World until Napoleon ceded the colony to the United States in 1803.

Before I discuss the revolutionary words and sentiments that emerged from the colonization of Louisiana, I will briefly outline the history of the colony, since it is little known outside specialist circles. The story of French colonization of the area along the Mississippi River began as a series of misfortunes. The vast territory that stretches from the source of the river in present-day Minnesota to the Gulf of Mexico was home to numerous

Native tribes, some of them decimated by what scientists call the Little Ice Age of the mid-seventeenth century. These included groups that migrated from place to place and sometimes joined together, such as the Iroquois to the north and the Tunica and the Chickasaw to the south. In the early seventeenth century, the French had made some incursions into eastern Canada, which they called Nouvelle France. Their first attempts at colonization ended in failure, but eventually a few settlements began to take hold, such as Trois Rivières and the town of Québec. From this base, France sent explorers west in hopes of finding a route to Asia, which would boost the lucrative trade in Chinese and Japanese commodities. They believed that there was a body of water, which they called the Mer de l'Ouest, that led to the Pacific Ocean.[7] The explorers they sent, first Jacques Marquette and Louis Jolliet, then René-Robert Cavelier de La Salle, never found the Mer de l'Ouest, but they did find a river, the Mississippi, that led to the Gulf of Mexico. After making this voyage, de La Salle returned to France to ask Louis XIV for permission to claim this land and to name it Louisiane in his honor. The king assented, and the French people began using this name interchangeably with that of the river running alongside it, the Mississippi.[8] De La Salle had tried to call it the Saint Louis River after a patron saint of France, but the name that persisted was Mississippi, which was reputedly derived from a Native word that meant "old father of waters."[9] On his second voyage, de La Salle failed to find the mouth of the Mississippi again and ended up killed by his own men somewhere in present-day Texas.

Then other French agents took over the settlement of Louisiana, among them the Canadian officer Jean-Baptiste Le Moyne de Bienville, who established the city of New Orleans around 1718, at the order of the city's namesake, Philippe, duc d'Orléans, who ruled France as regent during the minority of his nephew Louis XV. Meanwhile, the regent and his minister, the Scotsman John Law, caused the first major financial crash in France, the Mississippi Bubble, by first transforming government debt into bonds or paper money, then paper money into shares of stock in the Compagnie de l'Ouest (Mississippi Company), which administered the colony. The holders of these shares saw their value rise at a dizzying rate, until they realized that the colony was not profitable—specifically, neither gold nor silver was found there—so they tried to get rid of their shares. Neither the paper money nor the shares had enough gold or silver to back them, so panic and chaos ensued, and Louisiana's reputation suffered for decades to come. The Mississippi Company became a punchline for jokes about the perceived corruption of the duc d'Orléans and the financier John Law. For decades, it also made the French population skeptical of paper money; the memory of the Mississippi Bubble still haunted them, for instance, when the revolutionary government tried to issue *assignats,* or bills.[10]

At the same time, too few French people volunteered to settle the new colony, so the regent resorted to forcibly embarking prisoners—mostly nonviolent offenders, vagrants, and prostitutes—on ships that took them across the Atlantic.[11] Soon, rumors proliferated that innocent people were also being swept into the dragnet. By 1720, public outcries and financial turbulence had pushed the regent to order a definitive stop to the policy of forcing prisoners to go to Louisiana. However, the crisis of 1717–20 left a deep impression on the populace. Thirty years later, it was still very much alive in the collective memory, as evidenced by the riots of 1750, when a baseless rumor that the police were sending people to "le Mississippi" sent some Parisian mobs into a frenzy of violence.[12]

Meanwhile, the colony continued to survive, but barely. During this era and in the following years, a number of French officers negotiated with the Native tribes with varying success, but at some points the relationship broke down, notably during the bloody Natchez rebellion of 1729. Travelers described the settlement as a place of poverty and chaos, full of colonists who disregarded the rule of law and the admonitions of local Catholic clergy. By contrast, Natives feature in these accounts as wise, virtuous people whose lives were in many ways healthier than those of Frenchmen. In any case, the French government had yet to find a way to make the colony profitable. On the contrary, it incurred hefty military expenses in attempting to protect the territory from potential conflicts with Natives and with neighboring European powers. The French presence in the region was scant, but Louisiana received a population boost from the arrival of exiled French residents of Acadie in Canada, which had been taken over by the British. These Acadians, now known as Cajuns, made their home in the southern part of the colony.

In 1762, as part of the peace treaty of the Seven Years' War, the colony passed from French to Spanish control, much to the chagrin of French inhabitants. Members of the local city council, led by Attorney General Nicolas Chauvin de la Frénière, went as far as to mount an armed revolt in New Orleans in 1768, published manifestos demanding their rights as Frenchmen, and sent a delegation to Versailles. Louis XV ignored these actions, and the Spanish government had the rebels executed. Eventually, the residents of Louisiana accommodated themselves to the Spanish administration. The years under Spanish rule saw the popular governor Bernardo de Gálvez's military triumphs against the British and in support of the American Revolution in the years 1779–81. The Spanish period left its mark on the appearance of New Orleans; when the great fire of 1788 destroyed most buildings in the present-day French Quarter, they were rebuilt in the Spanish style, with the wrought-iron balconies that one associates with the city.

The revolutions that began in France in 1789 and in Saint-Domingue (present-day Haiti) in 1791 threatened to destabilize Louisiana, which still remained under the Spanish monarchical regime. During this era, members of the new French government and other metropolitan individuals still expressed anger at the ancien régime for mistreating the colony and, in fits of nostalgia, called for Louisiana's return to the French brotherhood as a way of repairing past wrongs. Agents from revolutionary France seriously discussed fomenting a revolution in Louisiana and bringing this land populated by their "brothers" in North America back under French rule. Their attempts to accomplish this were foiled by President George Washington, who wished to maintain neutrality, and by the ever-vigilant Spanish governor of Louisiana, the Baron de Carondelet.

In any case, shifting international alliances made Spain willingly hand back Louisiana to France under the secret treaties of San Ildefonso (1800) and Aranjuez (1801). At the time, Napoleon was in power, tenuously holding together the vast French empire. His military was stretched thin, especially by the nearby Haitian Revolution. Haitian émigrés, many of them pro-monarchy and pro-slavery, trickled into New Orleans during the 1790s, but they would not arrive in large numbers until 1809, when they doubled the size of the city's population. At the end of 1803, just months after Napoleon's agent Pierre-Clément de Laussat arrived in New Orleans to take possession of the colony, France negotiated with President Thomas Jefferson for the sale of this territory to the United States.

Although there was never a revolution in Louisiana, at least not in the traditional sense—as an independence movement or as an establishment of a new nation—this book explains some of the narrative traditions and other types of communication that inspired revolutionary sentiment and discourse in the colony and in the metropole. French subjects continuously grumbled about the government's handling of the colony, and they specifically blamed the Bourbon monarchy for its failings. While historians are justified when they warn against drawing simplistic lines of cause and effect between eighteenth-century texts and the French Revolution, it is still possible to see that certain grievances among the people, spurred on by certain spoken or written words, progressively wore away the ideological pillars that upheld the monarchy. By the time the mob attacked the Bastille, enough people had already lost their trust in the court and the clergy, had legitimate fears that certain abuses of power would be repeated, and had had their heads turned by false conspiracy theories about the ruling class's immorality for the ancien régime to collapse.

Current historians point out that until recently, eminent scholars of the Age of Revolutions, such as Eric Hobsbawm, R. R. Palmer, and Jacques Godechot, who published in the 1960s, focused exclusively on France, the United States, and sometimes Great Britain. Later, other scholars turned their attention to other parts of the world, to the Netherlands, Haiti, Venezuela, and so on, to show how they were influenced by the American and French Revolutions. However, as Lynn Hunt declares about twentieth-century historiography, "The arrow of influence always pointed outward, from mainland France, and especially from Paris, to other places, including the French colonies."[13] The notable exception is the Trinidadian scholar C. L. R. James, whose groundbreaking *Black Jacobins* (1938) showed the interplay between, on the one hand, Toussaint Louverture, Jean-Jacques Dessalines, and the Haitian people, and on the other, officials and protesters in metropolitan France, all of whose actions mutually affected each other's political destinies.

James pioneered the way historians currently look at the events around the Atlantic triangle. For example, David Geggus remarks, "Historians have increasingly recognized the colonial revolution as an autonomous force that helped to radicalize the French Revolution, rather than being merely a reflection of it."[14] Hunt also sees Enlightenment ideas traveling in both directions. "New notions and practices concerning individual autonomy and the inviolability of the body," that is, debates about slavery and citizenship, "took shape from the 1760s onward in the Atlantic world. They did not just radiate from a single intellectual centre such as Paris."[15] Another aspect of the colonies' effect on metropolitan politics was the John Law affair. Hunt notes,

> A deep suspicion of the deceptions of financial speculation and the corruptions of luxury always seemed to go hand in hand with discussions of colonial trade in France. Time and again, from the John Law affair in the early 1720s [actually 1710s] to its fraudulent liquidation in fall 1793, the Compagnie des Indes would become the flashpoint for worries about the moral fibre of the nation. The murky affair of 1793 proved to be arguably the biggest turning

point in the entire French Revolution: it brought down Fabre d'Eglantine, and by association, Georges Danton and his closest supporters. The Terror itself, then, is ultimately tied up with the Indes Company, but just how and to what extent?[16]

I delve into the John Law affair, in chapter 1. It was just one of the events involving the Louisiana colony that shaped the way metropolitans thought about government and, in turn, how European Enlightenment ideas helped colonists see their own place in the world.

In a circular way, events in Louisiana increased discontent in metropolitan France, which in turn spread Enlightenment ideas to the colony about citizens' rights, which made revolution imaginable. While scholars have long known that *philosophes* like Jean-Jacques Rousseau or Voltaire mined exploration journals for examples to prove their ideas, I also look at how influence worked in the other direction, that is, how French Enlightenment thought created a lens through which travelers and colonists viewed the colonial situation. We can see the influence of Enlightenment thought in, for example, the manifestos from the New Orleans revolt of 1768, written by New Orleanians who had received their education in France. Rumors about this revolt then inspired metropolitan Frenchmen, most famously the abbé Raynal, to use it as a pretext to question the very bases of monarchy and to demand that royal power depend on the consent of the governed, rather than on a king's whim or on belief in divine rights. While Enlightenment writers like Raynal and Rousseau may not have been trying to topple the monarchy—Voltaire had explicitly been against it—some of their readers went on to use their ideas to justify the French Revolution.

Thus the writings about Louisiana, produced both in the colony and in France, invite us to consider the links between the practice of colonialism and the emergence of the so-called public sphere. They ask us to give new theoretical consideration to the concept of the public itself and its investments in colonialism—literal investment in the form of money and shares of stock but also as identification with Frenchmen abroad. Metropolitans could imagine that they were observing the exercise of royal power over French subjects in its starkest form in this distant setting. Authors told stories that laid bare the arbitrary powers and abuses the government could exert on its people against their will. These texts established an implicit connection between histories of settler colonialism in the Americas and the fate of absolutism in Europe that has been largely overlooked in scholarship.

Because of the early misadventures of the colony that I mention in my brief history, *Louisiana* and *Mississippi* became catchwords for the abuses of absolutist monarchy—in other words, for a king's disregard for, even hostility toward, his subjects' life and liberty. At the beginning of the colony's French settlement, to be sent to Louisiana meant to be punished arbitrarily by an unjust system.[17] The kidnappings and the transfer of Louisiana to Spain without the consent of the colonists thus outraged French subjects both in the metropole and in the colony itself. They saw these actions as proof that the king was not living up to his paternalistic pact to nourish and protect his subjects, in return for their obedience. If the French had believed that they had rights as citizens, the events regarding Louisiana shattered their illusions. More likely, they had long been cynical about their leadership, and these events confirmed their convictions that they were powerless against a despotic regime. Would indignant subjects depose their leader who broke the social contract, as in the scenarios imagined by John Locke and Jean-Jacques Rousseau?

When I discuss opposition to the monarchy, I refer to the whole institution that traditionally demands unquestioning obedience to its laws, to its officials, and to Catholic dogma. The French monarchy specifically wielded powers to censor and imprison arbitrarily through the *lettre de cachet*. Raynal's rant about the mismanagement of Louisiana does not center on one single king but on kingship itself and its powers and privileges. Criticism of individual rulers during the period in which Louisiana was a colony certainly varied. Louis XIV, who gave his name to the colony but otherwise treated it mostly with indifference, appears relatively untouched in writings about Louisiana. His successor, the regent Philippe d'Orléans, receives the brunt of the scorn; people probably felt emboldened by the fact that he was not the divinely anointed heir to the throne. Of all the rulers of the colonial period, Philippe d'Orléans played the biggest role in developing Louisiana: financing, populating, and exploring the region and most notably establishing his eponymous city, New Orleans. While present-day historians see taking control of the Compagnie de l'Ouest and building the financial structures around it as not entirely bad ideas, French people of the eighteenth century saw his decisions as a total fiasco and bitterly satirized him for it. By contrast, the regent's successors Louis XV and Louis XVI appear rarely in writings about Louisiana. This is also the case with their Bourbon cousins who ruled Spain while the colony was under their control, Carlos III and Carlos IV. This scantness reflects their lack of involvement, good or bad, in the colony. As was typical for critiques of the government in the ancien régime, public virulence focused more on the royal entourage than on the sacred person of the king. Accordingly, the few critiques of Louis XV, for example, in post-revolutionary letters, blame his official mistress, the marquise de Pompadour, and his minister, the duc de Choiseul. These attacks were not inaccurate, since it was she who had Choiseul appointed, and both she and Choiseul made decisions about the Seven Years' War and about how the colonies, including Louisiana, would be traded with other European powers.

Under the power of the king, French people in the metropole and in the colonies considered themselves collectively one people. This was their legal status vis-à-vis the administration; family and commerce bound them together as well. The close identification is reflected in the name officials gave to the colony, Nouvelle France, which was divided into Canadian and Louisianian administrative units.[18] Many French travelers, administrators, and military men who were stationed in Louisiana later returned to France and wrote books about the area for readers who were becoming increasingly curious about these exotic lands.[19] Because the colonists and the metropolitans considered themselves one people, writers portrayed any governmental mistreatment of colonists as a strike against French subjects in general.[20]

The anxiety about being forcibly moved to another land or put under the power of a foreign king was a reminder of of the arbitrary nature of ancien régime government. In this scenario, the monarch was treating his subjects more like slaves than as citizens with free will and power of consent. While Montesquieu and other political theorists saw a continuum between monarchy, tyranny, and the enslavement of Africans, however, the colonists saw no moral conflict in demanding their rights while denying those of others, specifically Africans and some Native Americans. In fact, when French colonists spoke for themselves in the revolt of 1768, their status as citizens depended partly on their imagined superiority over non-Europeans, as if they were claiming that they were not slaves; the colonists believed they deserved to buy more slaves.[21]

In showing how the eighteenth-century Francophone imagination understood Louisiana to represent the French monarchy's abuses of power, this book is also about who controlled colonial information. The texts I cite, from multiple sources, for different audiences, and from a variety of genres, largely fall into two groups: those emerging from the ancien régime monarchy and those opposed to it. On the one hand, the imperial governments, first French and then Spanish, issued statements about a prosperous and orderly colony filled with gold and subservient Natives. On the other, skepticism simmered beneath the surface among colonists, people on the streets of Paris, *philosophes,* rogue administrators, and others. Some texts, such as the journal of the père Charlevoix, were commissioned by

Bourbon governments but secretly supported the opposing side. Writers who had been in Louisiana reported on much more dire conditions than royal propaganda was willing to admit: poverty, disease, lawlessness, subjugation to much more powerful Natives tribes, and the true condition of its capital, New Orleans, which was merely a small collection of rickety buildings on a muddy tract of land. Readers' fascination was combined with horror as they saw Louisiana described as an overseas outpost of the Bastille—a place where the king could whisk you away unnoticed as a punishment and where you would find certain death, if not from the harsh climate then from disease or Indigenous attacks.

When I discuss the opposition between Bourbon governments' discourse and public opinion, I do not presume that the latter is a monolith. It would be difficult to classify the different people who debunked or disbelieved official statements about Louisiana under the singular term *public opinion*. Since Jürgen Habermas established his conception of eighteenth-century "public opinion," scholars have noted how overly optimistic this theory was, since it was based on a presumption of universal rationality and equal access to the expression of one's ideas.[22] In fact, the population was far from united: even within one social order—for example, the clergy—political loyalties varied depending on where individuals placed themselves within an intricate web of patronage, factions, and personal convictions. There was a great deal of dissent within the ruling class itself, even within the circle of Philippe d'Orléans's advisors. This is why there were violent rivalries between the regent, Louis XIV's legitimized heirs, the members of the Parlement de Paris, and the bankers, to name only a few factions. Furthermore, rumors and satires did not necessarily emanate from the *peuple;* some works were commissioned from struggling writers by members of the elite.[23] My idea of public opinions, plural, refers more to Arlette Farge's search for ephemeral discourses that emerged from nongovernmental sources and circulated through rumor, songs, pamphlets, and books. She notes that "the people of Paris had opinions on what was happening" and that the government certainly tried to police these "grumbles and criticism. [. . .] While there was no public opinion, in the modern sense, in the eighteenth century, there were popular opinions, whose form, content and function developed under a monarchic system whose attitude gave them life even as it rejected them. It was amidst this curious tension that rumors arose, and perhaps at times gained a life of their own."[24]

Often the originators were unknown, which makes sense given that the regime could imprison people for criticizing the king or the church. Each of these ephemeral discourses—for example, the rumor about the regent's incestuous relationship with his daughter—does not represent any kind of consensus among all French royal subjects. It was an unproven bit of information that a large number of people believed or at least had heard of, and it contributed to their view of their leader as immoral and uncontrolled—which in the long run added to the increasing distrust of the institution of monarchy. But there were surely French subjects who liked the regent and supported his agenda. Like this rumor about the regent, discourse about the Bourbon kings' mistreatment of Louisiana also cannot be pinned to a single source, nor can we know for certain what percentage of the population believed it, though we have proof that the ideas were in circulation. Where my conception of public opinion differs from Arlette Farge's is that she focuses on the *peuple,* or the masses, while the audience I consider includes all levels of the social hierarchy.

My approach is similar to that of Raúl Coronado's discursive history, which is based on Foucault's idea that much information that we take for granted is not neutral but a creation by one side in an ideological battle that seeks to persuade others that it is the undisputed truth. All the parties in this type of battle try to establish their version of the truth to discredit those of their rivals. Foucault points out that one strategy in this type of battle is the interdiction of rivals' speech or writing, which was very much the case during the ancien régime.[25] Indeed, whenever people expressed doubts about the colony, they were playing with fire, since any criticism of policy implied skepticism about the wisdom and benevolence of the king. The government and the Catholic Church had the power to censor any verbal expressions, oral or written, and the king wielded the notorious *lettre de cachet* to imprison any of his subjects for the slightest reason, or for no reason at all. People in ancien régime France were accustomed to living under this type of threat regarding any controversial topic—religion, the royal family, parliamentary conflicts, or others. When it came to Louisiana, the French Bourbon regime simultaneously suppressed voices who disagreed with it and ignored calls for reforms that could have made the colony profitable. Nevertheless, French wits, diarists, explorers, and others did manage to evade official censorship, sometimes with satirical songs, rumors, and other oral media. Some writers published their books in countries with more liberal policies, such as the Netherlands. Even when writers had permission to publish in France, they could include hidden messages that put imperial policy into question, as in the case of Charlevoix and Le Page du Pratz.

Like Farge's and Coronado's sources, the majority of texts I studied do not fall under current definitions of classic literature or under the early modern category of belles lettres, but they do borrow techniques from novels and other popular genres of the time. My primary texts include administrative letters, royal proclamations, political manifestos, diary entries, satirical songs, and exploration reports. I also include some Enlightenment classics, most notably Raynal's *Histoire des deux Indes,* passages from Montesquieu's *De l'esprit des lois,* Diderot and d'Alembert's *Encyclopédie,* and the novel *Manon Lescaut.* The narrative modes of the assorted texts I deal with tell us much about the era they were written in, whether they can be described as *galanterie,* scientific observation, legalistic argumentation, *sensibilité,* or revolutionary oratory. To appeal to a wide audience, these writers expressed themselves through the fashionable modes of literary discourse of their day, adapted to colonial circumstances.

Who was the audience for these sources? Some of the manuscripts I cite are official correspondence between government officials, such as reports from the ground to the central ministries responsible for colonial affairs in France and Spain. They are not aimed at a general audience, but they are useful to us when they provide precious information about what the colonists, of all social stations and genders, are "murmuring" about, that is, how they are reacting to policies. This is the case with Governor Carondelet's anxious letters to the principe de la Paz, that is, the Spanish secretary of state, about rumored plans for slave revolts or dangerous signs of sympathy for the French Revolution among locals in the 1790s. At other times, government officials directly addressed the residents under their control, as when Carondelet issued a proclamation to Louisianians discouraging them from revolting and causing the type of violence reported from Saint-Domingue.

Other texts by private individuals, some of them employed by the government—for example, published descriptions of North America—were meant for the general public, that is, anyone who was literate and could buy or borrow the book.[26] A remarkable number of these descriptions were in the form of letters addressed to women, whether the addressee was actually a patroness of the author, as in Charlevoix's letters about Nouvelle France, or the letters were from a fictional gallant to a lady he was courting. Were writers responding to and encouraging women's investment (both financial and emotional) in this colonial enterprise? Or was the purpose of this trope to follow a literary trend of showing deference to the members of society who represented the most refined taste? In the case of the Ursuline nun Marie Hachard's letters, the gender roles were reversed: this was a woman writing letters, reporting to her male superior about her mission to establish a school in New Orleans. In spite of legal limitations to women's official power in the upper echelons of French society, the aesthetic of the ancien régime established a reign of politeness that allowed for women's unofficial influence in public affairs.[27] At the pinnacle of power, it was the king's official mistress, the marquise de Pompadour, who chose the minister, the duc de Choiseul, who would control colonial policy during the 1760s. Thus we see that both men and women were involved in the discussion about Louisiana, even if the majority of writings were by men.

Comparable to the relative paucity of women's voices, Indigenous voices, or the voices of the enslaved, appear rarely in the multiple archives I have consulted in New Orleans, France, and Spain. We do see the speeches and gestures of Native Americans eagerly recorded by travelers like Le Page du Pratz, who sometimes devotes dozens of pages to directly quoting speeches by leaders of the Natchez tribe, both male and female. But to what extent can we trust his understanding of the language, his fidelity in copying the words, or his agenda in choosing particular speeches to convey to us? The answer is uncertain. Historians have made discoveries about the lives and military strategies of the Native Americans in the colonial era, but primary written sources tend to originate from Europeans.

Meanwhile, Europeans in power put obstacles in the way of enslaved Africans who wished to learn to read and write, though some enslaved people eventually acquired literacy, along with freedom and property. However, their voices have not reached us as published texts authored in eighteenth-century Louisiana. In regard to Black residents, enslaved or free, Cécile Vidal has been able to find some of their words jotted down in legal documents and quoted in some Spanish official correspondence, which she presents in *Caribbean New Orleans: Empire, Race, and the Making of a Slave Society* (2019). Sophie White and a team of researchers have been able to revive voices of other Black and Indigenous residents of colonial Louisiana through legal testimony in the volume *Hearing Enslaved Voices: African and Indian Slave Testimony in British and French America, 1700–1848* (2020). In terms of material culture, White has been able to extract information about relations between Indigenous people and European colonists in Louisiana by examining remains of clothing and legal documents, such as inventories in *Wild Frenchmen and Frenchified Indians: Material Culture and Race in Colonial Louisiana* (2012). These are examples of valuable and groundbreaking research that expose aspects of life in the very mixed society of colonial Louisiana.

Like the unnamed people in Paris streets who grumbled or sang songs against their leaders, members of Native groups and of the African diaspora, as far as we know, did not author or publish books in this era, but their actions and words certainly played an important role in the events. Even when the White colonists insisted on distinguishing themselves from these other populations, their effort tells us much about their potential power to challenge European dominance, which at times was barely hanging on by a thread. In general, I believe that we should question the European assumption that the written text is *the* source of credible information that gets transmitted to posterity, because this was not the case for all populations. Native and African people in eighteenth-century Louisiana sometimes transmitted their memories to posterity through oral expression and performance. The Chickasaw, for instance, maintain their own orally transmitted version of eighteenth-century events such as battles or diplomatic negotiations with the Europeans, which we can glimpse in sources like the website of their cultural center. Outside the scope of academic work, we can observe how the legacy of the African diaspora permeates the living culture of New Orleans to this day, for example, in the musical tradition and in festival culture.[28] Joseph Roach saw festival culture as a paradigm of protest and parody that is just as worthy of study as the written European sources with which we literary scholars are familiar. In any case, while the voices of different populations make themselves heard in a variety of media, my present study is limited to verbal expressions about Louisiana that have been transmitted to us through writing.

In analyzing the rhetorical strategies of the eighteenth-century people who wrote about Louisiana, my approach is that of a literary scholar, though it is anchored by historical context. I am searching less for facts and more for the various ways these texts record people's opinions or attempt to persuade readers. In the case of Louisiana, persuasion was important because texts and spoken words affected how investors, government officials, and potential colonists saw the colony as a viable prospect, or they encouraged or discouraged revolutionary action among the populace. The texts require careful reading by someone who is familiar with the rhetorical tools, allusions, tropes, and genres specific to the eighteenth century. Historians like Farge and Robert Darnton have paved the way by finding new sources of information about life under the ancien régime, but a literary scholar can take texts and and reveal their hidden layers of imitation, sarcasm, parody, allusion, and circumlocution, for example. Given the scantness of biographical information about many of these texts in the archives, literary analysis can show us how the texts functioned internally and how they constructed an implied reader.

Writers choose certain styles and genres to please their readers but also to tap into these forms' built-in methods of persuasion. When a government-commissioned writer chooses a flirtatious "epistle to a lady" format for his description of Louisiana, he targets a certain audience who will be receptive to this type of writing. Also, he knows the readers' expectations about the narrative frame, turns of phrase, allusions to antiquity that signal refinement, and other features. The same can be said for exploration journals and political speeches. In other words, style *is* substance: authors' choices of genre, diction, and tropes tell us much about what they hope to accomplish. As Fredric Jameson argued in *The Political Unconscious* (1981), stylistic choices are inextricable from specific social and political positions.

My study of the language that emerged from this colonial situation builds upon the work of those researchers who established the historical facts about colonial Louisiana, as well as the researchers who are currently uncovering new material. The first people to document the events that shaped the area's early history were erudite amateurs with connections to the actual participants in historical events. The best-known are Charles Gayarré and the marquis François Barbé-Marbois in the nineteenth century. Later, professional historians began their research in the archives, most notably Marcel Giraud, whose *Histoire de la Louisiane française* is still the most thorough overview of primary sources concerning the colony while it was under French rule. The Louisiana-based scholars Jerah Johnson and Gwendolyn Midlo Hall established the bases for our knowledge about the African diaspora in the region. Since then, Cécile Vidal and Jennifer Spear have used legal archives to research the lives of Black Creoles in colonial times, while Jessica Marie Johnson has delved into the social circumstances of women of African descent in colonial New Orleans. Shannon Lee Dawdy and Emily Clark have done illuminating research on various aspects of life in colonial Louisiana, such as the lives of women in that colony. Daniel Usner and Sophie White have done groundbreaking work on the Native American tribes along the Mississippi, while Carl Brasseaux is the authority on the Cajun/Acadian populations. In terms of communication from the French government to colonial populations, I found the work of Kenneth J. Banks especially helpful: in *Chasing Empire across the Sea*, he explains how the top-down transmission of information and commands functioned in the colonial system. It gave me a framework for my complementary study of words of opposition that emerged from below. Gordon Sayre is one of the rare literary scholars in eighteenth-century Louisiana studies; his treatments of certain tropes of exploration journals in *Les Sauvages Américains* and his articles about particular explorers in Louisiana helped me navigate the sea of sources about Louisiana.[29] In terms of colonialism and parody, Joseph Roach's pioneering work in *Cities of the Dead* made me see the words of protest in colonial times as part of a whole tradition that lives on in New Orleans culture. I do not dwell on historians who have focused on the later eras, from the Louisiana Purchase (1803) to the present day, since this period is outside the scope of the present book.

My book largely follows chronological order, with the exception of a few texts of the Napoleonic era that I mention in several chapters. It is not a comprehensive history of the colony; instead, I choose moments in which words and rhetoric played key roles in its history. The first chapter, "The Regent's Seduction," deals with a clash of visions—the idealized one by the authorities and the more sinister one by skeptics—of the settlement of the Louisiana colony in the second decade of the eighteenth century. I begin with the stock market crash known as the Système de Law, or the Mississippi Bubble, caused by the French regent and his advisor John Law in 1720. While much of the scholarship emphasizes the traumatic nature of the event for European investors, it neglects one of Law's foundational assumptions: that Louisiana would one day make France rich. First, I focus on prospectuses that encouraged readers to invest in the Mississippi Company. These texts were coyly disguised as love letters and published in the *Mercure*, a popular literary journal that enjoyed the protection of the Bourbon regime. Under the pretext of flirting with a lady, the writer describes the Mississippi River valley as full of mineral riches and helpful Natives in order to entice readers. Then I look at darkly comic counternarratives. Some imitate the form of the *Mercure* articles but show a dire view of the colony. Others circulated in Paris by means of rumors, which are recorded in memoirs and song collections of the period. They tell stories of government agents arbitrarily kidnapping people off the streets and forcing them to settle in the deadly and desolate colony. Among the counternarratives, I include the novel *Manon Lescaut*, in which the protagonists' forced exile to New Orleans is a pivotal part of the plot.

Chapter 2, "Enlightenment Travelers," examines descriptions of Louisiana by explorers such as the père Charlevoix and Antoine-Simon Le Page du Pratz, published in the 1740s and 1750s. Even though these men were sent on missions to serve the strategic interests of the French government, their narratives may be read as Enlightenment-influenced critiques of the imperial project. For example, in his *Histoire de la Louisiane*, Le Page du Pratz recounts his life among the Natchez Indians. Although he enthusiastically praises their culture, he deplores certain practices, such as mass suicides after the death of a chief. I interpret these sections as reflections about some of the extremes to which religious credulity and the cult of monarchy can lead—ideas applicable not just in America but also in France. In this work, Le Page du Pratz follows the model of Enlightenment fictions by La Hontan and Montesquieu, who take on a foreigner's perspective in order to indirectly criticize their own French society. I examine these authors' covert attacks on some of the bases of absolutist monarchy, as well as their publication strategies to elude government censorship.

The third chapter, "Louisiana Finds Its Voice: The Revolt of 1768," concerns the transfer of Louisiana from the French to the Spanish empire as part of the peace treaty of the Seven Years' War. This change provoked a revolt in 1768, when the leading residents demanded the right of the colonists to remain French subjects. Their manifestos, which were some of the first products of their newly acquired printing press, demonstrate not only mastery of classical rhetoric applied to their colonial situation but also a new collective identity. At this point, the members of the local elite who wrote these texts portray themselves as connected to France through their blood and through their emotions. At the same time, they claim that they are ready to fight to protect their commercial interests, which are particular to their geographical location. They ally themselves with their fellow Swiss, German, and Acadian settlers and express a desire to maintain diplomatic ties to Native tribes such as the Illinois. Yet their desired status as royal subjects with rights involved the French and Spanish governments' acceding to their demands to import and exploit Africans: a mentality of White supremacy that was inherent to their self-identity. They see their metaphorical "slavery" to their imperial masters as unrelated to the actual condition of enslaved Africans.

Even though the revolt of 1768 had no immediate impact on French or Spanish imperial policy, it did produce emotional repercussions among French writers, which I trace in my fourth chapter, "The Sentimental Aftermath of the Revolt." Reactions to the suppressed revolt and the execution of its leaders include semifictional sentimental histories that fashion one of the main insurgents, La Frénière, as a novelistic or tragic hero. These histories, as well as a harangue in Raynal's *Histoire des deux Indes,* blame the loss of Louisiana on the unwillingness of the French king to live up to the role of the paternal figure touted by apologists for the monarchy. I show how the sentimental legacy of the revolt can be found in letters, printed speeches, and travel narratives by French authors until the time of the Louisiana Purchase. In all of these documents, tearful nostalgia for the lost Louisiana, following the trend in *sensibilité,* goes hand in hand with increasing anger toward the corrupt Bourbon monarchy.

The fifth chapter, "In the Age of Revolutions," focuses on the 1790s, when imperial Spain controlled Louisiana and Governor Carondelet attempted to stop what he considered the contagion of the French Revolution among the residents. I trace the circulation of revolutionary songs and seditious speech among members of various social groups in Louisiana—White landowners of French descent, free people of color, and enslaved people—who found a common interest: opposing the Spanish regime. Meanwhile, agents of the revolutionary French government such as Edmond Genêt attempted to provoke an uprising in Louisiana, through both military stratagems and emotional proclamations to the colonists. Even though this plot failed, as did a number of slave revolts, the unrest may have encouraged France and Spain to deliver Louisiana to the United States, lest they find themselves with another Haitian Revolution on their hands. My study ends in 1803 with the Louisiana Purchase.

In the conclusion, I demonstrate that Louisiana's special position vis-à-vis its successive imperial governments created a tradition of protest that is still very much alive. The language that characterizes this tradition is imaginative, playful, and tied to sociability and performance. As amusing and ultimately futile as these performances may be, however, they express a collective anger against their leaders, whom they see as both despotic and neglectful.

Then as now, words shaped the reputation of Louisiana, especially for outsiders. In turn, this reputation influences how the state is treated: whether people travel or move there, what the central government's policies will be toward it, how much money they invest in it. It remains a place that is not quite American, not quite French or Spanish, but whose very existence contests the powers and ideologies that are imposed from above.

1

The Regent's Seduction

In a letter published in the periodical *Le Nouveau Mercure* in February 1718, a marine officer addresses a lady in a tone of mock submission. The mere fact that they are in private correspondence with each other suggests that they are in the early stages of a courtship. In good form, she has evidently refused to listen to any directly amorous speeches but has "ordered" him to satisfy her curiosity about a current trend: investing in a little-known French territory across the Atlantic. The letter writer states, with facetious modesty, "And since you have often refused me the pleasure of discussing numerous interesting subjects with you, why then would you now listen patiently to that which is most boring?"[1] He then proceeds to describe the plants, minerals, Native American customs, and commercial potential of the colony for the next forty pages. His "obedience" to her commands is a conventionally acknowledged step in the process of seduction, as is her initial refusal to listen to "interesting things"—his declarations of love.

Seducing the Female Reader

While the *Mercure*'s editor assures us of its authenticity, the real import of the letter is not whether the officer will seduce the lady but whether the regent, Philippe d'Orléans, in collusion with his financial advisor, John Law, will seduce the French reading public. After all, this letter gives favorable publicity to the financial scheme that Law concocted and the regent backed. John Carpenter and Shannon Lee Dawdy have noted the *galant* tone of this promotional tract, which sought to attract settlers and investors to the Louisiana colony. Both scholars acknowledge that it is a bid for the attention of elite female readers. I would like to go further to explore the implications of this framing device—the letter to a lady—for the imagined relationship between the regent and his subjects. Subsequently, I will demonstrate how these attempts to "seduce" public opinion inspired counternarratives that showed public resistance to royal propaganda. Ultimately, the regent's scheme worked for a feverish moment but ended in a crash that substantially weakened the monarchy and the public faith that it relied on.

In reference to this letter from the *Mercure* and other promotional materials, Shannon Lee Dawdy remarks that in the accounts of Louisiana that appeared from 1717 to 1731, "two structural features of the writing from this period are remarkable: nearly all works were written in the epistolary form, and the majority were addressed to women [. . .] writing to a female correspondent allowed male writers to exhibit their gallantry."[2] While not all texts about Louisiana were addressed to women nor were they all examples of *galanterie,* Regency-era France did produce an unusual number of these flirtatious colonial tracts, compared with, say, seventeenth-century English descriptions of North America or Spanish explorers' journals. The latter more often presented religion as the main motivating factor, and the tone was far from coquettish.

Why did French tracts tend to address fictional readers or real patrons who were women? People of both genders invested money, but the address to a lady was a fashionable literary convention of the era. It was perhaps typical of this Regency period (1715–23), famous for its magnificently unbridled libertinage, that even colonial publicity tracts were permeated with the spirit of *galanterie*—the sophisticated, witty eroticism typified by, for example, the paintings of Antoine Watteau and the comedies of Marivaux. *Galanterie* had multiple meanings, from the most honorable to the most ribald. In the seventeenth century, *galanterie* could refer to the distinguished conduct of an admirable person, unrelated to love; it could refer to a person's worldly sophistication; increasingly in the eighteenth century, it could refer to the delicate, flirtatious tone taken by the elite, as reflected in their preferred literary genres; or it could be a euphemism for sexual promiscuity.[3] In this study, I concentrate on the latter two definitions. More generally during the ancien régime, *galanterie* added piquancy to otherwise dry topics of discussion, such as astronomy, in Fontenelle's *Entretiens sur la pluralité des mondes* (1686), or economic policy, in Galiani's *Dialogues sur le commerce des blés* (1770). These texts and hundreds of others made their material more palatable to the public by putting it in the form of conversations with a fictional lady, which added a certain amorous tension.

Delphine Denis states that the female reader to be charmed in *galant* literature often stood in for the implicit reader and the "correct" way to read: "By proposing a *female* reader as the ideal recipient, the *galant* text established her as the paradigm, not only of the right reception, not only of the sociocultural archetype of the worldly reader, to be educated and conquered—all of this is beyond doubt—but it also involved a specific approach to the literary exchange, conceived as a genuine strategy of seduction" (author's emphasis).[4] Accordingly, Madeleine de Scudéry, one of the most prominent novelists of seventeenth-century France, wrote that even when its primary aim was not to win someone's love, *galanterie* nevertheless "sometimes gets involved in the most serious things and gives an unexplainable charm to everything one says and everything one does."[5] Even when sexual conquest was not the ultimate aim, it served as a metaphor for persuasion in general. In the case of the Louisiana propaganda, the regent had a specific interest in persuading readers to invest in the Compagnie d'Occident, which managed the colony.

That figure of the ideal reader to be charmed could thus easily be transferred into the realm of political communication. In French, *séduire* has a more general meaning than in English—to persuade or charm—but it does not dissociate itself completely from its sexual connotation. As Christian Delporte explains in his study of the rhetoric used by statesmen, including Charles De Gaulle and John F. Kennedy, entitled *Une histoire de la séduction politique*, "Seduction is inseparable from political strategies to capture the favors of the people and to win their love, to seize power and to hold on to it."[6] He illustrates the idea of the people's "favors," a *galant* euphemism for sexual consent, with the image of "[public] opinion as a woman to be conquered," evoked by the famously charismatic Napoleon.[7] Accordingly, the implicit reader of the promotional tracts I discuss in this chapter takes the form of a lady whom the writer attempts to charm, or—the original meaning of *seduction*—to lead astray.

Fictions of the Mississippi Bubble

The regency of Philippe d'Orléans, after the death of Louis XIV and during the minority of Louis XV, acquired a scandalous reputation not only for its orgies but also for France's first major financial crash, known as *le Système de John Law*, or the Mississippi Bubble.[8] Its history has been skillfully documented by many scholars, most notably Edgar Faure and Antoin Murphy, but little has been made of the role of the Louisiana colony, which was a key component of the whole system.[9] To summarize: In the second decade of the eighteenth century France was low on gold reserves, which made the economy stagnant, and the government had issued bonds that it could not repay. To solve this problem, Philippe d'Orléans allowed the Scottish economist-adventurer John Law to implement a radical new financial plan.

Law had the regent create the Royal Bank, which issued paper money—for the first time in French history—that in theory represented the gold and silver that people deposited. These banknotes in turn would be exchangeable for shares of stock in the newly nationalized Compagnie d'Occident, whose mission was to look for gold mines in the new colony of Louisiana. If the company were successful, the shares of stock would be worth much more than their original price, so French people got into a frenzy of speculation. People even committed murders to acquire these shares. However, no gold was discovered, and the value of the stock quickly plummeted. Meanwhile, when people tried to recover their gold from the bank, the deeply debt-ridden government did not have enough specie to pay out all the notes and stock in circulation, which led to the disastrous crash of 1720.

The hope that Louisiana could supply desperately needed precious metals takes visual form in a portrait of the regent from before the crash, in which the engraver Bernard Picart shows the role that Louisiana was meant to play in his reign (fig. 1). In the left foreground we see a woman

Figure 1. Portrait of Philippe d'Orléans, regent, by Bernard Picart, 1720. The first three lines below the image read "Cessez de t'affliger, ô France! / Assez & trop longtems ont duré tes malheurs; / Tes trésors épuisés, ton Peuple sans finance" (Stop grieving, O France! / Your misfortunes have lasted enough and for too long; / Your treasures exhausted, your people without finance). (Bibliothèque nationale de France)

symbolizing France, looking distressed and holding an empty cornucopia. The verses below apostrophize her. However, there is new hope (which would be crushed soon after this image was printed): in the lower right-hand corner of the image, an angel holds a horn of plenty that pours gold coins over the map of North America, held by a Native American boy (fig. 2). The continuous line that one could draw from the top of the horn of plenty to the line on the map that represents the Mississippi suggests a vein of gold that would flow through this river to enrich France. (Ironically, it could also signify the opposite: that France would pour quantities of gold into North America, which would turn out to be a bad investment.) Meanwhile, the goddess Athena, identifiable through the owl, her martial helmet, and her Medusa-head shield, gestures toward this group, suggesting that wisdom dictates that this colonial enterprise be carried out. This image would contrast singularly with the satirical prints that Picart himself engraved a few months after the crash, in which folly, not wisdom, leads the way.[10]

Figure 2. Detail of portrait of Philippe d'Orléans. (Bibliothèque nationale de France)

Historians and many of Law's contemporaries saw that this financial scheme depended too much on imagined values—ultimately exposing the fictions (literary or otherwise) that are an integral part of a financial system. Charles Duclos remarks in his memoirs that "Law, seeing that he needed to give some foundation, at least a *fictional* one, to the stock, placed it on the supposed riches that would come out of the Mississippi" (emphasis added).[11] Law thus created a fiction, not only by suggesting that the stocks represented gold but by generally exploiting the blurry lines between truth and imagination, or between fact and fiction, in the minds of his contemporaries. For Law's system to work, he needed to appeal to the investors' imaginations; he needed to make them believe both in the French government's creditworthiness and in the narrative descriptions of future value, such as the treasures to be found in North America.

Mary Poovey, in her study of a parallel financial crash in England, the South Sea Bubble, argues that up to the early eighteenth century literature existed in a "fact/fiction continuum."[12] Novelists claimed that their works were based on true stories, while news contained fanciful elements. I would also point out that French "credit genres," as she calls them, such as colonial prospectuses, needed the tropes of novels in order to be more persuasive. The continuum, she explains, began to break down after the traumatic bursting of the two bubbles, as people demanded news, particularly financial news, that was verifiable.

The "fact/fiction continuum" also applied to financial systems. Poovey and other scholars point out the inherently imaginary value of legal tender, investments, and credit. For a bill or even a piece of gold to have value, a society must believe collectively that this arbitrary object is worth something. Banknotes are basically promises that someone makes to pay another person at a later time. As Jean-Michel Rey remarks about the John Law scheme, credit is "a financial transaction [. . .] that continually plays on a promise, therefore on the uncertainty of the future itself; a transaction reflected by a policy based on the 'fictional' character of currency."[13] In regard to Louisiana, Law's contemporary Duclos remarks, "It was, he said, *a promised land,* abundant in all kinds of food, in gold and silver mines" (emphasis added).[14] It is significant that, according to Duclos, the land had to be idealized, as expressed with a biblical reference to the Promised Land, or "terre de promission."[15] Even in 1727, the Ursuline nun Marie-Madeleine Hachard, who wrote a journal of her mission to New Orleans, referred to Louisiana as a "fortunate country that I long for as I do the Promised Land."[16]

While in the Old Testament, land was promised by God to the Jewish people, the concept of "promised" could also be applied to the deferral of debt, as in the English term *promissory note*. The word *promise* even appears in the *billets d'état*, the paper money issued by the Royal Bank: if we look at one of these bills, we can see that the bank "promises" to pay real coins ("livres tournois") in exchange for this piece of paper.[17] But since the government did not possess enough precious metals to back all the notes, the promise would be eternally deferred. The promise could be kept only if Louisiana produced gold and silver. For his whole system to work, John Law had to establish a belief that stock in the Compagnie d'Occident was valuable, or that it would become valuable in the future. Like many a real estate developer, he needed to use publicity to stir up enthusiasm for this investment.

Invitation au voyage: *Le Nouveau Mercure*

Encouraging reports about the French-claimed territory along the Mississippi River began to appear in the late seventeenth century and continued as the government nationalized the Compagnie d'Occident in 1717. These reports provided the basis for the promotional tracts that were distributed in Germany, the Netherlands, and other neighboring areas, as well as for the articles that appeared in the pages of the French journal *Le Nouveau Mercure* and several published descriptions of Louisiana.[18] To what extent explorers found it to their advantage to tell their government ministers what they wanted to hear and to what extent they had to hide unfavorable information, we will consider in a subsequent chapter.

Why did publicity tracts need to please their readers with rhetorical flourishes that they shared with novels? Why could they not merely state facts and figures? One such example does exist: a text entitled *A Full and Impartial Account of the Company of the Mississipi*, a bilingual text of seventy-nine pages, appeared with English and French pages facing each other. Evidently published just months before the crash of 1720, it plainly recounts John Law's plans using monetary figures, and it ends with excerpts from exploration journals that may be relevant to the investor. We can assume that this type of pamphlet targeted a different audience than did the gallant, seminovelistic texts I examine here. This *Full and Impartial Account* surely addressed the rational financier; it lacks the charm of the flirtatious colonization tracts, which probably addressed women and other less financially literate readers. The latter texts often refer to the desire not to bore their readers, who would probably yawn at calculations of stock values.

And what mass medium was better placed to reach the fans of *galanterie* than the journal *Le Nouveau Mercure*? Originally named *Le Mercure galant*, it was one of the earliest and most popular journals in ancien régime France.[19] While the other two major periodicals of the time, the *Gazette de France* and the *Journal des savants,* focused mainly on official court communiqués and on science, respectively, the *Mercure* was a collection of articles on a wide array of topics. It was often satirized by critics because it combined such disparate things, some serious and some frivolous: short stories, theater reviews, notices of military promotions, sheet music, descriptions of archeological discoveries, and other pieces.[20] Evidently a large audience of women and men found this content entertaining, and it catered to those elites who enjoyed the *galant* aesthetic as well as to readers who aspired to be part of this group.[21]

Unlike later dissident journals of the era such as the *Gazette d'Amsterdam,* the *Mercure* was published with the *privilège,* which meant that the royal censor approved it. From the time of its founding in 1672 to the Revolution, the publication disappeared and reappeared several times under variations of the title *Le Mercure galant*. It bore the title *Le Nouveau Mercure* from 1717 to 1721, which coincided with the era of the Mississippi Bubble and the crash. The editor for this period was François Buchet, described as a "former counselor and secretary of the king," which suggests further complicity between the journal and the government.[22] It is thus not improbable that since the journal depended on the government's permission to publish, the regent could have exerted his influence to help Law by imposing the publication of promotional tracts in it.

Scholars make this assumption, though they offer few details about the workings of the propaganda campaign. Michael Berkvam states, before his translation of these articles: "Law decided to use a form of indirect publicity to encourage colonization, and commissioned texts to be written in such a way as to present a rosy, attractive picture of what was, in fact, a very harsh reality. The best way to reach large segments of the French population, Law felt, was through newspapers and periodicals that were always eager to publish travel accounts."[23] Marcel Giraud also speculates, "Apparently, the panegyric, if not emanating directly from the Compagnie d'Occident, was written under its influence, since the living conditions during the period when the writer supposedly visited do not justify the description that he gives of the colony at all."[24] We can assume with Giraud and Berkvam that since the descriptions served the Compagnie's purposes so well, they must have been written for its advancement.

Several anonymous articles promoting Louisiana appeared in the *Nouveau Mercure*. Giraud lists them as appearing in the issues of September 1717, February and September 1718, February and March 1719, and January 1720.[25] I focus first on the one from the February 1718 issue since it is the longest, at forty-seven pages, and uses the most novelistic tropes. Its anonymous author makes particular efforts to give a truthful cast to what Giraud calls "pure trickery."[26] It notably uses the common framing device of eighteenth-century fiction: the editor of the *Mercure* prefaces the text by proclaiming that it is a letter that he came across by "a fortunate set of circumstances."[27] Because of these circumstances, the editor claims that "it may be assumed that because he had no reason to believe that his account would appear in print, he had no reason to hide the truth of what he saw."[28] Readers familiar with eighteenth-century novels are used to the editorial strategy of claiming that an obviously (to us) fictional narration was a genuine document that the editor had found. The problem with borrowing this particular trope from novels and coyly applying them to an informational tract was that for investors the distinction between truth and lies was blurred.

This playful editorial fiction has the same appeal that an epistolary novel might have for the reader—that of spying on personal correspondence. (This voyeuristic situation also replicates that of the reader who feels as if she is privy to "insider" knowledge of investment opportunities when reading certain tracts.) At the same time, the writer indirectly flatters the actual female readers, who would put themselves in the place of the fictional recipient of the letter. This situation is typical for the *Mercure,* whose very first issue, in 1672, began with the framing device of a fictional gentleman who obligingly promises a lady to send her news of the capital to amuse her, inventing a female member of the elite as the ideal reader.

In this article about the lands along the Mississippi, even though we cannot see how the fictional reader responds to the travel account, we receive hints of how the author expects her to react. First, with ladylike fear: in regard to the mere extent of the colony he writes, "Now I would like to begin a more general description of Louisiana. I beg of you, Madam, not to be astonished [or "scared"] by the size of this land."[29] When the narrator describes threatening animals, he worries "that these monsters may frighten you and that this journey through a still uncharted country may bore you."[30] In recounting a storm at sea, he quotes two lines from *Pharsalia,* a Roman epic poem by Lucan; by doing so, he shows that he is addressing an educated woman, but also one who scorns a bombastic display of erudition: "It did not go quite that far, Madam. I can already see you disgusted by my hyperbole."[31] While he admits that his experiences do not compare to Caesar's epic ones, he does encourage his reader to think of the colonization in terms of a novel: in regard to a priest who was stranded in the wilderness, he suggests, "Imagine for a moment, Madam, a Jesuit as the hero of a novel."[32] This gives us a clue that the narrator expects readers to blur the lines between fact and fiction.

Ultimately, the narrator of the letter reminds us of the implicit narrative pact of seduction. He jokingly boasts that the female reader will one day regard him "in the same way that the Israelites looked upon Joshua and Caleb when they returned from discovering the Land of Canaan"[33]—yet another reference to the Promised Land. But of course it would be too crude for a gentleman to demand her favors in return for entertaining her with his narrative. He thus ends the narrative by claiming, "Any esteem I might hope from you concerning my narration should be based not on its pleasing features, but on my devotion to you"—giving us the impression that at the end of his text he will lay himself at her feet in hopes that she will look upon him with newly admiring eyes.[34]

He shows his chivalric attentiveness throughout the text as he imagines leading her by the hand through various North American landscapes that are lush with fruit and flowers: "Allow me, Madam, to take you on an excursion of five hundred or six hundred leagues through an enchanting country. There we will walk in forests, our feet treading on grapes [grapevines] and wild indigo that await only cultivation. Elsewhere we will climb gentle slopes, cross immense prairies whose lushness and varieties of flowers will warm our hearts."[35] Passages such as these hark back to the classical *locus amoenus* of the Golden Age, which the poets of ancien régime France imitated in their pastoral poetry.[36] It is a place of primordial innocence, similar to a prelapsarian Eden, where humans can live off nature's generosity with minimal effort.

This passage also makes use of another popular trope of this era, of fictional lovers who invite their ladies to walk with them through pleasant landscapes. Alain Viala, in his overview of the literature of *galanterie,* states: "As for subjects, everything was possible: a voyage, a beautiful place."[37] Although any topic is possible, the voyage is the first that he mentions, surely because it is so common. It is most famously visualized in Watteau's *Pèlerinage à l'île de Cythère* of 1717. We can presume from Watteau's reference to Cythère, which is home to a cult devoted to Aphrodite, that the invitation to a voyage is an allegory of an amorous affair. Baudelaire would refer to this tradition more than a century later in his poem "Invitation au voyage." While the *locus amoenus* trope connoted innocence, the gallant voyage trope had more sexual connotations, though both evoked a welcoming, mild vision of nature in which visitors lived without having to work very hard (or the work was done by others and conveniently hidden from the visitors).

In the fictional letter about Louisiana, the lady's purported curiosity, to which the narrator is responding by writing his description of a foreign land, can indicate her propensity to be led astray. He remarks, "I gladly accept the task of guiding you by making known to you a land worthy of your curiosity"[38] and "If you are interested in mines [*Si vous êtes curieuse des mines*], as I know you are."[39] This curiosity that the writer mentions has several moral implications. According to Neil Kenny, curiosity was both a virtue and a vice in early modern France. On the one hand, an explorer or scientist who sought to make discoveries (though not beyond human limitations) could be seen as laudable. However, Kenny tells us that Catholic orators such as Bossuet compared "concupiscence of the eyes" to "concupiscence of the flesh," finding them to be equally bad.[40] The guilty kind of curiosity was especially attributed to women, as illustrated by figures such as Eve and Pandora. In the exemplary fiction of the era, "the curiosity of women was usually distinctively female [. . .] In particular, it was often accompanied by the related vices of disobedience, lack of chastity, and loose speech."[41] Curiosity and lapses of chastity are hinted at in the *Mercure* letters about Louisiana: the lady is curious about the officer's travels, so she requests a description, which he will presumably use as a pretext to enter into correspondence with her. As I quoted earlier, he asks, "And since you have often refused me the pleasure of discussing numerous interesting subjects with you, why then would you now listen patiently to that which is most boring?"[42] In the context of ancien régime seduction, readers know that listening and refusing to listen indicate degrees of a lady's receptiveness to a gentleman's courtship.

Specifically in the colonial context, the woman's curiosity makes her enjoy hearing about life on other continents. Jonathan Lamb evokes the image of Desdemona, which he takes from Shaftesbury's rant against travel narratives, as the paradigmatic reader who is seduced by Othello's tales of exotic lands to the extent of losing her judgment and falling in love with the storyteller. Lamb tells us that Shaftesbury uses the example of Desdemona to critique "the female relish for outlandish and superstitious yarns" and more generally to express that "a first person narrative capable of providing a vivid and detailed eyewitness account of marvelous places [. . .] can fascinate a reader out of her skepticism."[43] Likewise, the gallant officer of the *Mercure* encourages the lady to sin, metaphorically seducing her with his words but also aided by her concupiscence—for gold and for knowledge.

The deception contained in the *Mercure* articles can be seen in subtle rhetorical tricks. For example, in the 1718 letter the narrator assures the lady that precious metals can indeed be found: "We will travel together in the Natchitoches Land [. . .] we will visit the mountains along the Arkansas, that has its headwaters in New Mexico and in which we will certainly find silver nuggets. [. . .] I will point out to you that these mountains are in the same chain as those of New Mexico where the Spanish extract immense riches. These mountains will surely be just as bountiful for us."[44] This translation simplifies the last sentence, but it is worthwhile to look at the original French version: "il est impossible qu'elles ne soient pas aussi fécondes" (it is impossible that they would not be as bountiful). This double negative does finally add up to a positive statement, but it is one example of deliberate lack of clarity in these statements. In this whole passage, instead of declaring outright that there are gold mines, the author presents a chain of reasoning that sounds logical but is in fact false.

Other rhetorical tricks appear in other *Mercure* articles about Louisiana, including one in the September 1717 issue that both hints at extraordinary things and sows the seeds of uncertainty. The Natives "would also *lead us to believe* that there are gold and silver mines there, and there is a rock made up of very precious stone on which they must use their arrow points in order to extract a kind of green stone that is very hard and very beautiful, *much like* the emeralds they use to decorate their upper lips which are pierced for that purpose" (emphasis added).[45] This giant boulder, which could be made of emerald or studded with emeralds, would surely fire the imagination of the *Mercure*'s readers.[46] They would largely be the same readers who would have delighted in Sindbad's discovery of treasures in faraway lands in *1001 Nights,* a highly popular work that was published in the same era, between 1704 and 1717. Literary works like *1001 Nights* and fairy tales involving fabulous treasures were considered especially popular with women readers.[47] In these narrations, female characters act sometimes out of curiosity and sometimes out of greed for rare and visually beautiful objects. The fascination for jewels and precious metals in fiction perhaps reflects France's real situation at the time, even among the elite, namely, the desperate lack of gold and silver to support the French economy.

Like Sindbad in *1001 Nights,* the adventurer-storyteller in the *Mercure* cannot verify the extraordinary sights he has seen; listeners simply have to take his word for it. In fact, he does not even claim that his stories are true, but merely reports what the Natives "font entendre" (let be known). With these rhetorical sleights of hand, he avoids being held accountable for his statements. This narrative uncertainty also emphasizes how information is relayed through a chain of oral reports across lands that few Europeans had ever seen. We see that ultimately these written accounts contained orally transmitted knowledge of unverified status, which in many cases turned out to be simply rumors and wishful thinking. As Gordon Sayre remarks, "The successful explorer in Louisiana was [...] the one who kept the myths alive, who sustained and redirected the hopes entertained by metropolitan investors and policy makers."[48] The government thus had every interest in proving that gold and jewels existed in Louisiana, even if they had to rely on vague, thirdhand, or outright false reports.

The account from the *Mercure* claimed that not only gold and emeralds but another luxury product, silk, might be there for the taking.[49] Originally, the French went as far as the Mississippi River only because they were convinced that just west of their Canadian settlements they could find a quick sea route to Asia and its lucrative trade.[50] Optimistically, the February 1718 letter reports that the "Mer du Japon" (Sea of Japan) is nearby and that in any case silk could be produced in North America easily. The writer reported that there were many mulberry trees, on which silkworms feed, though he had not seen these firsthand: "I consulted with various *voyageurs* [roaming fur traders] and learned that they found silkworm cocoons that reproduced naturally."[51] And true to the pastoral tradition of romanticizing the work of rural laborers, this report presumes that the work of transforming mulberry trees into silk will be done by happy, compliant Native Americans: "The mulberry trees are very plentiful and need no special care [...] since silk does not require any difficult or exhausting care, I am convinced that however opposed to work they might be, it would not be hard to train the Natives for this work, especially if they realize that through it, they can satisfy their needs and their wants [and their curiosity]. Thus, for just a few trinkets, we could get from them the most valuable merchandise in Europe."[52] He again creates the image of a *locus amoenus,* a happy landscape that provides food and luxuries in abundance, requiring no toil from the visitors. And the locals are in this case mere supporting players in the imagined idyll of the officer and the lady, much like the shepherds of pastoral poetry. These fictional languid, compliant Natives contrast singularly with the actual powerful ones that the French had to submit to diplomatically and militarily, as the officer admits in another part of his account.

To make the Louisiana landscape appealing, the narrator of the *Mercure* letter tries to minimize any of the real dangers that European explorers endured. There is no mention of the illnesses, harsh climate, or starvation that afflicted travelers. In terms of Natives and animal life, the text admits dangers but also reassures the reader of ultimate domination by the French. He describes several animals, such as bison, bears, and alligators, while also assuring his reader that they are not dangerous. "The only things we have to fear are some snakes," in particular rattlesnakes, he warns, but the description of their "small, interlocking scales" is more alluring than frightening, plus these rattles serve as an announcement of their presence: "Without this warning, they would be extremely dangerous."[53] Alligators are slow-moving and not poisonous like snakes; they can eat people, but Natives eat them in turn. In regard to the dangers that the Natives present, the narrator does refer to an incident in which a French priest was "massacré" by some Chitimachas; however, he claims that the French triumphed over formidable odds under the leadership of Lieutenant Bienville to punish the Natives for their perfidy, even enslaving some of them.[54] The Chitimachas recount their side of the conflict differently, claiming that they killed the priest in response to "slave raids and French aggressions"; after a conflict that lasted from 1706 to 1718, their chief made peace with Bienville.[55] By contrast, the French narrative tells a story of French officers who subdued any threats, human or animal, to pave the way for colonists to enjoy the territory safely.

Even when describing harsh realities, the narrator prettifies his text by using stereotypically *galant* turns of phrase. Remarking on the diplomatic difficulties of the French exploration parties led by the military officer Bienville, he sprinkles some *précieux* words: "How does one stand up and win over *an infinity* of savage nations, whose friendship and submission always have our presents as a goal and which were *incessantly* solicited by the liberalities of our neighbors?" (emphasis added).[56] Hyperboles like *infinity* and *incessantly*, as well as rhetorical questions, were identified by critics of *galanterie* as typically *précieux* language.[57] Even though he does not portray the Natives as behaving in a *galant* way in regard to love, the narrator uses *galant* expressions to describe their customs. For example, marriages are simple transactions, executed in the plainest terms: "A savage is hardly amused to sigh for the girl he likes";[58] he does not "soupirer" (sigh) as a refined French courtier does. "Marriage among the savages is not, as it is for us, the most serious matter in life," writes the narrator, recalling salon debates about the advantages and disadvantages of marriage for women.[59] So even while evoking the non-*galant* loves of the Natives, the narrator nevertheless mentions the words that will get the attention of the reader who wants to read *galant* words.

While looking at all these efforts to please the reader, we should bear in mind the inherent deception of *galanterie*. In most ancien régime love stories, the promises made during the courtship turn out to be perfidious lies.[60] We see this type of manipulation in works ranging from Molière's comedy *Dom Juan* to the epistolary novel *Les liaisons dangereuses*, to take a few famous examples. Like Don Juan's conquests, those who would fall for the colonial prospectuses' promises would end up ruined. We may recall that the etymology of the word *séduire* contains the ideas of both duplicity and traveling: it means to lead away from the right path. The topographical literal meaning and the moral metaphor can be applied to this description of Louisiana. When the narrator of the February 1718 letter announces, "Here, then, Madam, is an expanse of inhabitable lands but the mind swims [*l'imagination se perd*] when one tries to comprehend it."[61] The imagination does indeed lose its way, just as the lady could be "lost" in the moral sense and the readers who are persuaded to invest in the colony will lose their money.

Louisiana for Ladies

The *Mercure* article of February 1718 was followed by a number of similar fictional epistles about Louisiana, which can lead to confusion because of their often overlapping content.[62] The following similar texts appeared in print:

> Chevalier de Bonrepos, *Description du Mississipi* (1720)
> Anonymous, *Relation de la Louisiane, ou Mississipi, écrite à une dame, par un officier de Marine* (1724).
> *Journal d'un voyage à la Louisiane, fait en 1720, par M***, Capitaine de Vaisseau du Roi* (1768), attributed to Vallette de Laudun.

The legal concept of plagiarism did not come into being until copyright laws were established in the late eighteenth century, so authors unapologetically copied whole sections of other books and published them under their own names.[63] The second text I list was merely a reprint of the *Mercure* letter from February 1718, with a few word changes in the first two paragraphs.[64] I examine the first text in this section and the third text in a subsequent section that deals with negative accounts of the Louisiana colony. Let us consider how these texts elaborate on the original frame of the "epistle to a lady," which allows the government to make its propaganda appealing to a wide audience.

The 1720 book by the fictional chevalier de Bonrepos was printed with the approval of the royal censor, as we see on the title page, which bears the words "Avec permission." The historian John Carpenter muses that although we have no direct proof that the regent commissioned this publication, it is clear that it is part of the "machine de propagande"[65] that benefited the Law scheme. "Whether the author of this book was on the payroll of the Compagnie d'Occident or not, his book exploits the lies and exaggerations that had accumulated in the course of thirty-eight years [...] the author is no more than a member of a great commercial movement, supported by the King and by the State, and who aimed to destroy all truthful knowledge of the colony."[66] Furthermore, the author writes this description of Louisiana in a way that would appeal to the fans of *galanterie,* that is, women, the financially illiterate, the elite, and the aspiring elite. Carpenter describes it as "a sort of manual of the way to speak about Louisiana in salons or in society," written in a manner that is "simple, clear, and a little bit puerile."[67]

The suggestive fact that the text is addressed, as we can see on the title page, to a certain "Mademoiselle D***," is perhaps attenuated by the narrator's indication that she is his cousin. Although romance between cousins was not considered shocking at the time, the emphasis here is not so much seduction as an attempt to describe the Mississippi's flora and fauna in a way that is not boring to a stereotypical young woman of high society. The tone recalls what Viala had gleaned from seventeenth-century authors like Scudéry and Bouhours: that *galanterie* can refer to a way to talk about serious topics that elegant company can enjoy. In this case, it serves the sales pitch by the government, which has an interest in persuading readers to invest in the colony.

The narrator begins by congratulating his cousin on being interested in something other than malicious gossip among her coterie. This worthy topic, the Mississippi colony, he states optimistically, is "the occupation of so many social circles, as they are hopeful for the immense profits that the kingdom should draw from commerce there."[68] He combines flattery with the "bandwagon fallacy," used in modern advertising: the idea that his cousin should be interested in Louisiana because many other people are. He uses another sales technique toward the end of the text: "The French are so beloved there, that to become masters, they have only to want to establish themselves in that country, following the example of so many others; I would not counsel you to allow this wonderful chance to pass you by."[69] Like a good salesman, the author closes his pitch with a call to action, but on the very last page he returns to the narrative situation so that he can continue the illusion that it is a gentleman writing to his dear cousin: "I end this letter by testifying that I will always have the sensible pleasure of being useful to you in some way and that no one is more touched than I by the little sorrows that you feel at the absence of your friend, who may well hide from the world to spend the rest of her days in the convent where she has retired."[70] He alludes to this mysterious circumstance—his cousin's sadness at the absence of her friend, who has joined a convent—that recalls the plot of a novel.

In the body of the text, he echoes the officer in the *Mercure* letter by mentioning jewels and precious metals to attract the attention of his reader. He even uses the same comparison to the Peruvian gold mines, writing that "recently they have discovered two gold mines, which will doubtless make the kingdom of France as rich as Peru."[71] Regarding the Natchez, he remarks that "their highest revenue comes from pearl diving," enticing the young lady with pearls as the writer of the *Mercure* enticed his reader with emeralds.[72]

Aside from appealing to his readers' greed, the author uses terms from *galanterie* or *préciosité* in a self-mocking way, surely to make his cousin smile. For example, the Ohio River contains fish that are "délicats," and it has none of "those nasty crocodiles who are so terrible and so dangerous to the poor humans."[73] The facetious use of subjective words like *vilains* (nasty) and *pauvres humains* (poor humans) for otherwise scientific facts evokes the way adults talk to children. Other animals appear in terms of their deliciousness: about beavers, for example, the "savages" are "fort friands de leur peau" (strongly crave their skin).[74] The word *friand* belongs less to the ethnological register than to that of Parisian elite culture, since the definition takes its distance from actual hunger to describe something like a refined preference for certain delicacies.[75]

Like *friand*, the word *inconstance* (fickleness) seems inappropriately dainty for a decidedly nondainty situation. The narrator uses it to refer to the nomadic lifestyle of the Natives, as if they were inconstant in love, a ubiquitous concern for fictional characters of eighteenth-century literature.

In regard to the Miami, who lived on the upper Mississippi, he writes: "Monsieur de la Salle, to stabilize the fickleness of this people, which is pretty natural to Americans, and to affirm the authority of the King, had a fort built on the shore of their river."[76] De la Salle's strategic military actions are perhaps more palatable to the young lady if she imagines the Miami being unfaithful in love. Native mores and ways of life are thus seen through a rococo lens, as in the "Sauvages" episode of Rameau's 1735 opera *Les Indes galantes*, in which a Native North American woman must choose between three suitors, one from her own people, a Spaniard, and a Frenchman. These depictions turn the brutal reality of colonialism into coquetry.

Some descriptions of Native life perhaps encourage the fictional reader to think that these foreigners follow the same social conventions that she does. The narrator depicts Native Americans as being not unlike French courtiers, who enjoy hunting as a pastime rather than a necessity.[77] The French colonists "will soon pull them away from their idleness and the laziness in which they live, since they have almost no other exercise than hunting, fishing, and war, which is always cruel," he writes.[78] The narrator also promises his cousin to "entertain you with a hunt, which they engage in from time to time," an event that a gentleman would organize for a lady he is trying to please.[79] The idyllic leisure that he evokes is even indicated in his very choice of pseudonym, *Bonrepos,* meaning "good rest."

At the same time, he also presents an imperialist fantasy of submissive peoples eager to serve the French for nothing in return. He specifies that the Chickasaw Nation live along the Ohio River, "receiving foreigners perfectly well, and especially the French, to whom they granted most graciously the permission to build a fort that would serve as a warehouse and a residence in this country that is so beautiful and so charming."[80] Like the claim in the *Mercure* letter that silk would be easily obtained, free labor by Natives is part of the pastoral fantasy. The narrator thus prettifies Native life in the playful tone that destabilizes his own meaning. Is he mocking his own use of euphemisms for harsh realities? or is he presenting facts in a manner that is understandable to the ladies? The fashionable tone in this era hovers over the line between sincerity and insincerity, or between discrediting oneself and teasing the reader. The instability of his statements protects the narrator from accusations of outright lying.

Mentions of the parts of Native life that Parisian aristocrats might find revolting, such as scalping, are quickly followed by reassurances that the French will make everything better. First, the narrator mentions that "the savages would not consider themselves victorious unless they brought back to their chief the skin of the head of their enemies, along with their hair."[81] Then, even though the French were well used to public torture and executions as well as frequent wars, he reassures his cousin that they have a civilizing influence on Native Americans: "We should admit nevertheless that since these savages placed themselves under the protection of the king, the Iroquois have lost much of their brutality [...]. Thus the French having humanized them a little, it is to be hoped that the colonies [sic] that we send there at present will make docile peoples out of them."[82] To relieve the reader's potential horror, he even makes a little joke: after describing their temple, which is a repository of scalps and decapitated heads, he remarks, "All of it makes a strange *cassolette*, and in these places one would need the perfumes and herbs of Arabia, which these poor savages are missing as much as I am."[83] He jocularly uses the word *cassolette*, the name of a dish for burning scents, for the room that smells of decomposing human flesh. Following *galant* decorum, rather than mentioning a stench, he relies on pleasant words to express the good smells that are missing.

With increasing insistence, the narrator emphasizes the good effect that French colonization will have on the behavior of these Natives. His narration is meant not only to please his fictional reader and actual readers who resemble her but also to flatter the regent and his entourage, as we can see from passages such as these: "Monsieur de la Salle, wishing to make these different nations that he traveled through accustomed to recognize the French court, changed the names of these great lakes that we have spoken of and gave them names: one, the Lake of Orleans, the other the Lake of Condé, etc."[84] Toward the end of the text, the future prosperity of the colony and the Natives' submission to the French monarchy are intertwined: "It would be impossible to conceive of the richness and the beauty of all these lands inhabited by so many peoples who nearly all have already submitted to our young monarch; there, abundance reigns, in grains as in fruits and in cattle."[85] The newly established city of New Orleans, which will later be described in other terms, is mentioned optimistically as having "almost eight hundred inhabitable and comfortable houses."[86] Another claim that will be disproven summarily by subsequent texts is that "that famous Company, to which none of the other foreign trade companies can be compared, does not take anyone by force and does not even want to engage those who offer themselves for more than three years."[87] It is almost comical that the writer feels the need to state that colonists are not sent by force; the mere mention of this fact indicates that he needs to counter rumors to that effect, as we will see.

While some people did fall for the propaganda for the Law scheme, others remained skeptical or openly defiant, even before the crash. Marcel Giraud finds proof in ship logs and government reports that only a very small number of people set sail for the colonies in spite of Law's campaign. Other sources, such as the memoirs, journals, and satirical songs of the epoch, show that the French, far from passive consumers of information, expressed a great deal of doubt about their regent's policies. Fictional letters like the ones I have discussed obviously attempted to create what we now call "buzz," or enthusiasm for a product among consumers, instigated by positive and disinterested reports from their own peers.[88] Then as now, buzz tends to emerge spontaneously from actual word of mouth, and companies often struggle uselessly to create it artificially.[89] In spite of their clever rhetoric, the *Mercure* and prospectuses failed to influence many Europeans to settle in Louisiana; evidently, other sources' negative news about the colonizing project found more resonance among the public.[90]

Vallette de Laudun

The travel account entitled *Journal d'un voyage à la Louisiane, fait en 1720, par M***, Capitaine de Vaisseau du Roi*, attributed to Captain Vallette de Laudun, appeared in 1768. One would expect to find messages in this text similar to those in the *Nouveau Mercure* and in the Bonrepos text discussed above because of their comparable narrative frame and the closeness of their purported dates of composition. However, when the Vallette de Laudun text appeared in print, the Louisiana colony was already in Spanish hands, so the French government was no longer interested in promoting it.[91] Because it shares some passages with the other two texts, they could have been written by the same author. If so, the change in political circumstances would explain their different messages, specifically Vallette de Laudun's newly unconstrained right to criticize the whole Louisiana enterprise.

In the *avertissement,* or foreword, the author explains his choice of genre, which points to his work's teetering on the margin between fact and fiction. In the voice of the editor, he notes that this narrative is "in the epistolary form, which it has in common with other accounts," notably that of the abbé de Choisy's *Voyage de Siam* (1687).[92] Choisy had already been evoked as a literary model in the 1717 *Mercure* letter as "M.L.D.C.," or *Monsieur l'abbé de Choisy.* What Vallette de Laudun hopes to imitate from the *Voyage de Siam,* he states, is its "badinage" (wit) and "gaieté" (gaiety); in his view, it "could amuse more productively than so many bad novels."[93] Although he claims that the letters are "purement historiques," he writes that "the officer who for his own amusement wrote every day, even about the smallest incidents, presumed that the letters would be read by the lady for whom he had undertaken this task, in the same spirit in which one presents them to the public."[94] This creates the illusion that we are peeking into a private correspondence, confirmed by the first letter, in which the officer says "this will pass between you and me and will not be seen by anyone else."[95] Again, this is a common subterfuge in epistolary novels of the period.

The letters begin with the officer's lighthearted and chivalric compliments to his addressee. He playfully proposes a sort of contract with her: since she wants him to recount his travels in the manner of the abbé de Choisy but he claims his talents are not up to the task, he says she must keep their correspondence private and she must be grateful to him even if he fails to be witty enough. These two demands imply a degree of intimacy, in the novelistic conventions of the era: if she agrees to this pact of secrecy, the lady already compromises her virtue to a certain degree. In another letter, the officer maintains a chivalric and slightly self-mocking pose: "Adieu Madam, I promise you on the faith of an errant knight not to talk about our country without having made your name known to the Illinois, the Hurons, and the Iroquois."[96] To please her further, he constantly refers in the rest of the letters to his selection of details that might amuse her and to the suppression of others that would bore her.

The most notable feature of this travel account is that the narrator evokes the delightful illusions about the Mississippi created by Law's prospectuses, but he compares them with his disappointing encounters with the actual place. Upon his arrival in the city of New Orleans, he conjures up the image of arriving in a glorious procession, past women waving from balconies and crowds following him (which sounds uncannily like a modern-day Mardi Gras parade), but then he admits that it is a lie. As Dawdy and Carpenter have noted, he reveals the depressing truth that there are only sixteen soldiers, no people at all on the balconies, and only a few wooden houses: "In short, this island is almost deserted" (some explorers referred to New Orleans as an island).[97] He thus contradicts Bonrepos's claim that there were already eight hundred houses there in 1720. He makes further reference to the disappointment that the colony brought to the French, with a description of the sand on the islands of the Gulf Coast, which he said was "so fine and so brilliant that one could take it to be the gold powder of the Land of Quincampoix."[98] He reminds readers of the Mississippi Bubble, since the rue Quincampoix was the street on which Law's offices were located and the name became synonymous with false riches.

Not only was New Orleans undeveloped and the gold a mere illusion but the other inhabitants of Louisiana also did not exactly live in a pastoral idyll, as the *Mercure* had suggested. In regard to the Natives, he remarks, in a style that parodies aristocratic understatement: "The Chickasaw, who until now had been our friends, are growing tired of being agreeable people [*gens de bien*] and are threatening to declare war on us."[99] He describes the other French residents using the word *galanterie,* but in a different sense of the word: "Besides, it is said that the European women who are transplanted into this country become sterile here. [...] I think instead that the women they send here are so unhealthy and so worn out by the gallantries they've had that they were sterile even before their departure."[100] As we will see, a certain number of prostitutes incarcerated in France had been forcibly exiled to Louisiana. The word *galanterie* could also be used this way, as a euphemism for seedy sexual activity. Thus the elegant flirtation of the *Mercure* articles degenerates into a mention of prostitutes so diseased that they have become infertile, an apt metaphor for the trajectory of the Law scheme, from promising to hopeless.[101]

Toward the end of his narrative, the officer muses on the failure of the plans for colonization. He traces the value of Law's paper money to the shares of stock in the Compagnie de l'Occident to the actual terrain of Louisiana and finds that at the end of the chain there is a void. He sees that even if there were mines, it would be impossible to extract precious metals, because of the lack of manpower. He declares himself "fallen from all my hopes. I believed, as everyone did, that the shares derived their origin from here."[102] On his return voyage, as he approaches Europe, he is dismayed to hear the news of the plague in Marseille and the crash of Law's system. The narrative that had started in such a lighthearted tone ends not with a reunion with his lady, since the plague keeps him from landing, but with somber reflections on the "saddest trip ever made."[103]

Resistance through Songs and Rumors

It is possible that Vallette de Laudun wrote this text in 1720 and self-censored it until 1768 or that he wrote it later with a revisionist perspective. Even in the second decade of the eighteenth century, however, wits were already satirizing the hopes that the government tried to inspire in this little-known North American colony. One song from 1717 entitled "La Compagnie d'Occident" mocks all its aspirations:

The country is not inhabited
It will soon be frequented
Maybe one hundred years from now. [...]

They will dig in the mines
For surely they'll find some
If Nature put something there.

Our banknotes will be paid,
Because the funds are guaranteed
On the gold that they will have produced. [...]

Finally, everything will prosper there,
And France we will desert
  Tralala
To populate the Mississippi
  Tralala.

Le pays n'est pas habité,
Il sera bientôt fréquenté;
Peut-être dans cent ans d'ici. [...]

Les mines l'on y fouillera,
Car sans doute on en trouvera,
Si la nature y en a mis.

Nos billets vont être payés,
Car les fonds en sont assurés,
Sur l'or qu'elles auront produit. [...]

Enfin tout y prospérera,
Et la France on désertera
  Landerirette,
Pour peupler le Mississipi.
  Landeriri.[104]

The song parrots back and exaggerates the propaganda that the government has been feeding the people, only to show its absurdity (though, ironically, the first stanza would become true). Not only does it mock the government's wishes to fill the area with inhabitants but it specifically refers to its hopes that gold mines will be found to provide specie to back up the paper money that it issued.[105] Research by scholars such as Robert Darnton and Henri Duranton has proven how important this genre of political satire was in influencing and expressing public opinion in eighteenth-century France, while the authorities tried to suppress it. As I show later in the case of one exiled man, songs expressed French people's fears about Louisiana and suspicions about the reliability of their leaders, which in the long run weakened the monarchy itself.

At the same time that there were rumors of gold in Louisiana, reported in the pro-colonial propaganda, rumors circulating in France told the opposite story, of kidnappings, deprivation, and death. The oral nature of the communication makes all the facts reported especially unstable and unverifiable; they tell us less about the events reported and more about what the public was willing to believe because of previously held suspicions.[106] The anonymity of the sources also made their origin difficult to trace, most importantly for the government, which tried to punish the creators of this counterpropaganda.[107] Nevertheless, French monarchs dispatched police to find out who had written these songs that cast their policies in a negative light. Darnton argues that even though the ancien régime was not a democracy, kings were still ever vigilant regarding the ups and downs of their popularity because they drew some legitimacy from the idea that they were beloved by their people.

John Law's system depended on public faith to set the value of its shares, but just as he tried to build up this faith through positive reports, Law and his royal patron were not fully in control of the information, as we can see from songs and other oral sources. For example, I previously mentioned how the favorable reports in the *Mercure* assured readers of the submissiveness of the Natives, but according to the memoirs of the royal librarian Jean Buvat, rumors told the opposite story: in an entry from March 1719 he states, "Some rumors from the isles of the Mississippi asserted that more than fifteen hundred French people of both sexes had been hacked to death by the region's savages, who had arrived in great numbers to surprise them in their new homes."[108] Even though this information was secondhand (via "avis," or rumors), it still had the potential to damage the image of the colony. A few months later, in August, after the shares had enjoyed a good reputation, Buvat recounted, "The shares, which were worth five hundred livres for a profit of one hundred livres, went down by fifty livres, which one attributed to the rumor circulating that the Spanish had ravaged the Mississippi."[109] We see evidence here of rumor having an immediate impact on monetary value and more generally on Law's whole system. The reputation of Louisiana would suffer more as time went on.

Since the propaganda for the investment in and settlement of Louisiana, expressed in terms of tender seduction, failed to win over French people, the government turned to more brutal measures. Like a novelistic villain, the regent began by wooing his subjects with false promises and in the end resorted to violence.

The Quoniam Case

The word *seduction,* as I discussed earlier, has inherently dangerous connotations, since it is derived from the verb "to lead astray." The image of the chevalier leading the lady reader into the idyllic forests of Louisiana to find jewels and friendly Natives is ultimately a deceptive *invitation au voyage*. We do not know if he seduces and abandons her in the end, but we do know that the Law scheme ended in disaster, bankrupting investors and stranding colonists in a dangerous territory. The regent, in turn, was able to seduce some of his subjects only up to the moment when they realized they had been duped. When French people largely refused to volunteer to settle Louisiana, he turned to kidnapping, which was also the last resort of desperate seducers of eighteenth-century literature. Rumors exaggerated the extent of these disappearances, which were exemplified perfectly in one conspiracy theory that linked the regent's reputation for sexual excesses and the abuses of absolutist monarchy. I present the case of a man named Quoniam in order to contrast the government's attempts to persuade the public that Louisiana was a paradise with a generalized suspicion among the French that Louisiana was a trap, a faraway version of the Bastille, where the king or regent could exile anyone at his will.

Many people today know the novel *Manon Lescaut,* but the lesser-known, supposedly true story of Quoniam also deals with forced exile to Louisiana, this one narrated in a comic-historical mode. In the year 1717 a man named Quoniam, owner of a rotisserie, was traveling with his wife from Paris to Montlhéry. Suddenly, armed men attacked the carriage and seized Quoniam, but they allowed his wife to return home peacefully. The rumor arose that Mrs. Quoniam had orchestrated the kidnapping, along with her unnamed lover, to send the poor husband off to exile in the Mississippi colony. This anecdote comes to us through memoirs and gazettes of the time, and we see it commemorated in a number of satirical songs, for instance:

> The charming roaster's wife
> For her boyfriend's sake,
> Sends, so she can be happy,
> Her man to the Mississippi.[110]

As is the nature of rumors, the story of this unfortunate roaster takes on various guises.[111] The first known mention of this was in the year 1717, specifically October 27, in a letter from the marquis de Balleroy: "The only news is that of a roaster named Monsieur Quoniam. The poor man had, to his misfortune, married a very pretty woman: a man of great credit fell in love with her; no one knows who it is [. . .] it happened that there were people who kidnapped the husband and let the wife return to Paris."[112] In this early account, any mention of Louisiana is notably absent.[113] Yet the place of exile later becomes an indispensable part of the anecdote—and the word *Mississippi* becomes necessary for the rhyme.[114] If Quoniam really existed and was indeed "disappeared" (as in the authoritarian regimes of the twentieth century), it still has not been proven that he was sent to the Louisiana colony. He could have languished in the Bastille or in Vincennes, as did many other victims of secret arrests by *lettres de cachet*.

In the story of Quoniam, the identity of his wife's lover is particularly subject to speculation. One song insinuates that "This woman certainly has credit / A minister has served her well / My lord his secretary as well."[115] Another song, entitled "L'aventure de Quoniam," suggests merely that the lover is "a big gentleman" (un gros monsieur) and an important "galant homme" who "spends magnificent amounts."[116] The editor of the *Chansonnier Clairambault*, in which this song is archived, remarks, in a note to this song, that the man in question is the "sieur Marie," secretary to the intendant d'Angervilliers, which matches the description of the lover's titles in this song. This annotation, however, was made after the fact; the songs themselves only refer to the lover's identity in the vaguest of terms.

The memoirs of the era, on the other hand, dare to name names, probably because the private nature of these writings made their authors less fearful of imprisonment. The *premier commissaire de police*, Pierre Narbonne, recounts the episode in his memoirs and names the lover as Coche, a valet in the service of the regent.[117] Edgar Faure puts forward another possible identity for the lover—that of Philippe d'Orléans himself! In a footnote to his *Banqueroute de Law* he quotes from a police report: "Madam Quoniam allegedly presented her daughter to the Regent, who became interested in her and who sent away Quoniam, not as a husband but as a father."[118] We see the story being transformed to include the head of the French state in the intrigue.

The idea of the guilty regent persists into the next century, in an obviously fictional text, the *Mémoires du cardinal Dubois,* allegedly written by Paul Lacroix, one of Philippe d'Orléans's most important ministers. This source presents a particularly convoluted version of the Quoniam story; at one point the narrator, the pseudo-Dubois, addresses the reader directly to deny any allegations that he himself was the lover. Instead, he accuses several of his contemporaries, such as the famous seducer the duc de Richelieu, who, he claims, negotiated the transaction between the roaster's wife and an important man. "I have recounted this somewhat unimportant fact because my enemies have placed the blame on me [...] but I do not have the misfortune of this poor husband on my conscience. Ravannes, who was not yet Councillor of State, is capable of having done the deed [...]. Furthermore, Massillon, the confessor of the Quoniam woman, refused to clear my doubts. What if it were His Royal Highness Himself!"[119] It is obvious that all the versions of the Quoniam story have a tenuous relationship to provable, historical reality, since they contain varying amounts of fact, rumor, and imagination. What is important within the context of John Law's system is to examine how a simple anecdote such as Quoniam's cuckolding can be transformed in the minds of French people into an expression of indignation against the regent and his colonial policies.

No one could report for certain who the lover of Mrs. Quoniam was, but all the presumed individuals, whether humble or exalted, had some relation to the head of state. Even if it were only his valet who was guilty, the regent himself was the one who disposed of the infamous *lettre de cachet* and the one who could command soldiers to seize an innocent man off the street and hide him away forever. It is therefore not surprising that people blamed Philippe d'Orléans in some way for the disappearance of Quoniam the roaster. His *galanterie,* instead of staying within the bounds of noble, decorous behavior, as in the *galant* novels of Madeleine de Scudéry, was perceived as descending to the vulgar situation of being the rival of a roaster. What was worse for his subjects was that he had allegedly resorted to abusing his powers—a morally repugnant transgression in the eyes of many French subjects.

In many ways, one could see this tale of cuckoldry as merely the kind of tale that the French have typically recounted for one another's amusement since the medieval *fabliaux.* As in these texts about such love triangles, the husband is portrayed not as a tragic figure but as a fool—like Arnolphe in *L'école des femmes* or like Charles Bovary. As expected, the songs about Quoniam fully exploit the comic possibilities of lowbrow language to mock the man's profession, giving double meanings to terms like *larder les jambons* (basting hams) and *embrocher la viande* (skewering meat). In fact, given the generic conventions of the era, the story of a roaster could *only* be recounted in a comic mode. Nevertheless, we can see beneath the careless tone of these songs a sense of bitterness about the injustices of the world. In the following song, for instance, tears alternate with joyful nonsense syllables:

> Well now, let's all cry over the misfortune
> Of that amiable roaster
> Lan la derirette
> Gone to the Mississippi
> Lan la deriri.[120]

We could assume that the silly refrain puts the events into a comic frame and dismiss any possibility of taking the rest of the song seriously. On the other hand, we could see the careless singing as representing a sense of absurdity, which is the only relief available to the powerless when contemplating the bitter injustices of their society. We can compare the tone of these songs to the deceptively lighthearted tone taken by La Fontaine in his poems addressing the serious matter of despotism.

Whether it is sincere or sarcastic, a certain sympathy for the husband is visible in almost every song. One example is from his point of view and uses the popular eighteenth-century poetic form of *apobaterion,* or the "adieux":

> Adieu, wife, children, and household,
> I wish you all the best.
> I am being embarked on a voyage
> that will be long.
> To get rid of the husband,
> They're sending me to Mississippi.[121]

Like nearly all of the songs about Quoniam, this one ends with a warning to husbands in general:

> Husbands who know this story,
> Think of yourselves,
> And do not take pride
> In being jealous.

> Otherwise you will also go,
> Against your wishes, to Mississippi.[122]

One could read between these lines a critique of the government, since they remind listeners that anyone is vulnerable to arbitrary arrest in an absolutist monarchy. It was precisely the cuckolding of a humble man because of the sexual caprice of a man of higher birth, an example of *galanterie* gone wrong, that would provoke the rage of characters like Figaro several decades later.

While these songs' message may be rendered ambiguous by their comic tone, there is other evidence that the contemporaries of the Quoniam couple did not take the incidents lightly. For example, the marquis de Balleroy mentions that while the wife tried to take over the missing husband's business, "all the neighbors pursued her with all the stones, mud, and all sorts of trash with which they filled the shop, since everyone was persuaded that she took part in the kidnapping of her husband."[123] There is a sense of indignation in one song:

> As for the beautiful roaster's wife,
> That everyone murmurs about,
> They treat her as a miserable being,
> All of Paris says she's in the wrong.[124]

A note from the editor of the song collection explains, "It appears that her shop had to be guarded by soldiers to protect the *beautiful roaster's wife* against public anger" (emphasis in the original).[125] In these versions of the story, the wife suffers physical and verbal attacks and social ostracism, while the guilty lover is only whispered about, perhaps because he has successfully hidden his identity, or perhaps because he is too powerful to attack directly, except through satire. In these songs about Quoniam, we can see a public's anxieties that are specific to this place and time, namely, the fear that the regent's unbounded sexuality, the earthier side of *galanterie*, will lead him to sacrifice some of his subjects to Louisiana. The Quoniam affair thus reveals French people's fear, be it expressed in comic or tragic terms, that they were living in an absolutist state with an unworthy leader who was simultaneously imposing a colonial project and a financial system that they simply did not understand.

To a certain extent, people were justified in fearing arbitrary arrest and exile to Louisiana. As mentioned above, while the French government sent out explorers in search of gold and other natural resources to this area, the

Compagnie d'Occident sought to also populate the area. Marcel Giraud calculates a tiny population of only 550 settlers in the era just before John Law took over as director of the company.[126] To increase that number, the regent had recourse to some extreme measures, which he later rescinded. At first, he ordered the expatriation of certain convicts: those who had committed nonviolent crimes and were still healthy and capable of manual labor, namely, deserters and *faux-saulniers*. Later, a wider net was cast to include women imprisoned in the Hôpital de la Salpêtrière for prostitution. Girard and Faure tell us how some *archers* were designated as special troops for these arrests; they were identifiable by their *bandoulières*, or shoulder straps.[127] However, these archers, who allegedly received payment for each person arrested, soon became overzealous and started arresting all kinds of people who did not fit the specified categories. Word began circulating of these arbitrary arrests and of the riots by the imprisoned prostitutes—as we can see even in various memoirs of the era, including those of the duc de Saint-Simon. Based on Giraud's documentation, people were right to fear arrest, since prisoners died in extraordinary numbers, from starvation or disease, while on the road, in temporary holding pens in France, or once they reached the dangerous environment of southern Louisiana.

This situation that disturbed French people was expressed in various forms, not just songs; for example, in the 1720 play by Lesage, *Arlequin roi des Ogres*, the title character is shipwrecked on an island.[128] When locals ask him to identify himself, he says, "My name is Harlequin, adventurer. I come from Paris. I left there with two hundred young members of the elite, male as well as female, whom the police had selected with discernment to go establish respectable families in the Mississippi."[129] Arlequin uses archly positive language to describe a baleful situation, while the audience is supposed to understand the opposite, as in the song "La Compagnie d'Occident," mentioned above. It mocks the language of the government, which people simply do not believe.

Aside from lack of faith in the authorities' statements, a central question in this Quoniam affair is whether the government of Philippe d'Orléans acted in a legal or extralegal manner. According to the regent, certain types of persons—namely, people already convicted of a crime—were subject to exile, while others would be left in peace. According to rumor, however, all kinds of innocent people were seized at random and sent to a near-certain death by the Mississippi. The principle that would have been violated by the forced exile to Louisiana, and by the *lettres de cachet* in general, would have been *la liberté publique*, the right to move freely without being arrested.

In a document dating from April 29, 1720, a clerk for the Parlement records an instance of popular resistance to the *archers* who tried to arrest people and send them to Louisiana: "all the populace was fiercely against those people, and with reason, because it was a denial of *la liberté publique* not to be able to leave one's home without being arrested to be sent to Mississippi."[130] Did French subjects have the right not to be arrested arbitrarily? In fact, the English had their tradition of habeas corpus, but there was no equivalent law on the books in France.

It is surely appropriate that abuses of power and popular resistance in the Regency era should be imagined in terms of sex, namely, in the cuckolding of Quoniam and the targeting of prostitutes to settle the Louisiana colony. After all, the best-known aspect of the regent's reputation was his licentiousness. As in the present day, the majority of the French people have tolerated sexual transgressions in their leaders—up to a point. For example, Dominique Strauss-Kahn's libidinous behavior was ignored by voters for years, but his presidential aspirations collapsed when mere hedonism started to look like an uncontrollable compulsion and he crossed the line into criminal activity. In the case of the regent Philippe d'Orléans, rumors of his debauchery have survived so long that even now scholars attempt to correct some of the more exaggerated ones.[131] His perceived dissipation was such that many accused him of committing incest with his own daughter, the duchesse de Berry. We must also remember that the rumors of incest with his daughter were completely unproven, so the facts that they emerged at all and gained so much popularity are probably more expressions of the French public's general distrust of him as a leader than anything else.

The analogy between the ruler of a nation and the father of a family was an important one among theorists of absolutist monarchy. If, in the minds of the public, the paternalism of absolutist monarchy lost its protective, nurturing aspect, then surely only the coercive part would remain. Therefore, if one believed that the regent was cuckolding a family man, then he was symbolically perverting the paternalistic pact that bound him to his subjects.[132] Furthermore, since the regent's role as father of his own family had fallen into disrepute through rumors of incest, would his role as father to his people also fall by analogy? What these two negative images of the regent have in common is the idea that he seeks not to protect his dependents but to exploit them for his personal pleasure: his daughter as well as the women of the kingdom. As for his male subjects, the Quoniam anecdote reminds them that the regent has the power to symbolically emasculate them by taking away their own paternal rights, just as he allegedly replaced the roaster in his sexual role vis-à-vis his wife and took away his child, property, and home.

The idea that the regent, his intendants, or his servants could make use of state power, via the soldiers who kidnapped Quoniam, expresses a fear among the public of arbitrary power. If the story were true, then the lover would have employed state troops as his own private hit men in the service of his personal vices, which not even Louis XIV had dared to do. These arrests were only one kind of application of the notorious *lettres de cachet*, a powerful tool at the king's and the regent's command.[133] These allowed the monarch to unilaterally and secretly seize his subjects and put them in prison for any amount of time, without a trial or any justification.[134] These letters became one of the targets of popular rage in the revolutionary era, but the songs and rumors about Quoniam show us a much earlier instance that exposes public anxieties about arbitrary arrests.

Manon Lescaut: The Death of *Galanterie*

Until now I have mostly discussed texts that may be familiar to Louisiana scholars but are likely not known to the general public. In canonical literature, the most popular work that deals with this colony is the 1731 novel *Manon Lescaut,* by the abbé Prévost. It is a tale of gallantry gone wrong, or the rapid degeneration from the highest ideal of *galanterie,* something recognizable from chivalric romance, to its most debased form, a euphemism for prostitution. The two main characters, Manon, an alluring but amoral young woman, and the chevalier des Grieux, a naïve seminary student, fall in love at first sight and then run away together. When he is disowned by his parents, they try to live in Paris through various schemes. To the chevalier's horror, Manon eagerly turns to prostitution, for which she is ultimately arrested by the regent's troops and sent to the Louisiana colony. The devoted Des Grieux accompanies her to the colony, where she dies in a quasi-saintly way; he then returns to France and tells his story to the narrator.

The actions in the plot would normally call for a picaresque style, but since the story is told from Des Grieux's point of view, it is cast in a sentimental, tragic mode. Ironically, the chevalier's adventures are reminiscent of medieval romance, as suggested by his title of "knight." However, mundane concerns about money, other people's dishonesty, and his mistress's inconstancy repeatedly attack his idealism. He tries to live as a Tristan or a Lancelot, but he is more like Don Quixote, whose knightly enthusiasm is out of place in his society. His tender speeches and heroic sacrifices for

Manon would also be prime examples of *galanterie* as in the seventeenth-century ideal of the perfect suitor. In the end, Louisiana is the place where *galanterie* goes to die—literally, because Manon, the character who inspires everyone's desires, ceases to live, but also symbolically, because even before her death, romantic *galanterie* is completely debased.

It is especially appropriate that their love story ends in the colony of Louisiana, because it represents not so much disillusion (since Des Grieux never loses his ideals) but the sad contrast between ideal and reality. In this novel, as in the texts that counter the government propaganda about Louisiana as the Promised Land, a hostile environment and human corruption are the truths the travelers have to face. Upon their arrival in "Le Nouvel Orléans," Des Grieux and Manon are initially shocked at the primitive state of the settlement: "We were surprised to discover, as we advanced, that what people had praised to us until now as a fine city was nothing but an assemblage of some poor shacks."[135] This description echoes the text by Vallette de Laudun, for example, which exposes the sorry state of the settlement in spite of the hype created by propaganda.

However, this desolation isolates the couple from the temptations of Paris, which leads to a purified, renewed version of their love. Their speeches of self-sacrifice to each other meet Des Grieux's ideal of pure love, which is the old-fashioned ideal of *galanterie,* as in the Carte de Tendre. This moment makes him reflect: "It is to New Orleans that one must come, I often said to Manon, when one wants to savor the sweetness of love. It is here that one loves without self-interest, without jealousy, without inconstancy."[136] He then contrasts the emotional development he experiences in this colony with his country's political failure in the same place: "Our compatriots come to look for gold; they do not imagine that we have found much more valuable treasures here."[137] This situation does not last: a local administrator later tries to seduce Manon, which makes the couple escape the New Orleans settlement, but Manon dies along the way and then Des Grieux returns to France.

Did Prévost choose this setting for the end of Manon's adventures in order to subvert the regent's colonial project? Or was it simply a faraway place with a bad reputation that suited the needs of the story? On the one hand, we can see Prévost as a critic of the French government; for instance, *Manon* was banned in France in 1733 because it was seen as insulting to powerful people. Jean Sgard specifies that "these barely veiled allusions [. . .] to the Regent, to the police lieutenant d'Argenson," would "shock the respectable world."[138] And this was not the first time Prévost wrote unfavorable things about the French government. His first novel, *Les aventures de Pomponius* (1722), was an erotic satire of the regent. Sgard also sees anti-government sentiments in Prévost's descriptions of Louis XIV's wars and their effects on the population of Artois, the northern province where Prévost grew up, in his works such as *Mémoires de Montcal* (1741). Even the name he gave to himself, Prévost d'Exiles, suggests that the condition of exile was part of his identity and that rather than pledging loyalty to France, he felt stateless.

On the other hand, one could see the setting for the end of *Manon* as not containing any particular political message. The forced settlement of prostitutes in Louisiana was simply one of the biggest stories of this period, and perhaps Prévost believed it contained a lot of potential for the display of novelistic emotions. One could say the same of this author's ambivalent treatment of John Law as a minor character in the larger narrative that *Manon* is a part of, *Mémoires et aventures d'un homme de qualité*. He portrays Law as an intelligent man who falls in love successively with two women who lead him to a life of crime and greed.

The Louisiana setting might simply have been an exotic place to take his readers, without even attempting to describe the place accurately. Many modern readers note how absurdly erroneous the description of the terrain is: when the two protagonists escape and try to reach the English colonies, they encounter, just two leagues away from New Orleans, "a vast plain, without being able to find a single tree to cover us" and "a countryside covered with sand."[139] Both landscape features are highly unlikely, if impossible, to reach within walking distance of the city. As in the Quoniam story, the most important feature of this terrain is that it is not Paris. A dichotomy must be created between Paris, the center of high society, and the "desert," in the sense of a biblical place of exile.[140]

Whether or not Prévost had a political goal in highlighting the desolation of the Louisiana colony, the effect of this novel, one of the most popular of the eighteenth century even now, was to solidify the area's bad reputation. In contrast, the 1801 novel *Atala*, by Chateaubriand, imitated the end of *Manon* in many ways—both involve tragic young lovers who wander the inaccurately described wilderness of Louisiana until the young woman dies, and the male lover lives to tell the tale. However, Chateaubriand's equally famous story elevated the Louisiana setting back to a *locus amoenus*. He did not do it to support the French government's schemes, as the *Mercure* articles of the 1710s had; in fact, Chateaubriand was himself in exile from France when he wrote this novel, and he opposed Napoleon, who controlled the government at the time. His treatment of Louisiana in *Atala* was more an expression of nostalgia and other Romantic-era yearnings than of a clear political position. In any case, for his own reasons, Chateaubriand brought the idealized Louisiana back into public consciousness, thus closing the circle of the reputation of this colony.

What the texts in this chapter demonstrate is that the regent and Law tried to control the information that went out to the public, but members of the public made up their own minds. We can see evidence of popular resistance in unofficial sources, mostly word of mouth, that found their way into memoirs and journals. If people disbelieved official sources, however, they did not necessarily turn to the truth—a phenomenon we know only too well in our current era of conspiracy theories. Sometimes they simply seized upon another exaggeration or untruth that they found more satisfying. As Arlette Farge remarks in *Dire et mal dire*, "It was hard to control the effect of images that were flung at the public, and in fact the populace had their own way of appropriating myths [...] the people [...] hijacked the meaning of something that had been roughly forced on them from above."[141] Many French people thus remained skeptical of the official pronouncements and preferred to believe sources that were perhaps even less trustworthy.

The deformation or invention of the Quoniam events in particular illustrates Jean-Noël Kapferer's theories about rumors. Not only do they change to fit the preexisting opinions of listeners but they proliferate in the absence of trust in the official sources of information. To what extent can we interpret grumbling *bruits* (rumors) as seditious to the monarchy? In the eighteenth century as in the present time, Jean-Noël Kapferer reminds us, "*A rumor constitutes a relation to authority* [...]. It often involves oppositional speech: it remains unconvinced by official disclaimers, as if 'official' and 'credible' did not go hand in hand. [...] As information that runs alongside and at times counter to official information, rumors constitute a counter-power, i.e., a sort of check on power" (emphasis in the original).[142]

The Quoniam affair certainly could be seen as an expression of public resistance to the regent's policies. As Thomas Kaiser explains, this whole episode of the Mississippi Bubble made a permanent mark on the history of the French monarchy: "Law's System tested the limits of the king's capacity to establish credibility in the eyes of his subjects and, hence, provides a major case study in the politics of French absolutism."[143] Perhaps thinking of twentieth-century despotic regimes, Kaiser links the use of force and the spread of propaganda through Law's pamphlets: "The more Law threatened the ordinary citizen with the loss of his possessions and personal liberty, it seemed, the more Law sought to justify this 'despotism.'"[144] As a consequence of the perceived despotism of the regent, spurred by Law, the French monarchy lost prestige, and more precisely "credit," in both the financial and moral senses.

2

Enlightenment Travelers

Scientific Description as a Critique of Monarchy

After France made its claim on Louisiana in the late seventeenth century, a number of explorers traveled through this area and documented their experiences for the reading pleasure of their readers back home. In this chapter I demonstrate how exploration journals, whose initial purpose was to serve the government, became a tool for covertly attacking the ideology of the government itself. Le Page du Pratz, as well as some of his predecessors in the exploration of Louisiana, subtly embedded in supposedly objective scientific descriptions various critiques of colonial policy. In this way, they prodded at the religious and political faith the ancien régime relied on to stay in power. Their writings were revolutionary in a subtle way, not openly critiquing the regime but, like some the Enlightenment *philosophes,* sowing the seeds of doubt that would come to fruition decades later.

Truth, Lies, and Publication Strategies

Scholars have focused on the content of explorers' accounts of Louisiana, but few have considered how their position vis-à-vis the government, which was both patron and censor, influenced their writing. What explorers included and excluded in their texts, how openly or subtly they expressed certain ideas, and when they had their texts published were all affected by their relationship to the authorities. For example, researchers discuss the favorable publicity that several writers, including Le Page du Pratz, Bossu, and Le Mascrier (all published in the 1740s to 1760s) gave to Louisiana,[1] but my question is, to what extent were they obligated to do so?

The Ministère de la Marine sent agents not to freely gather whatever information there was on the ground but rather to confirm its hopes of finding gold mines or a quick route to Asia. The information provided by explorers became a valuable commodity in itself, thus maintaining an "information economy."[2] Inevitably, some voyagers, for example François Le

Maire, obliged their employers by saying what they wanted to hear, whether it was true or not. However, other explorers found ways to express their skepticism about the colonial project and, even more daringly considering the possible consequences, about their sacrosanct institutions back home.

Probably the most well-known example of this type of rhetorical rebellion was performed by the Baron de Lahontan, as many scholars have noted. Although the region he deals with is a different part of Nouvelle France than Louisiana, I evoke his writing because it serves as a model of Enlightenment-style dissent against imperial policy that officers in Louisiana could have followed but dared not to. He was sent as a military officer to Canada but then openly broke ties with his superiors. No longer beholden to the French interests in the region, he wrote critical and even satirical texts based on his North American experiences. Readers familiar with Enlightenment wit will recognize his rhetorical strategies: he blends fact and fiction to expose the lies of government propaganda and to advance his own progressive ideology. Lahontan created a skeptical, anti-imperialist vision that would, not surprisingly, keep him outside the circles of French royal favor for the rest of his life. In fact, he brazenly dedicated his books and offered his services to other monarchs, namely, those of England and of Denmark.

Another voyager, the père Charlevoix, who traveled from Canada down the whole length of the Mississippi to the Gulf of Mexico, used different tactics to critique the French takeover of the area. A Jesuit employed by the government to explore the commercial possibilities of the region, he wrote two texts, one fulfilling his mission and the other critiquing it in a set of informal letters to a friend. We can see a marked difference in the way this Jesuit justifies his two narrations. At the beginning of the official report entitled *Histoire et description générale de la Nouvelle France,* he writes that his purpose is to "please the public" and, speaking with polite modesty, "render a service to my native country."[3] In the subsequent paragraph, he gives a third, much longer reason for writing: "If I owe myself to the State as a citizen, my profession also obliges me to serve the Church [...] I have also resolved to undertake this work, in the desire to make known the mercies of the Lord, and the triumph of religion over that small number of the elect, predestined before all ages, amid so many savage tribes, which, till the French entered their country, had lain buried in the thickest darkness of infidelity."[4] He asserts, then, that a major purpose of his voyage was to proselytize, thus imitating the message and the wording of his fellow religious explorers in Canada, such as Marie de l'Incarnation or Louis Hennepin.

By contrast, Charlevoix's more informal account of the same trip, *Journal d'un voyage fait par ordre du roy*, in the form of letters to the duchesse de Lesdiguières, contains no such mention of missionary goals. Interestingly, he follows the pattern of the texts I examined in the previous chapter, that of the letters to a lady. In the second letter, he even makes an allusion to the *Voyage de Siam*, by the abbé de Choisy. I mentioned that text in chapter 1 in regard to several flirtatious description of Louisiana, so perhaps Choisy provided a common model for an entertaining travelogue. Charlevoix's letters, if they are not especially flirtatious, are at least worldly and polite, taking the tone that an aristocratic lady would expect. They begin with "Madame, You wished for me to write to you regularly, at every opportunity I could find, and I promised to do so because I cannot refuse you anything."[5] Although he is trying to please, it is also important for him to remain respectful, since the duchesse de Lesdiguières is a real person, unlike the addressees of the previous texts I mentioned, and she is a woman of social standing from a prominent family.[6]

Another way in which the official *Histoire* and the informal *Journal* differ is in the attitudes toward the government's plans in Nouvelle France. For example, in the second letter of the *Journal*, Charlevoix mocks the French desire to find gold mines. First, he contemplates the bounty of fish, specifically cod, in Canada and remarks: "These, Madame, are true mines that are worth more and require much less expense than those of Peru and Mexico."[7] Like Raynal some sixty years later, Charlevoix laments that the government disdains the true richness of the continent—for example, in sources of food—and searches instead for chimerical gold or silver mines. In the same letter, Charlevoix tells a joke about misplaced greed, as well as misplaced faith in God. In reference to the Isle of Anticosti he writes:

> There was a rumor several years ago that a silver mine had been discovered on it, and for lack of miners a goldsmith was sent from Quebec, where I was at the time, to test it. But he did not get very far. He soon realized, from the speech of the person who had informed him of it, that the mine existed only in the injured brain of this man, who recommended incessantly that he have confidence in God. He considered that if trust in God could miraculously cause a mine to be found, it was not necessary to go to Anticosti, and he turned back.[8]

Charlevoix mocks the madman who believes in the existence of mines, but this same madman also exhorts people to have faith in God. If the mines are imaginary, should listeners assume that God is also the illusion of an "injured brain"? The comparison echoes some of the jokes about John Law comparing the belief that paper money could be transformed into gold to the belief in the Eucharist—does not skepticism for one suggest a dangerous skepticism for the other?

In regard to the publication of both texts by Charlevoix, there was apparently some speculation among scholars about why they appeared in 1744, more than twenty years after the voyage itself.[9] In the nineteenth century, for example, the diplomat François Barbé-Marbois looked back at these descriptions of Nouvelle France and remarked, "The letters of this Jesuit were addressed to the duchesse des Lesdiguières; they were kept quite secret. If they had been published then, the colony would undoubtedly have had a different destiny; but this correspondence did not see the light until twenty-five years later."[10] Barbé-Marbois saw the suppression of unfavorable information about Louisiana as part of the government's project to encourage people to invest and settle there. Similarly, in a discussion of the deaths of colonists under the Law scheme, Barbé-Marbois remarks on how the government tried to cover up information: "It was easy to hide from the public the countless calamities to which those Frenchmen fell victim. Communication with the metropole was rare, correspondence nonexistent or mysterious."[11] He regrets that there were no periodicals at the time that could "expose the truth and, by informing the people, inform the governments themselves."[12] However, he declares that there were some "enlightened" individuals who dared to expose the failures of French colonization in Louisiana: "Still, some enlightened and wise men brought a healthy sense of judgment to the state of affairs of this country. Father Charlevoix, Jesuit, was traveling through it in 1720, 1721, 1722. The extreme discretion of the order he belonged to did not permit him to say everything; but what he says is sincere, especially in the narration of what he saw."[13] Barbé-Marbois, who had served in Philadelphia and Saint-Domingue under the ancien régime, surely had extensive knowledge of his government's policy of suppressing information from the colonies.[14] He was thus able to see how Charlevoix found a balance between telling what he saw and protecting himself from persecution.

The strategy of writing two texts, an official one that favored government interests and another, less formal in style, that revealed doubts about the whole colonization project, was not used only by Charlevoix but also by another visitor to the Mississippi River valley, the military officer Dumont de Montigny. One experience taught him that he should not be overly sincere in writing an official report to the government. He recounts in his memoir that during his first voyage to Louisiana, from 1719 to 1721, other officers confiscated his papers: "M. de Saint Martin, the second director of the Company [...] issued an order from the king that all passengers and others—sailors, officers, whoever was in the ship—must deliver to him all the letters that we had carried out of the country we were coming from so that they could be inspected [...]. All this was to see whether we were speaking ill of the country."[15] Dumont managed to keep his letters private by claiming (falsely) that he was the godson of the war minister, Le Blanc.[16]

These explorers' canniness is understandable when we consider that someone who openly described Louisiana as a bad prospect could indeed be punished for his frankness. In one case, a former governor of Louisiana, Antoine Laumet de Lamothe-Cadillac,[17] was imprisoned for spreading information that was unfavorable to the Compagnie d'Occident's project. He had been governor of upper Louisiana and founder of Detroit, but after conflicts with a number of people in the Iroquois territory, he was appointed governor of the lower part of the Mississippi in 1712.[18] He arrived in 1713 and remained there until 1717. Upon arriving on the Gulf Coast, in complete disregard for the success of the Compagnie d'Occident, Lamothe issued a long memorandum to the minister of the marine, the comte de Pontchartrain. This document, from October 26, 1713, is almost comical in its annihilation of practically any hopes for this area. He covers the meager agriculture, the disgraced inhabitants, and the crumbling buildings. At l'Ile Dauphine, he writes, there is a sad little fort, a "*Salmigondis* where one understands nothing,"[19] that is rotting away; no vegetables can grow on this terrain; there is a little tobacco, but it is full of vermin; there is a little wheat, but it is all wet and the grains contain no flour. As for the few inhabitants, he remarks, "According to the proverb 'Bad country, bad people,' one can say that they are a heap of the dregs of Canada, jail birds with no respect for religion or for government, addicted to vice."[20] There may be mulberry trees, Lamothe admits, but they need "at least ten years"[21] to grow the silkworms and to train the inhabitants in the manufacture of silk thread. This potential source of income, which never materialized, was mentioned in the *Mercure* article discussed in the previous chapter. As he describes the pathetic fruits of the island—dry grapes and a three-foot-tall plum tree—he particularly attacks his predecessors who lied to the government about the fertility of the area: "That is the 'terrestrial paradise' of Mr. D'Artaguiette and of several others, the 'Pomona' of M. De Rémonville and the 'Fortunate Isles' of Mr. De Ma[n]deville and of Mr. Philippe; their memoranda and their relations are pure fables. They have spoken about what they have not seen at all and they have too readily believed what was told them."[22] He directly mocks the idea promoted by government propaganda that Louisiana is a paradise, the land of Pomona, Roman goddess of orchards.

Repeating the word *fables* to show the favorable views of Louisiana as fictions or lies, Lamothe expressed through the Superior Council of Louisiana on July 1, 1716, that "the colony of Louisiana is a monster that has no form of government. The deplorable condition in which it finds itself is a result of the little attention that has been paid to his [Lamothe's] memoranda and of the fact that the fables of those who have depicted this country as very excellent have been preferred. He has examined all of it and protests that he has never seen any that was worse."[23] After submitting these reports, he returned to France and was suddenly imprisoned. While he had perhaps alienated those he worked with by his acerbic manner, the specific reason given for his imprisonment is that he spoke badly of Louisiana. Documents from the Bastille label him and his son as "suspected of inconsiderate speech against the government and the state."[24] They remained in prison from September 27, 1717, to February 8, 1718. The document further specifies that they were "suspected of having spoken inappropriately against the government about the state of the colonies, accused also of having worked on memoranda contrary to the good of the state."[25] It alleges that Lamothe sinned both via the spoken word (*discours*) and via the written word (*mémoires*). The marquis de Dangeau notes this arrest in his journal on Saturday, October 2, 1717: "La Motte, who had commanded in the Mississippi at the time when Crozat was in charge [before the regent nationalized the Compagnie in 1717], was put in the Bastille these last few days for having spoken badly of the settlement that they want to establish there under the banner of the Compagnie d'Occident."[26] The year 1717 is suggestive: perhaps Lamothe's words were dangerously close to counteracting the claims that appeared the same year in the *Mercure*. Unfortunately for him, Lamothe's opinions, which he was imprudent enough to voice so publicly, are examples of the "disruptions in the reporting hierarchy"[27] or "disunity" among the governing elites, which, as Kenneth Banks tells us, "could lead to a serious challenge to their authority."[28] Lamothe's silencing, through the punishment of imprisonment and disgrace, proves how dangerous information could be.

Considering these cases that showed the consequences of critiquing the colonial project and considering that many travelers depended on their government for their income and their careers in general, it is not surprising that so few were openly critical. Nevertheless, expression of doubt about

Louisiana's prospects sometimes slipped through the hands of France's censors. Other pessimistic accounts, such as the one attributed to Valette de Laudun, appeared anonymously, perhaps printed outside France, and after France had transferred the colony to Spain. Meanwhile, critiques were also voiced in satirical songs, whose authors were difficult, if not impossible, to trace. As Michel Foucault remarked, in this premodern era to name an author was to be able to arrest him.[29]

Many explorers were obligated by their government to put their name to their writing, however, so they found other rhetorical strategies to avoid trouble. A very typical strategy for telling the truth and not getting punished in this Enlightenment era was to write a report that seemed favorable on the surface but hid indirect critiques. I argue that this was the approach taken by one traveler in Louisiana, Le Page du Pratz. His text begins as a report in support of French government interests but then it strays from the path (literally and figuratively) to embark on a whole different voyage led by personal curiosity.

Le Page du Pratz's Enlightenment

Antoine-Simon Le Page du Pratz was an engineer who also cultivated a concession close to the new capital of the colony, New Orleans. He was so fascinated by the region that he moved farther inland to live among the Natchez Indians. In his text, he claims to have become fluent in the Natchez language and to have spent time interviewing members of this tribe and neighboring ones to get a solid understanding of their religion, government, and other aspects of their culture. Life imitates art when he conducts these conversations much like Lahontan's famous but surely fantastical debates with the Huron Adario. He documents these experiences in his three-volume *Histoire de la Louisiane,* first published in 1758, which combines the genres of personal memoir and ethnographic treatise; it also contains descriptions of flora, fauna, and geography.[30] His accounts of the Natchez tribe, especially the unraveling of a Native rebellion against the French, influenced later authors such as the abbé Raynal and Chateaubriand.

It has been well documented that Le Page du Pratz's text bears marks of Enlightenment writing and in turn provided material for the polemical treatises of better-known Enlightenment writers. In fact, this is a wide-ranging phenomenon from the late seventeenth century onwards, when we can see an exchange between a number of explorers and Enlightenment philosophers, who both influence each other in a circular way. Lahontan (as well as the Jesuit missionaries in China, for example) opened up new vistas to philosophers like Voltaire and Rousseau, who could now imagine a critique of the absurdities of their own society through the eyes of a fictional "straight man" in the shape of a virtuous foreigner. For instance, surely based on La Hontan, Voltaire presented a good Huron in *L'Ingénu* and, more briefly, a comically reasonable "lady from the Mississippi" who advocated for cannibalism in the article "Anthropophages" of his *Philosophical Dictionary*. Meanwhile, Le Page du Pratz, writing in the 1720s and publishing in 1758, also expresses opinions that are in line with the Enlightenment. For example, he is open about his religious skepticism, his cultural relativism, his penchant for physiocratic economic theories, and his belief that truth is attained through empirical observation.

Shannon Lee Dawdy calls Le Page du Pratz's approach "Enlightenment from the ground up" and demonstrates the mutual influence of this explorer and the major *philosophes*.[31] She notes similarities between the messages of Le Page du Pratz and of the abbé Raynal, who was the author of the hugely successful *Histoire des deux Indes* (1770–80), a critical history of colonialism from an Enlightenment point of view. In terms of their polemical nature, Raynal is "less diplomatic" than Le Page du Pratz, Dawdy claims. This is certainly true of Raynal's passages concerning, for example, Catholic oppression, the greed of the French court, and how both stunted the growth of the Louisiana colony.[32] She attributes the difference in approach to the fact that Raynal wrote when France had already ceded Louisiana to Spain in 1762. This is certainly an important factor, but I believe that still others made Le Page du Pratz more circumspect.

Le Page du Pratz evidently decided on a strategy to express his progressive ideas in a discreet way, while retaining his status vis-à-vis the government. For example, he proudly called himself a "royal engineer, civil and hydraulic architect" on a map that he published.[33] Raynal, on the other hand, was an armchair philosopher, and while he had benefited from the patronage of members of the court at Versailles at certain times in his career, he decided to break from official patronage by writing from a more radical stance. Under these circumstances, he chose to be more daring in his condemnation of European imperialism. He surely knew the explosive nature of his *Histoire des deux Indes,* so he had it published anonymously and outside France.[34] Soon, the work was banned and put on the Index—the Inquisition's list of banned books—and Raynal was forced into exile, consequences that Le Page du Pratz managed to avoid as far as we know.

In order to publish legally, like all French authors of the ancien régime, Le Page du Pratz had to submit his text to a government censor, who would grant or deny him the *privilège,* the royal approval. It was indeed published *avec privilège,* specifically for the following reasons provided by the officials Guétard and Le Bègue, and then approved by P. G. Le Mercier, syndic.

> I have read, by order of my lord the Chancellor, a manuscript entitled *Histoire de la Louisiane,* by M. le Page du Pratz. The history of a land that is as interesting to France as Louisiana can only be favorably received by the public, and it seems to me that it must be even more so because the author resided for a long time in this land, he lived with the savages, he himself saw the majority of the events that he reports, which has put him in a state to note, verify, or destroy the notions that we already had about this vast area.[35]

This official's justification indicates to us that the royal court accepted him as a safe, not subversive, author. The wording echoes Le Page du Pratz's preface, in which he claims that his text is useful to the public and his authority is based on firsthand experience.

In the preface, Le Page du Pratz gives more extensive reasons why his book will be useful to the public. Unlike the missionary Charlevoix, who announces the conversion of Natives as his primary goal (at least in his official *Histoire,* not the *Journal*), Le Page du Pratz the engineer is more openly secular about his purposes. From the very first page, he declares that he writes out of patriotism, specifically a commercial kind of patriotism: "In the interest of my country, I have discovered in these distant regions new natural resources, which human industry can transform into a surplus of commodities."[36] In this passage, he accomplishes several things. First, he declares his devotion to his country's *interest,* a word that had a stronger emotional connotation in the eighteenth century and also referred to a general awareness of someone's advantage. Second, he declares that his wish to advance his country's interests involves exposing the commercial potential of the regions he has explored. And third, with his reference to nature and human industry leading to abundance, he declares his adherence to the newly emerging economic theory of physiocracy, which is closely tied to Enlightenment thought.[37]

He then makes the standard declaration that all explorers make, that in contrast to all his predecessors he is telling the truth. Once again, he attributes his truthfulness to his being a patriot: "The false judgments that people have made about this part of America seem to invite a good patriot to correct their ideas and to give the right ones."[38] Furthermore, he claims to defend the reputation of the Mississippi area, which reflects on the good name of the king. He even declares that he prefers the name Louisiana to Mississippi, presumably flattering Louis XV because it is based on his predecessor Louis XIV's name. "We know every unfavorable thing that people have said and thought about the Mississippi, a name that the common man likes to give to this land, although the first and the true one is that of Louisiana, which I confer upon it."[39] He promises not only the impartial truth but a truth that is favorable, perhaps actively distancing himself from others, such as Lamothe-Cadillac, who previously described the region thus: "It is thus absolutely necessary to destroy these false judgments occasioned by unfaithful accounts, often full of malignity and almost always of ignorance [...]. You will see not only with what impartiality I considered Louisiana but also with what attentiveness I examined its products."[40] He calls unfavorable accounts of Louisiana *infidèles* (unfaithful), perhaps not only to the truth but also to their royal patron. Finally, he claims most hyperbolically, "I will consider myself happy and fully compensated for the troubles and cares that my research has cost me if this story can be useful in the service of the king and to the commercial advantage of my home country, because all my life I have had no other ambition nor other desires than to be able to render myself useful in the service of the king and the state."[41] Clearly, the effect of this flattery would be that his text was published with royal permission and that he remained in favor at court rather than suffering persecution.

In spite of these protestations of loyalty to the king, Le Page du Pratz still manages to take his place in a line of critics from Charlevoix to Raynal. All these writers begin by attacking the French government's get-rich-quick scheme to find gold as a ruinous illusion, advocating instead for the development of agricultural wealth in the Louisiana colony, which is the physiocratic approach. As time passes, each successive writer becomes bolder: Charlevoix hints at skepticism, then Le Page du Pratz clearly shows the advantage of the empirical approach over blind faith, then Raynal puts into doubt the infallibility of the king and the nature of religious faith. By the time Raynal wrote, these ideas would shake the foundations of the absolutist monarchy. I discuss Raynal later in this chapter; but first, I discuss the subversive nature of Le Page du Pratz's writing. I focus in turn on several aspects of his writing that embody Enlightenment ideas: empiricism, religious skepticism, and criticism of tyranny.

Scientific Phenomena

In this section I focus on Le Page du Pratz's descriptions of nature, which ridicule anything other than an empirical approach. Rather than relying on past knowledge or on pure rationalism, as scientists of the past had done, or attributing phenomena to supernatural causes, as religious writers had done, Enlightenment thinkers placed a new emphasis on sensory observation and personal experience. Such is Le Page du Pratz's method, but he also plays with readers' expectations of the fantasy element, the *merveilleux*, which had been a staple of travel literature of the past. He evokes phenomena that he can easily exploit to create a sense of wonder, but then he pointedly demystifies it.

At the very beginning, for example, before his ship has even landed in the Americas, he describes a family of fish unknown to Europeans, namely, the flying fish (Exocoetidae). His justification for writing about this family is in keeping with the goal of his *histoire:* to provide information about the commercial possibilities of the colony. Another justification for writing his book is unstated but implied throughout: to contribute to European scientific knowledge about animals, plants, and other things that can be found in North America. Both goals are met in this one-page description of the flying fish and its traditional predator, the bonito. In addition, this passage gives Le Page du Pratz the opportunity to give us a lesson about credulity. He insists on the idea of believability when he states that "I consider myself obligated to give a description of it to disabuse the incredulous people, such as those I have found in Paris and in the provinces"[42] and when he establishes his authority by insisting, "I am a first-hand witness."[43] He thus claims that those who do not believe his accounts of his firsthand experiences are wrong—they are overly incredulous.

In his description, he first explains the propulsion mechanisms of the fish that make it seem like it is flying, so that the mystery suggested by its name is dispelled. Second, after observing the flying fish and the bonito, he recounts one instance in which the ship's captain was hit in the back by a flying fish that jumped onto the deck. At first, the captain thought someone had hit him from the back, but then he and Le Page du Pratz saw the fish and shared a laugh. A few details that Le Page du Pratz gives, that it happened at night under the moonlight and that he himself had been awake because he couldn't sleep, may have encouraged him to narrate the story in a mysterious, ghostly way. But he refuses this mode and prefers the scientific approach—and the "laughter" of both the captain and the narrator helps to dispel any ghostly atmosphere. The captain's first impulse after discovering the truth was a scientific one, to preserve the fish in brandy in order to "show it in France to those who do not believe the voyagers on this matter."[44] The purpose of the captain's action parallels that of Le Page du Pratz's act of narration: to give people back home factual proof of a previously unknown phenomenon. They act like men of the Enlightenment, establishing their believability through an eyewitness account and by preserving a specimen, lightly mocking those whose incredulity would be misplaced.

After mocking undue skepticism, they in turn mock credulity. Immediately after recounting the episode of the captain episode, Le Page du Pratz describes how sailors catch bonito by crafting fake flying fish. "The bonito, fooled by this bait, wanting to swallow the toy that it takes for a fish, finds itself caught."[45] The reader, looking at this succession of anecdotes, will come to the conclusion that false illusions are to be laughed at and worthy of only dumb fish. The important lesson is that one has to develop the ability, or the critical reason, to know the difference between truth and lies.

According to the prefaces of various eighteenth-century authors such as Charlevoix, travel writing had acquired a reputation for dubious descriptions of extraordinary, even supernatural things. These authors claimed to take their distance from accounts of monsters or treasure troves; they wished to focus instead on observable, verifiable facts, at the risk of focusing on the disappointingly mundane. According to Jorge Cañizares-Esguerra, "Travel literature was becoming firmly associated with the taste of a populace enamored of marvels and false curiosities."[46] Le Page du Pratz, for example, refers to the Spanish explorer De Soto's accounts as "romanesque" (novelistic),[47] though he strategically spares French explorers and declines to explain what the false claims were.

By contrast, the new breed of Enlightenment-influenced compilers of travel literature—and I would add actual travelers like Le Page du Pratz—were what Cañizares-Esguerra calls "philosophical travelers," who "began to call into question the authority and reliability of the sources that historians and chroniclers had traditionally used."[48] By writing from their "philosophical" point of view, they sought to train their public in a new skeptical method of reading: "The new art of reading also coincided with the rise of the 'philosophical traveler,' who, unlike his counterparts in the past, was not satisfied with collecting tales of wonder."[49] Le Page du Pratz exemplifies this approach: he addressed his readers' expectations of the extraordinary only to tease them; by this means he could teach them an Enlightenment lesson about the folly of imagination. In other words, he used narrative technique to battle against the exoticizing imagination and to teach his readers how to approach travel accounts with a critical viewpoint.

To demonstrate his technique of teasing his reader with the promise of fantastic stories, I give two further examples, one of a rumored oyster tree and another of a meteor. In both cases, Le Page du Pratz draws the reader in by almost promising a supernatural event. Then he immediately undercuts this suspense by anticipating the reaction of gullible people and counteracts it with an Enlightenment-influenced scientific approach.

First, the oyster tree. After describing the taste and the measurements of Louisiana oysters, Le Page du Pratz breaches a related topic: "Having spoken of the oysters of Louisiana, we will say a word about those of Saint-Domingue, which one finds hanging off trees; I believe that one can call them branched oysters."[50] After confronting us with such an unusual spectacle—these "branched oysters," perhaps hybrid animal-plants, a combination of sea and land creatures like we've never seen before—he then taunts us by anticipating how we will react. "The critics," he says, "will imagine having an easy time with this item," perhaps suggesting that those with a skeptical outlook will laugh at him or accuse him of lying.[51]

He then recounts his firsthand experience chronologically. He is at first surprised to see oysters hanging from trees, "something I could not easily conceive."[52] Immediately, however, the vice captain of his ship gives a perfectly rational explanation: the oysters get caught in the bushes during high tide; then the water recedes, leaving the oysters in the branches. We can see that what Le Page du Pratz called *trees* have now been transformed into *bushes;* so he exaggerated the height of the plants in order to create a more surprising effect. After the logical explanation, he triumphantly states, "That is the supposed phenomenon; may no one accuse me of fraudulent deception [*imposture*] concerning my branched oysters; I am even sure that no one will contest this fact, which is known by sailors; in any case, it is both natural and possible."[53] He supports his claim to truth by mentioning the sailors—other eyewitnesses who have seen the same sights and can corroborate what he says.

He further tries to boost his own credibility by contrasting this more "verisimilar" claim about oyster trees with a less believable rumor regarding oysters, that cats can open and then eat them while the oysters remain underwater. "By contrast, if I said the cats of Louisiana fish for oysters and that having put one of their paws into the shell, which closes immediately, they stay in this position [. . .] if I spoke that way, you would be authorized not to believe me."⁵⁴ His emphatic tone and the example of something he would not claim because it is too improbable (the cats opening the oysters) is supposed to make his previous claim, about the oyster trees, that much more believable. He continues by inviting his readers to read his text with a critical eye: "In truth, I cannot imagine how an author can be so bold as to make a gift to the public of inventions that are as impertinent as they are impossible. Personally, I willingly accept my own condemnation if you can find the slightest contradiction in what I report. I do not haphazardly advance something unless I am certain of it; I profess to say what I know, and nothing more."⁵⁵ He even offers to accept their "condemnation" if he ever presents anything that is contradictory, assuring them that he describes nothing that he has not seen with his own eyes. In other words, he expects his readers to be Enlightenment readers, to rely on his empirical approach to phenomena and to also use their reason to judge whether it is trustworthy.

There are many other passages in which he describes flora, fauna, and climactic events, which he represents to his reading public with a contrast between the fantastical and the so-called natural. In these passages, he often uses the words *monstrous* and *monster* to pique the readers' interest and make them think of mythical creatures, only to present them with the description of a simple rattlesnake or an alligator. Even when Le Page du Pratz has no explanation of a phenomenon, he refuses to submit to fantastical explanations and retains his Enlightenment forbearance before the mysteries of nature. For instance, he recounts seeing a strange sight in the sky that we can now recognize as a bright type of meteor called a fireball. Once again, he begins by anticipating the reactions of the credulous and the incredulous—"I saw a phenomenon that frightened the superstitious"⁵⁶—and then remarks that "the phenomenon was perceived toward the end by many people who saw it with terror."⁵⁷ He admits that he had never seen anything like it. It was a trumpet-shaped light in the night sky, then something like a cannonball that shot from it with a hissing sound. He makes sure to describe it as objectively as possible, with approximate measurements and cardinal points. Instead of speculating on the nature of such an unusual sight, he restrains his imagination and defers to "scholars" who "will be able to exert their talents to discover the causes."⁵⁸

One cannot help but compare this passage to the multitudinous myths that surrounded Halley's comet, which appeared in 1680 and to which Paul Hazard devotes part of his classic intellectual history of the early Enlightenment, *La crise de la conscience européenne*. Hazard tells us that before the advent of critical thinkers like Pierre Bayle, the populace attached various irrational interpretations to astronomical phenomena: "Comets are omens, said credulous people, omens sent from above to announce some great punishment deserved by men."[59] Unlike the masses of the previous generation, Le Page du Pratz refuses to read something supernatural into what must have been an astonishing sight.

Even as he refrains from overinterpreting what he observes in a superstitious way, he also avoids the other extreme, giving a comprehensive scientific-philosophical explanation when he lacks information. Instead, he simply states his ignorance of the fireball's causes, without indulging in any speculation. This position of temporary ignorance is what d'Alembert would approvingly call the *esprit systématique* a few years later in the "Discours préliminaire" of the *Encyclopédie,* as opposed to the *esprit de système.*[60] In the face of something unknown, a proper Enlightenment attitude would have been to admit ignorance but to try to understand gradually using logic and observation, whereas the *esprit de système* would artificially claim to somehow fit all phenomena into its schema explaining everything in existence, as the metaphysicists of the past had done. Even before Diderot and d'Alembert labeled these two ways of thinking, John Locke made this comparison, as Hazard reminds us. Le Page du Pratz, then, like a man of the Enlightenment, suspends his understanding until he finds out more about the light he saw in the sky. It would seem that the exotic setting in a faraway land would almost justify some elevation of his observations into something supernatural—but he declines to take his readers there. Nevertheless, he still teases his readers by appearing to build up to a stereotypical traveler's account of an extraordinary sight. His two plausible goals are to please them by adorning what would otherwise be an overly dry narrative of scientific observations and, more likely, to use this anticipated pleasure to teach his readers how to read like good Enlightenment skeptics. Le Page du Pratz takes advantage of the sensationalism that readers allegedly expect from the exotic adventure narrative but transforms it to serve his own purpose.

While these instances of playing with readers' expectations may seem innocent, the implications were in fact dangerous for the Bourbon regime. The censors who approved this text apparently did not see that skepticism about scientific phenomena could spread to other areas of thought. For example, Le Page du Pratz questioned the government's very goals for exploring Louisiana—to find not just gold but also the mythical Mer de l'Ouest. Although explorers before and after Le Page du Pratz searched in vain for this sea, he questions its very existence and whether France should even be looking for it. "As for me," he ventures, "I am strongly inclined to think that it exists only in the imagination";[61] and if that is true, why search for "chimerical advantages" when the country at hand is so fertile? he asks. "Let us profit from what we have at hand; is real usefulness not preferable to the chimerical advantages that one would have to search for far and wide and that may never exist?"[62] This was the line of argumentation taken by Charlevoix and later by the abbé Raynal. As Paul Mapp observes about the European governments' obstinate "self-deception" in looking for the Mer de l'Ouest, the explorers they sent "deliberately misled French officials and the gullible readers of tall tales" and ignored the "possibility that they were strategically omitting, restating, exaggerating, and even fabricating" information.[63] Le Page du Pratz does fulfill his patriotic duty, as he claimed in his preface, by telling the truth, but if the government were to take this idea seriously, it would have to come to terms with its twisted relationship to truth-telling and positive propaganda.

Cañizares-Esguerra sees a similarly conflicted relationship between Spain's Bourbon regime and the explorers and philosophers it employed to bring information about the colonies. While Spain took pride that its writers were at the forefront of intellectual methods, these new methods also carried latent dangers for the public faith on which the government relied. "The reaction in Spain to these new historiographical developments was one of ambivalence. On the one hand, the lure of 'modernity' moved many authors to reject traditional Spanish historiography on the land and peoples of the New World. On the other hand, Spaniards understood that questioning the credibility of Iberian sources could not be dissociated from the Protestant assault on Spanish colonialism."[64] In other words, the "philosophical traveler" could not entirely be a loyal, but hopefully the governments would not notice. To return to Le Page du Pratz's case, let us see how he dared to take his skepticism into more dangerous territory.

On Religion

As Le Page du Pratz chides the French reading public and government for their credulity, he seems ready to present the Natchez Indians as their polemical opposite, for the sake of a neat rhetorical structure. At first, the Natchez do appear in an extremely favorable light when he describes the refinement of their manners, their dignified and honest way of speaking, their advanced medicine, and their uncorrupted relationship to nature. He famously refuses to apply the common French term *sauvages* to them, preferring to call them *naturels* because they are "men who know how to make very good use of their reason," better than "certain civilized nations."[65] Once he ensconces himself in the tribe and starts to learn more about their religion, though, he begins to show their less favorable side. His critique, and sometimes mockery, of their beliefs may seem to contradict his general respect for this tribe. However, I believe that this approach serves as a covert attack on his own countrymen's faith, while refusing to idealize the Natchez as a perfect society—both typical Enlightenment literary strategies. In other words, he neither claims French superiority nor gives up his right to look critically at the Natchez.

Sometimes Le Page du Pratz directly challenges both Catholic and Natchez beliefs, albeit diplomatically. For instance, after he asks the Natchez about the origin of the neighboring Chatkas tribe, he reports that "they responded to me that they came out from under the earth."[66] But to assure us that he does not take this extraordinary statement too seriously, he interprets it for his readers as a metaphor used "to express the surprise with which people had seen them appear all of a sudden."[67] He may seem to accept the fiction when face-to-face with the Natchez, but he expresses his skepticism in an aside to the reader.

In another moment, he has to decide how to confront a Catholic priest who evokes a scientific claim that he, Le Page du Pratz, knows is wrong. First, the author pacifies potential censors by praising this priest with words like *charitable* and *erudite:* "Among the number of those charitable neighbors was the Reverend Father de Ville; this worthy cleric was full of erudition and he was a member of a society that produced such a great number of scholars that his knowledge was not a matter of astonishment for me."[68] He then assures us about his own humble attitude toward this cleric, who had the power to denounce him for heresy if it came to that: "I made it my duty to listen much and to ask questions rather than make decisions."[69] It is then an exceptional occasion when the père de Ville asks Le Page du Pratz, as someone who has studied math (and presumably science), about the conflict between the heliocentric model of the solar system advanced by scientists and the geocentric one that is part of church doctrine. This way, Le Page du Pratz presents himself not as seeking out controversy but as having this question imposed on him. Still, it was his choice to include this conversation in his book, so he clearly had a reason for mentioning it at all.[70]

His diplomatic way of defending heliocentrism involves a recourse to physics. He states that if Joshua was able to stop the sun, as is written in the Bible, in the tenth chapter of Joshua, it was because God knew the sun was the center of the system, which was easier to stop than a body revolving at a distance from the center. "Since God was the inventor of this machine, he knew all the parts and the mechanism perfectly well, and he inspired Joshua to stop the machine of the world through its first moving body; that is, since the sun was at the center of the world and turning on itself, it gave movement to all the other parts of the universe; so, out of prudence, a wise man and a clever physicist would stop their machine by means of the first moving part rather than by means of a more distant part, which should have a faster movement."[71] In other words, a God well versed in mechanics would choose the more efficient of two possible actions. Ultimately, Le Page du Pratz defends the heliocentric model and claims that the priest walks away satisfied that scripture and physics are reconciled. It is a particularly meaningful topic for Le Page du Pratz to address, since heliocentrism was a particular cause célèbre for Enlightenment philosophers, who looked back at the way the Inquisition had punished Galileo for his observations in 1634. By the eighteenth century, the Catholic Church had accepted heliocentrism, but evoking the topic still recalled the past errors of religious authorities.

It is perhaps more provocative that the imagery Le Page du Pratz uses to describe God is precisely that of deism, the belief most prevalent among Enlightenment thinkers such as Voltaire. "'One cannot doubt,' I told him, 'that the universe is a machine, whose parts are all intimately connected to each other,'" says Le Page du Pratz,[72] and as he said in the previous passage, "God was the inventor of this machine." However, in deism the point of describing the universe as a machine is to exclude the possibility of divine intervention, since the God/mechanic who initially created the machine lets it function on its own. When the case of Joshua's stopping of the sun comes up in the conversation, the author does not even touch upon the believability of the miracle itself—whether it is possible to stop the sun. He chooses to leave this idea intact, surely to avoid trouble with any authorities who would see any doubts as blasphemy. So we see Le Page du Pratz advance some Enlightenment positions such as heliocentrism, the metaphor of the universe as a machine, and faith in science, while taking care not to tread on some sensitive areas.

In other parts of the *Histoire de la Louisiane*, Le Page du Pratz expresses skepticism in the comic mode. As in the incident of the supposedly flying fish, laughter serves at times to puncture a false belief or a feeling of religious awe. In one instance, he recounts an anecdote that could be seen as mocking the sanctity of the Catholic Church. A Spanish contingent of soldiers, civilians, and one priest, he tells us, were captured by the Missouri tribe, which killed them all except the priest, whom they kept around so that he would teach them horse-riding techniques. At some point, the priest escaped and left his church vestments. The Missouri took these garments and put them on when they went on a diplomatic mission to the French settlement.

> As soon as they were close to the French settlement, they adorned themselves, each with one of the pieces from the chapel: the one who wore the most beautiful chasuble directly on his skin marched in front; those who wore chasubles followed him, then came the stole wearers, followed by those who had maniples on their necks; after these, you could see three or four Natives dressed in albs, others in surplices; the acolytes, against common usage, marched at the end of *this new-style procession,* not considering themselves overdressed if they carried in hand, while dancing to the rhythm, a cross or a candleholder.[73] (emphasis added)

Le Page du Pratz describes this spectacle in a clearly comic mode. Certain juxtapositions strike him as bizarre, and he invites the readers to agree: one Native wears a chasuble directly on his bare skin; they walk as in a parody of a Catholic procession, but dancing in their Native style. One Missouri has adapted a paten, a metal plate used to hold the Eucharist, into a necklace: "one of them had found the secret of piercing the paten, which he wore as a neck pendant."[74] The author expresses his amusement by referring to this travesty as "this new-style procession" and "this mascarade troupe of a new style"[75] as if it were a deliberately parodic theatrical troupe or a European carnival parade. The author also invites the readers directly to react: "Imagine the ridiculous spectacle that could offer to your eyes the bizarre order of this procession as I have described it";[76] and he mentions that French people who were present laughed at the sight. One spectator at first was concerned that the Missouri's possession of these objects meant that a group of Frenchmen had been killed, but when he found out that it was Spaniards who had been killed, "his sorrow disappeared; he had a hard time keeping from laughing like the others."[77]

By choosing this anecdote, which actually begins pretty violently, Le Page du Pratz avoids accusations of anti-patriotism. His laughter about some mishaps of Spanish colonialism make this story seem innocently comical, but in reality it could apply to any imperial power, including his own. In this episode, the humor comes from the desacralization of church garments and objects, which normally worshippers should behold with awe or at least respect. What the Missouri do is show that these are merely objects that can be turned into carnival costumes.[78] When Le Page du Pratz describes the Missouri treating church vestments like any other clothes, hilarity ensues, and this hilarity deflates the supposed sacredness of these objects. By focusing on the cultural cross-dressing and not, for example, on the massacre that preceded it, Le Page du Pratz manages to satirize both European colonizers and some of the common rituals of the Catholic Church.

By contrast, Jesuit letters about exploring the Natchez areas include one that describes a similar event, but the victims were French. In the words of the père Le Petit in Louisiana, "Before the Chactas [Choctaw] decided to attack the Natchez, they went to carry the peace pipe to them. They were received in quite a new way: they found them, along with their horses, adorned with chasubles and altar frontals. Many wore patens at their necks, they drank and offered drinks of brandy in chalices and ciboriums. The Chactas themselves, when they had pillaged our enemies, renewed this sacrilegious profanation by using our sacred ornaments and vessels for their dances and their games."[79] Since the letter concerns the writer's own nationality and religious order, it of course has no humorous overtone.

My final example of Le Page du Pratz's use of laughter in order to provoke skepticism about religion is part of his lengthy and otherwise respectful dialogue with the religious leader of the Natchez, the guardian of the temple. In describing their series of conversations, he puts himself in a situation similar to that of the character Lahontan in the Baron de Lahontan's *Dialogues avec un sauvage* (1704). In Lahontan's fictional dialogue, the author's mouthpiece pretends to defend the French project of converting the Hurons to Catholicism, but he really acts as a rhetorically weaker adversary to the much more convincing Huron. Similarly, Le Page du Pratz sets the scene by claiming, not very convincingly, that he considers the Catholic religion a priori more true than the Native American ones. He states, "I endeavored to cultivate our relationship, without contravening the superiority that we naturally have over them through our intelligence, our science, and our arts."[80] One might presume that he is referring to science, but he establishes in the first volume that Natchez medicine is far more effective than French. He then specifically mentions religious superiority, after explaining the Natchez system of the two great spirits, one male and one female, who are served by minor spirits. Perhaps to make it clear that he does not seem to be advocating for this system, Le Page du Pratz reassures us, "I did not neglect to correct his ideas on this subject or on that of aerial spirits and the prayers that the Natchez addressed to them, nor did I neglect to bring him to the truth that our religion teaches and that the sacred books transmitted to us. He listened with great attention and promised me to teach everything I told him to the elders of his nation."[81] The guardian's response seems more polite and dismissive than anything else, and indeed the matter of converting the Natchez to Catholicism never comes up again.

In the course of their dialogues, Le Page du Pratz learns that the main part of the Natchez religion involves maintaining the fires eternally burning inside their temples. Legend has it that the Great Spirits descended from the sun itself to speak to the Natchez; they gave the tribe their rules of morality and governance and commanded them to build temples in which eternal fires would burn. The people fear that if the fire ever goes out, a great calamity will befall them. According to the guardian, a man once fell asleep and let the fire go out momentarily; he rekindled it, but this negligence had already caused an illness to spread through the tribe. The guardian further expresses his belief in these supernatural causes and effects when he worries that a recent hurricane was a bad omen: "This extraordinary event seemed to announce something sinister to him; and firmly persuaded, as the populace is, that the extinction of the sacred fire invariably leads to the death of many men, it had made him dread that this second accident, added to the first, would cause the whole nation to perish."[82] Instead of trying to persuade him verbally to abandon his faith, Le Page du Pratz plays a joke on him. "I will not hide the astonishment into which I threw him by saying that nothing was less extraordinary than to make fire descend from the sky and that I was capable of doing it as often as I pleased. His surprise was extreme. 'It is beyond me,' he said, 'is it possible that a mortal could bring down the fire from the sun?'"[83] Taking out his magnifying glass and a piece of tinder, he pretends to perform the supernatural feat of making a fire: "I pronounced, in a firm tone, the word *Caheuch*, which means *come*, as if I commanded the fire to descend. In an instant the tinder smoked, I blew, and fire appeared, to the great astonishment of the Great Sun [the chief] and of all his followers, some of whom trembled, and their prince did not appear any more reassured."[84] As the leader of the tribe who witnesses this event, Great Sun asks whether any man can make fire with these awe-inspiring instruments. Magnanimously, the Frenchman assures him that "every man can" and even teaches him to do it. "I assured him so much that he decided to try it himself."[85] Although the Natchez tremble visibly and believe they are in the presence of something supernatural, in fact Le Page du Pratz is not only showing them fire-making techniques but also practicing the scientific method that the Enlightenment popularized. Any experiment should be able to be re-created by anyone. Still, he does not entirely disenchant the experience:—he secretly mocks the Grand Soleil by having him pronounce the same word he did, *caheuch,* as if it were a magic word.

Le Page du Pratz's ambivalence between respecting this tribe and mocking their beliefs is evident in the following passages. On the one hand, he admits that "I had much difficulty keeping myself from laughing; but it was in my interest to maintain a mysterious air,"[86] and he ultimately persuades them to give him a considerable amount of food in return for the magnifying glass. At another moment, he reports, that while "they had a meeting" to decide what to offer him for the instrument, "I took advantage of these moments to go to my field, as if I had something to take care of, but really to go there and laugh all I wanted over the scene that I had just caused."[87] He also quotes several long and solemn speeches by the Natchez leader and adds sarcastically that "he promised me to say nothing about it to the French, out of fear that they would resent me for giving up such a precious object."[88] The exaggerated status given to what is, to the author, an everyday object is the contradiction necessary to create the comic tone.

At the same time, Le Page du Pratz does not try to make them look like complete fools. He suggests that the readers imagine how they would react to something they had never seen before. "Put yourselves in their place for a moment: if we had had as little education as these peoples and if we had never seen anything as extraordinary of any kind [...] we would certainly be as surprised as they are, the first time they see truly surprising things."[89] The comparison between the Natives, whom he describes as equal if not superior to his countrymen, and his countrymen suggests an indirect invitation to reflect upon Europeans' tendencies to ascribe supernatural powers to phenomena they do not understand.

As in the descriptions of the fireball and the oyster tree, with cats that open oysters, Le Page du Pratz is teaching readers how to be skeptical. Paradoxically, he needs false impressions and errors in order to keep his readers' attention. Without them, a purely factual narrative risks being boring. In particular, the laughter of various personages, of the author himself, and of the readers, which he openly anticipates, accomplishes several goals: it is an indication that the text is in the comic mode, and as the opposite of the sacred, it attacks the solemnity required by the religious faiths in question, without direct argumentation against these religions.

Monarchy

Teaching his readers to be skeptical was one way in which Le Page du Pratz's report subtly undermined some pillars of absolutist monarchy. By exposing the illusions on which the Natchez religion relied, he attacked an easy target, but what would have stopped readers from applying the same disenchanting perspective to their own religion? And we should recall that one of the most important attributes of the French monarchy was the Catholic faith; the pope, after all, had designated the French king as *le Roi très chrétien*, defender of the religion. Aside from attacking religious dogma, skepticism could threaten the monarchy in other ways. The state was the guarantor of all investments in Nouvelle France, since the Compagnie d'Occident had been nationalized. Even in the aftermath of the Mississippi Bubble, to doubt the success of the French mission was risky because it exposed the dishonesty of government propaganda. This, in my opinion, is the most obvious reason why the publication of the texts by Charlevoix and Le Page du Pratz, both written around 1720, was delayed for more than twenty years.

Yet another subtle attack on the monarchy by Le Page du Pratz, under the cover of a "patriotic" travel narrative, was his account of the Natchez's political organization and customs, whose excesses could be interpreted as reflecting those of the French monarchy. In showing the Indigenous people as willing victims of despotism, Le Page du Pratz's strategy was opposite to that of his predecessor Lahontan, who had praised the freedom of northern tribes. However, both could lead the reader to the same conclusion: aversion to despotism.

The frontispiece of Lahontan's *Nouveaux voyages dans l'Amérique septentrionale* had famously featured an image of a Huron who defied political subjection. Réal Ouellet and Alain Beaulieu comment on this image: "An engraving represents him, with a bow and arrow in hand, stepping on the scepter and the code of laws, symbols of royal and scriptural authority. Above his head, a shocking slogan summarizes well the subsequent developments of his critique: *Et leges et sceptra terit* (He treads on both the law and the scepter)."[90] By contrast, as may scholars have noted, Le Page du Pratz describes the Natchez as very much subject to a sovereign and to a religion. "The sovereigns were despotic and had a long time ago established the gruesome custom of having a number of their people die along with them."[91] "These peoples were raised in such perfect submission to their sovereign that the authority that they exert over them is a true despotism that can be compared only to those of the first Ottoman emperors."[92] In contrast to the

Canadian tribes, which were reputedly more democratic, Louisiana tribes became, for European readers, examples of oppression by ruler. To what extent was this view accurate? According to Daniel Usner, "Natchez political organization was not static but it adapted to circumstances and in relation to other groups"; it was indeed "one of the few centralized chiefdoms left in the Lower Mississippi Valley by the eighteenth century," in contrast to tribes whose government was more dispersed.[93] Whether or not this government was more despotic, Enlightenment *philosophes* in particular used the Natchez as handy examples for their rhetorical purposes. Le Page du Pratz, however, was not their only source of information. The *Encyclopédie,* for example, associates the Natchez specifically with a despotic system in the entry "Natchez" (mistakenly printed as "Matchez") and with Louisiana more generally in the entry "Despotisme." Both articles were written by the chevalier de Jaucourt, and both borrow material from Montesquieu's *De l'esprit des lois* (1748), which in turn quotes from the Jesuit letters concerning their missions around the world, published as *Lettres édifiantes et curieuses* (1702–76).

One of these two borrowings from Jesuit sources is found in the article "Despotisme": after giving examples of Asian and Middle Eastern rulers, Jaucourt turns to North America: "When the savages of Louisiana want some fruit, they cut the tree at the base and pick the fruit."[94] The point of this anecdote within the context of the article is that, Jaucourt explains, under despotic rule the monarch owns all property, so his people neglect to work the land: "In countries where the prince declares himself heir and owner of his subjects' assets, the result is necessarily the abandonment of the cultivation of the land: everything becomes wilderness, everything there is deserted."[95] And Jaucourt credits his fellow Enlightenment philosopher Montesquieu for this example: "'There you have the despotic government,' says the author of *The Spirit of the Laws.*"[96] And indeed, the passage in question is found in *De l'esprit des lois;* however, it was useful for Jaucourt to explain the connection between the wasteful tree-cutting and despotism, because in Montesquieu's text that passage sits isolated as its own minuscule chapter, which I quote in full:

> *Idea of despotism.*
> When the savages of Louisiana want some fruit, they cut the tree at the base and pick the fruit. There you have a despotic government.[97]

There is no clear connection between this story and the political lesson we are supposed to draw from it in Montesquieu. And if we look further into its original source, we see that in fact it illustrates the disadvantages of anarchy, not of despotism.

The quotation from Montesquieu refers to the *Lettres édifiantes,* specifically the 1712 letter in which the père Marest, Jesuit, describes the Illinois tribe in disapproving terms. It is extremely difficult to convert these Natives into Christians, he says, because "first we must make them into men." They are "absolute masters of themselves, without being subjected to any law"; consequently "the independence in which they live subjugates them to the most brutal passions."[98] And once the Jesuit establishes that these Natives live without government or laws, he mentions that "our savages are not accustomed to pick fruit from trees; they believe it is better to cut down the trees themselves: this is the reason why there are almost no fruit trees in the vicinity of the villages."[99] However, it is unclear whether this passage is meant to illustrate the complete chaos in which they live or is simply a description of the terrain that explains the absence of fruit trees near settlements. The latter is a more likely explanation, given that the passage appears ten pages after the discussion of their lack of government but immediately after the descriptions of the available fruits and pecans.

The second quotation about Louisiana Natives in the *Encyclopédie,* under "Matchez," concerns the Natchez tribe specifically: "If one is to believe the accounts, the government of these savage peoples is despotic. Their chief disposes of the property of all his subjects and makes them work at his whim. They cannot even refuse him their head."[100] Because the word *despotism* is so closely tied in eighteenth-century thought with "Oriental" (Middle Eastern and Asian) governments, the references to this part of the world are numerous, even in this article about North American Natives. In regard to the Great Sun, "you would say he is the great Sesostris," an Egyptian king, and "this chief is treated in his hut to the ceremonies that one would conduct for an emperor of Japan or China."[101] Why this recourse to Oriental despotism, when there were much nearer examples at hand? Because French philosophers were punished if they discussed the excesses of monarchical rule in their own country or even in Europe.

Much of this *Encyclopédie* article "Matchez" is copied from the chapter "Force de la superstition" in *De l'esprit des lois.*[102] In this chapter, Montesquieu muses about "a people of Louisiana named the Natchez": "Their chief disposes of the property of all his subjects and makes them work at his whim [...]. The prejudices of superstition are superior to all other prejudices and its reasons superior to all other reasons. Thus even though the savage peoples do not naturally know despotism, this one knows it. They worship the sun, and if their chief had not imagined that he was the brother of the sun, they would have found him to be just another wretch like them."[103] We can presume that Jaucourt thought the idea that it was superstition that kept people under the power of their leader, because he had persuaded them that his status was divinely ordained, was important enough to repeat. In reality, he was merely an ordinary man. Clearly, this idea was not just specific to Oriental despotism but also to the king of France, who supposedly ruled by divine right since, according to legend, his ancestor Clovis received the anointing oil from the Holy Spirit in the form of a bird. Also, *philosophes* like Jaucourt and Montesquieu had lived under the shadow of the previous king, Louis XIV, who took the sun as his emblem, though without the literal meaning it had among the Natchez.[104]

Montesquieu took his information once again from the Jesuit *Lettres édifiantes,* this time a letter by père Le Petit. What strikes Le Petit as the most terrible aspect of the despotism of the Natchez is the ritual of mass suicide that follows the death of a chief. He links superstition with despotism in that it allows the chief to keep his people in thrall: "The credulity of people maintain him in the despotic authority that he gives himself."[105] As a result, "One of the main articles of their religion, especially for the servants of the big chief, is to honor his funeral rites by dying with him to go serve him in the next world [. . .] as soon as a presumptive heir is born to the big chief, each family who has a nursing infant must pay homage to him. Among all these children, a certain number of them is chosen to serve the young prince [. . .] if he dies, all the servants self-immolate with joy in order to follow their master."[106] Le Petit points out that in this polygamist society the chief's wives also sacrifice themselves and their children. Specifically, after the chief's brothers and sisters have let themselves be killed, the chief's wives are next in line. They are exempted if they are nursing a baby, but some of these women "strangle their children themselves in order not to lose the right to self-immolate on the spot, according to the ordinary ceremonies and just as the law commands."[107] Paradoxically, however, this evidence Le Petit gives of "despotism" is not true to the definition of the word, which involves a ruler who disregards laws and traditions for an arbitrary rule. In the *Encyclopédie* article "Despotisme," Jaucourt copies Montesquieu's idea that "the principle of despotic states is that one single prince governs according to his will, without any law at all that dominates him, other than his whims."[108] But in the accounts of Natchez rites, it is nowhere implied that the chief departs from the time-honored traditions, as horrifying as they may be to Europeans. In the passage above, Le Petit even mentions that these women kill themselves and their children "according to the ordinary ceremonies" and "just as the law commands," not at all according to the caprice of their leader.

How, then, do we interpret the attention devoted to these scenes of ritual mass suicide in the pages of Le Petit and of Le Page du Pratz (and other explorers), which in turn become examples of so-called despotism in Enlightenment political theory? Are they exaggerated visions of a monarchy taken to an excessive point? Are they indirect critiques—unconscious on the part of the religious Le Petit (though Jesuits had a contentious relationship to European monarchs) but more conscious on the part of the secular Le Page du Pratz—of monarchy in general? Are the deaths actually metaphors for what the subjects of a king give up for him—money, rights, liberties?

What does Le Page du Pratz contribute to these reflections about Natchez mass suicides? In his extended discussion of the topic, two Enlightenment principles are at conflict: on the one hand, the reformer in him tries to persuade the Natchez to change their tradition; on the other hand, the cultural relativist in him represents to us their point of view. First, he gives us the chilling details of the rituals in which members of the chief's entourage and close family submit to being killed by their own family members. He also deplores the number of people the tribe loses each time a chief dies, and we know from current scholarship that at this point, this tribe's number had been severely reduced in the preceding centuries. Le Page du Pratz then recounts his conversation with one of the chief's wives and, if we are to believe him, transcribes the woman's long speech in defense of her own suicide. She appears to us readers as a dignified, rational person, which destabilizes our certainty about right and wrong.

Some forty years later, when the Revolution was approaching, Raynal would be much more explicit in his secondhand account of the Natchez ruler, making parallels between him and Louis XIV more obvious. "Among these nations, the most remarkable was that of the Natchez. It obeyed a man named Great Sun [...]. Governing, war, religion: everything depended on him. Perhaps the whole globe could not have offered a more absolute sovereign."[109] The concerns about the "la police" (which at this time also meant "governing") and religion seem more relevant to the French king than to the Natchez one, since the Natchez had only one religion, while the Bourbons often persecuted Protestants and dissidents. Also, Louis XIV established the first modern police force to serve at his will.

Raynal follows this remark with an ambiguously worded description of what happens to the royal entourage at the death of their leader: "When he died, he or his wife, it was necessary for many of their subjects to end their career, to go serve them in the other world."[110] On the surface, if Raynal is describing what happens to the Natchez, it is obvious that he is using *carrière* fancifully to mean the course of the person's life, which ends, as we know, in ritual suicide. However, *carrière* can also have the more common meaning of work trajectory, so this sentence would refer to the ambitions of French courtiers; the "other world" might be exile in the provinces, a common punishment for the partisans of a ruler who dies.

The culminating point of this section is when Raynal discusses to what excesses citizens go to prove their loyalty to their despot:

> The religion of the Natchez limited itself to the adoration of the sun, but this belief was accompanied by a lot of worship and consequently followed by bad effects. However, there was only one temple for the whole nation. It caught fire one day from the flame that was maintained perpetually or at least habitually, and there was general consternation. They made vain efforts to stop the fire. Some mothers threw their children into it, and the fire finally went out. Praise for these barbarian heroines was pronounced the next day by the despotic pontiff. That is how he reigned. One is astonished that such a poor and savage people is so subjugated, but superstition explains everything that reason finds inconceivable. It alone could take liberty away from men who have little else to lose than their liberty.[111]

In this passage, Raynal can show how superstition and blind loyalty lead to actions that go against reason and natural feelings like maternal love.

Whether or not the Natchez's mass suicides were a consequence of living in a despotic state, the presence of this tribe in Enlightenment political thought did not necessarily match the historical reality. From archeological and documentary evidence, Jayur Mehta finds that the principal Natchez Sun may have held something like absolute power in De Soto's time, circa 1540, but by the eighteenth century, even before the 1729 revolt, this monarch was severely weakened. Mehta points out also that the Natchez were a more heterogeneous people and a looser political confederation than French explorers portrayed them to be.[112] If this is so, then Le Page du Pratz and other Frenchmen's exaggerated visions of this tribe surely came from their projections, based on their own experience, of what a monarchy was.

Raynal Defies Censorship

I will not delve into other aspects of Le Page du Pratz's writing since other scholars have already covered his depiction of the 1729 Native uprising and his inhumane description of enslaved Africans. My aim in this chapter has been to demonstrate how travelers to Louisiana negotiated reporting what they saw as the truth and protecting their position vis-à-vis the government, which had the power to punish them. After Louisiana was no longer French, a transfer that I discuss in the next chapter, the most extreme criticism of Louisiana policy appeared in print, by Raynal. This Enlightenment author attacked the folly of looking for gold in the Mississippi valley in the first place, then agreed with Charlevoix that the cultivation of natural resources could have made the colony prosperous, but it had been neglected. Unlike Charlevoix and Le Page du Pratz, Raynal allows himself to rant openly about the exclusion of Protestants in the French colonies. He rails against both the king and the Catholic Church for preventing a host of useful citizens from improving Louisiana. He even dares to apostrophize the king:

> And you, blind tyrant! because your priests do not have the persuasive arts that would make their reasons triumph; because they cannot erase from the spirit of the innocents the profound traces that education etched there; because these do not want to be cowardly, nor hypocritical, nor ignoble; because they prefer to obey their God rather than you, you have to dispossess them, to put them in chains, to burn them, to hang them, to drag their cadavers over a rack. [...]
> [...] The misfortune of the state was that the superstition of Louis XIV, that the weakness of the regent, made them reject these proposals.[113]

Raynal's bold, direct reproaches to the king of France and to the clergy illustrate how far Charlevoix and Le Page du Pratz could have gone, but then they would have suffered consequences. Rather than being imprisoned as the undiplomatic governor Lamothe-Cadillac was or exiled as Lahontan and Raynal were, the explorers treated in this chapter let readers understand their Enlightenment ideas, while still managing to survive in the ancien régime.

3

Louisiana Finds Its Voice

The Revolt of 1768

The preceding chapters describe an antagonistic dialogue between government propaganda and a counterdiscourse that includes satirical songs and covert critiques. In the 1760s, a bolder form of counterdiscourse emerges, this time from the colonists themselves, who publicly resist imperial orders. These Louisiana residents wrote manifestos in an attempt to have some say about who owned the colony and about who would impose their version of the truth. Their revolt in 1768 is now nearly forgotten except by historians of Louisiana, yet their actions and their written demands can be seen as a daring intermediary step between the political theory of the Enlightenment and the final overthrow of imperial monarchy that would occur later in the American, Haitian, and French revolutions. Once the insurgents had carried out their revolt and waited for the imperial governments' response, they "actually considered an end to their colonial situation and proclaiming their independence." "They were the first settlers to envision such a radical measure," Cécile Vidal remarks.[1] In this chapter, I recount the events that led up to the revolt, how the insurgents expressed their grievances and their political role vis-à-vis the king, and finally how the revolt was put down, but not forgotten.

First, the background. The Seven Years' War (1756–63), also known as the French and Indian War, redrew the map of European possessions in North America. In the peace treaties, France abandoned claims to Louisiana: from this point on, the area east of the Mississippi River belonged to Britain and the area west of the river, along with the city of New Orleans, belonged to Spain. There is a general agreement among historians that France renounced Louisiana and most of Canada because these lands were not only expensive to defend against Indians and neighboring European powers but also far from profitable. The colonies that France did hold on to were the sugar-producing Caribbean islands of Saint-Domingue, Guadeloupe, Martinique, and Santa Lucia and two small Canadian islands,

Saint-Pierre and Miquelon. The European powers agreed to this division in the secret Treaty of Fontainebleau, signed on November 3, 1762, and in the publicly promulgated Treaty of Paris, signed on February 15, 1763. It now remained for the king of France to inform the inhabitants of Louisiana that they were no longer French subjects. His letter, dated April 21, 1764, reached Louisiana on September 10 of that year.

The letter was not received well by the inhabitants. The colony was already in a state of unrest for various reasons, mostly related to its desperate lack of cash, French food staples, and other supplies. Until then, colonists had also lacked security against Native raids and existed in a state of near lawlessness.[2] The news of the cession caused such indignation among the inhabitants that they assembled to discuss how to persuade France to reverse its decision. This was the beginning of the revolt that would be violently put down only in 1769. At an assembly in January 1765, several people emerged as leaders, notably the attorney general, Nicolas Chauvin de La Frénière; the commissary, Nicolas Foucault; and Jean Milhet, the wealthiest merchant of the city. They met as members of the local governing body, the Conseil Supérieur (Superior Council), which now assumed a more powerful role than the French government had originally granted it.

After a long delay following the signing of the peace treaties, Spain appointed Antonio de Ulloa, a scientist of great renown, as the new governor of Spanish Louisiana. This reclusive intellectual with little charisma was ultimately a terrible choice for the position.[3] The Spanish government's misjudgment was compounded by another error, that of sending with him a scant military escort of approximately ninety men. When he arrived in March 1766, he delayed the ceremony of official transfer until more troops arrived, which resulted in a period of uncertain leadership: was Louisiana still French, or was it already under Spanish rule? The rebels would exploit this state of affairs in order to claim that they had not broken any Spanish law, since no Spanish government had been officially instituted.

On January 20, 1767, Ulloa decided to take formal possession of Louisiana, but in a secret ceremony at La Balise, a French fortress at the tip of what is now Plaquemines Parish.[4] The secrecy of this act would later be mentioned by rebels as a sign of despotism. Ulloa then remained in La Balise to wait for his fiancée, a Peruvian noblewoman who did not speak French, to arrive. After their wedding, they led a reclusive life, especially during her ensuing pregnancy, and they even worshipped at their private chapel. Locals would interpret the couple's absence from public view as disdain for the French. (By contrast, later Spanish officers and administrators would marry French Creole women, thus cementing the social connection between the two populations.) Ulloa's behavior further incensed an already angry population, and plans for an armed insurrection began to take shape.

After the Superior Council issued a number of letters of protest to the French government without receiving satisfaction, conspirators such as Joseph Villeré went to the countryside, into enclaves of German farmers and of newly arrived Acadians, to persuade them to rally in New Orleans on the designated day.[5] These threatening crowds marched into the city on October 28 and 29, 1768, yelling "Vive le Roi de France, vive Louis le bien-aimé!," cheering for Louis XV, who was known as the "Well-Beloved." At this time, Ulloa, along with his wife and baby, immediately retreated to a ship that would eventually take them to Cuba; from there, another would take them to Spain. The distressed former French governor, Charles-Philippe Aubry, described the events in a report to Versailles as "a general conspiracy" and "a general revolt of all the inhabitants of the colony, against the government and its nation, which broke out suddenly on October 28 and 29."[6] In more detail, he recounts that "there were about nine hundred armed men from both the city and the countryside, led by all the militia officers, with a white banner that they displayed in one place, all yelling together 'Long live France' and saying that they did not want any other king. They even appeared disposed to make the Spanish fear for their lives, if their demands had not been listened to."[7] The banner mentioned was surely the white flag with gold fleur-de-lys that represented France under the Bourbon regime, though a blue flag with gold fleur-de-lys sometimes also represented pre-revolutionary France. Their strategy was apparently to show passionate loyalty to the king of France, while defying his decision to give up the territory to Spain.

After Ulloa's retreat, the rebels celebrated victory and prepared a delegation to represent their interests at Versailles. They issued a proclamation in which they justified their actions to the king of France. Several sources specify that an initial document was published by the official printer, Denis Braud, and signed by more than five hundred citizens but that it was later amended and reprinted. This new version was taken to France by a delegation sent by the Superior Council. The mission to Versailles was unsuccessful, for the delegates from Louisiana were not even able to see the king himself. The *Gazette d'Amsterdam* sympathetically reports from Paris on May 5 that the "deputies of the residents of Louisiana, commissioned to take the tears and the respectful supplications of the colony to the foot of the throne, [. . .] have orders to express the unanimous vow of their fellow citizens to live and die as *Frenchmen*" (emphasis in the original).[8] However, this journal also reports the same week that the Louis XV and his entourage had left Versailles to spend several weeks at the palace of Marly. The deputies then resorted to asking prominent nobles to intercede for them with the king "so that His Majesty deigns to take them under his protection and always see them as his faithful subjects."[9] Meanwhile, the duc de Choiseul, chief minister, considered their request and after some initial hesitation decided to maintain the primacy of the Pacte de Famille (Family Pact) with Bourbon Spain over the demands of the colonists.

The historian John P. Moore remarks that even though the delegation failed to persuade the French government to keep Louisiana under French rule, it did stir up a measure of sympathy among some French merchants, journalists, and *philosophes*. We see remnants of this feeling during the next few decades, most notably in Raynal's *Histoire des deux Indes* but also in the memoirs of French officials who traveled to Louisiana, such as Baudry de Lozières and Champigny, and even up to the Napoleonic era, especially in the writings of future governor Pierre-Clément de Laussat, as I explore in subsequent chapters.

Meanwhile, the Spanish government considered various possible responses to the crisis, finally deciding to send the Irish-Spanish general Alejandro O'Reilly to take control of the situation. King Carlos III gave him a free hand in establishing order and granted a contingent of about twenty-one hundred soldiers to accompany him. Upon their arrival in August 1769, O'Reilly called for an investigation and trials for the rebels. He had twelve of them executed, including the purported leader, La Frénière. Thus began the era of uncontested Spanish rule in Louisiana, which lasted a little more than thirty years.

These events have been extensively documented by the historians John P. Moore, Alcée Fortier, Marc de Villiers du Terrage, Vicente Rodríguez Casado, and Carl Brasseaux, among others. As Carl Brasseaux remarks, in reading accounts of the rebellion it is necessary to disentangle the pro-Spanish from the pro-French primary sources, even in more recent scholarship.[10] Most historians who write about these events depend on Charles Gayarré's 1846 *Histoire de la Louisiane*,[11] even though he is heavily biased toward the interests of his ancestor Esteban Gayarré, a Spanish military officer who was present during the rebellion. Furthermore, Charles Gayarré quotes from documents of the period without giving any references, thus making them impossible to confirm. Meanwhile, other narrations of the events obviously favor the colonists, such as the 1904 account by Alcée Fortier, who very subjectively asserts that the colonists "resisted oppression, and their spirit was highly patriotic. They were not impelled by fear of losing their commerce, but primarily by love for France, and then by a worthy spirit of independence. We, their descendants, admire their feelings and admire their heroism."[12] Other historians dispute Fortier's idealistic belief that the rebels were motivated by patriotism. John P. Moore, for example, explains the events as largely motivated by economic interest. Whatever the true intentions of these rebels may have been, it is still important, as Vidal argued recently, to examine how they presented themselves and how they attempted to persuade others to favor their cause.[13]

As I demonstrated in chapter 1, in the early years of the colony, especially in the 1720s, people who traveled to Louisiana, those who feared to be sent there, and those who invested in the colony expressed skepticism toward the government's information machine. They used satire to disrupt the government propaganda about a prosperous colony inhabited by happy settlers. Four decades later, rebellious settlers tried to seize control of the colonial narrative by other means. They spoke for themselves, using their eloquence to persuade the king to meet their demands and manipulating information in order to gather more support among the public.

The Beginnings of Colonial Eloquence

The fact that the rebels expressed themselves collectively, in correct French, and with rational argumentation was in itself a novelty for this colony. Until this point, the voices "heard" from Louisiana had belonged to French travelers or other people based in France. When we look in the archives, we see that individuals who lived in the colony itself sent handwritten letters to French officials, for example, merely to claim a piece of property or to request a pension: it was not a collective expression concerning anything political. As we saw in the previous chapter, Native American oral eloquence had been showcased by Le Page du Pratz, and it had made a mark in works of fiction and nonfiction of the past decades, but it was reported in secondhand fashion. What was new about the eloquence that emerged from the 1768 revolt was that it came from the colonists, it appeared in published form, and it addressed the general public.[14] The manifestos of the rebellion, issued by the Superior Council, claimed to represent all Louisianians, at least those of European descent. With regard to the Farge-esque "voix du peuple," it is significant that the first version of the manifesto was reportedly signed by more than five hundred inhabitants. If this was true, one could assume that the council did speak for some sort of collectivity.

The colony had come a long way since the second decade of the eighteenth century, when, as Marcel Giraud states, it was nearly impossible to fill certain administrative posts for lack of educated individuals. "In Louisiana, where education is not widespread, where the population has no means of instruction,"[15] the governor had to recruit practically illiterate people for the offices of judge, notary, and clerk of court. By the 1760s, however, members of the Louisiana elite had achieved a level of education beyond mere literacy. As we will see in their entreaties to the king, they were able not only to use standard spelling (a rarity at the time) and legal argumentation but also to elaborate rhetorical tropes and an awareness of the new, subversive ideas in political theory. Vidal remarks, "Drawing on Hugo Grotius, Samuel von Pufendorf, and, most of all, Emer de Vattel," one of their manifestos "contained a long philosophical, juridical, and political argument intended to justify the insurgents' actions on the basis of natural law."[16] These were the same theorists whose ideas about a contractual relationship between the king and his people were popularized by authors such as Montesquieu and Rousseau.

Also by the 1760s, we see the first generation of native-born colonists, whose families had amassed some amount of wealth and privilege, occupying the seats of local power. As Vidal points out, "When Louisiana was ceded to Spain and Great Britain in 1762–63, the first generation of Creole elites, that is, those born locally, had just started to inherit the property of their parents and to occupy the posts of responsibility in the colony, in the place of the officers who were natives of the metropole."[17] These Louisianians' social ascent made it possible for them to take a stand politically and to justify their resistance verbally. At this juncture, the members of the Louisiana elite had to ask themselves whether it was in their interest to label themselves as a group distinct from the metropolitan French. Vidal explains that "with 'Louisianais,' the insurgents conceived of an ethno-label that not only expressed how their relationship to the place where they lived had evolved but that also allowed for the development of a new kind of patriotism, independent from the metropole, should the crown refuse to grant their demands. At the same time, their decision not to call themselves Creoles signaled a desire to continue to claim their Frenchness."[18] Another decision was to identify themselves as *Louisianais,* while excluding other residents who were of Native or African descent. Vidal remarks that slaves, for example, "were not included in this process of identification, which only served to strengthen the cohesion of whites," as we will see in their writings.[19]

The story of Nicolas Chauvin de La Frénière the younger perfectly exemplifies the rise of the Louisiana-born elites. His father and three uncles had been French Canadian *voyageurs,* or roaming fur traders, named Chauvin, who accompanied the royal administrator Pierre Le Moyne d'Iberville to Louisiana.[20] These four Chauvin brothers took on additional names in order to distinguish among themselves. Nicolas the elder, who had reputedly trained as a miller, took the name Chauvin de la Frénière. He was appointed to the Superior Council in 1717, but several French officials objected to his scant education.[21] Marcel Giraud finds in letters from Governor Lamothe-Cadillac and the *ordonnateur,* Hubert, that they "deplore [...] the need to give the role of councilors" to people like the "'former miller's apprentice' La Fresnière, who is practically illiterate and not worthy of the dignity of a Superior Council."[22] Nevertheless, La Frénière took a seat on the council and remained there for many years.

When Bienville established New Orleans, the Chauvin brothers were granted plots of land, which they transformed into prosperous farms. Chauvin de La Frénière married in 1724 and had a son, the future rebel leader, also named Nicolas, whom he sent to France to be trained in the law. La Frénière the younger returned and became attorney general, or *procureur général,* of Louisiana in 1763. In two generations, then, we see one family go from wandering the forests to enjoying a position of relative wealth, education, and power. Far from representing an isolated example of social ascent, La Frénière was part of an interrelated group of families that rose together through marriage and business ties. As Emilie Leumas demonstrates, many members of this nascent elite played major roles in the insurrection.[23] This situation recalls Wim Klooster's observation about revolutions, that they were led not by the populaces but by local elites, though he does not include Louisiana in his comparative study.[24]

Now that the rebels were educated enough to speak out for the first time, they also had the ability to print their opinions and therefore distribute them to a larger audience, including a metropolitan one. Denis Braud, a New Orleans merchant, had come forward in 1764 to request royal permission to be Louisiana's first official printer, presumably to issue decrees for the government. He received approval, but, ironically, the earliest texts of his that have survived are the rebel manifestos.[25] During the 1769 crackdown, O'Reilly had Braud arrested along with the leaders of the insurrection. Significantly, Braud's role in the rebellion was ambiguous enough for him to be acquitted: he claimed that he had merely printed what local officials ordered him to print.[26] After the rebellion, the printing press once again returned to the use that the French government had surely originally intended, which was to promulgate its own decrees to the people, in a top-down form of communication. For the brief period of 1768–69, however, the printing press accomplished what modern scholars see as its revolutionary role during the late eighteenth century, which was to subvert government discourse.

In the Rebels' Words

In the period just before the revolt, then, we see letters and reports documenting the emergence of public oratory in Louisiana by leaders such as La Frénière. These speeches given in the Superior Council became solidified, so to speak, in the printed manifestos. Of the numerous statements issued by the council before and after the march on New Orleans, one handwritten and two printed ones still remain accessible to us.

1. The manuscript "Très-humbles représentations qu'adressent au Roi notre très-honoré et souverain seigneur, les gens tenant conseil supérieur à la Nouvelle-Orléans" (Most humble remonstrances that the people who conduct the Superior Council in New Orleans address to the king, our very honored and sovereign lord).
2. The printed text that has no title but begins with the words "Louis, par la grâce de Dieu" (Louis, by the grace of God).
3. The printed *Mémoire des habitans et négocians, de la Louysiane sur l'événement du 29 octobre 1768* (Statement by the residents and merchants of Louisiana on the event of October 29, 1768).[27]

Texts 2 and 3 are printed together. The published texts were at once appeals to the French government and open letters to the public. The purported reader is Louis XV, but the fact that many more copies were printed and distributed means that the true intended readership was more extensive. For example, copies of the *Mémoire des habitans* can be found in many libraries in North America, Nantes, Poitiers, and Paris. This distribution, as well as written reactions to the manifestos, suggests that the rebels' complaints reached a wide range of readers, including English speakers and people in the French provinces.

I will analyze the use of rhetoric in the *Mémoire,* with occasional reference to the other statements. This text is given the most weight by historians, and it was treated by O'Reilly as the most dangerous, perhaps because it was the most widely disseminated. It has no attributed author, though Governor Aubry and others pointed to La Frénière.[28] From the first sentence of the *Mémoire,* the language of emotion seizes the reader's attention: "Ocular witnesses of the calamities that afflict us, the magistrates of the Superior Council of Louisiana have not been able to refuse any longer to listen to the plaintive cries of an oppressed people."[29] The elevated register would surely recall, to readers of the period, the language of classic French tragedies. We can see not only the style but also the imagery of this beginning as attempts to appeal to the readers' *sensibilité*. The first sentence draws attention to the collective narrators, who are the members of the council and who refer to themselves in the third person as "magistrates," who are distinct from the rest of the *peuple*. Using figurative language, the "magistrates" present themselves as the rational but worried caretakers of the baby-like people, who are clamoring for the love of their parent, the king of France. They continue: "Their diligent cares were not limited to calming the anxieties of a groaning people. They have also authorized them to carry their supplications and their desires to the foot of the throne, being well persuaded that the compassionate look of their natural sovereign would rest upon such devoted subjects and that their respectful love for their monarch would not be rejected by his beneficent Majesty, the image on earth for his people of the preserving Being."[30] Even though later in the text the authors intersperse passages of more sober argumentation to prove their own legal competence, they place emotional expressions like the ones above especially at the beginning and end of the *Mémoire*. Several of the themes announced in this passage recur in other writings related to the revolt of 1768. In particular, we will see how the rebels manipulate the words *love, natural,* and *father* to fit their circumstances.[31]

The emotion of love between children and fathers is particularly important in the context of European monarchy because it had been invoked in treatises to justify a king's power over his subjects. As Fanny Cosandey and Robert Descimon remark, the "extrapolation or analogy" was "an essential reference to the natural and reciprocal love between the prince-fathers and the subjects-children."[32] The relationship had both affectionate and punitive implications. The Louisiana rebels were both submissive and subversive by throwing back to their leaders the language of paternalism once used by apologists of absolutist monarchy, from Jean Bodin to Jacques-Bénigne Bossuet.[33] When the Louisianians are "claiming back our laws, our country, our sovereign, to vow to him the perseverance of our love"[34] they are demanding the love that was promised in traditional royal discourse but also reminding Louis XV of his duties.

In contrast to the language of emotion and the father-child metaphor in the letters that the council addressed to the king, the documents relating to the transfer issued by the king and his ministers express no love for the people. Instead, more sentiments are expressed in the peace treaty between Sa Majesté Très Chrétienne (i.e., the king of France) and Su Majestad Católica (i.e., the king of Spain), these cousins from the House of Bourbon who were bound by diplomatic agreement and by blood in the Pacte de Famille. In the secret Treaty of Fontainebleau, by which the French offered Louisiana to the Spanish, the first alleged motive for the transfer is not to end the Seven Years' War but "tender friendship": "The most Christian King, with the firm resolution to strengthen more and more and to perpetuate the ties of tender friendship that unite him to the most Catholic King, his cousin [. . .]"[35] Meanwhile, in the same document, the French subjects living in Louisiana are only mentioned briefly at the end, in terms of their "evacuation," or presumably that of the military outposts.[36] The official response from King Carlos III of Spain uses affectionate language equal to that of Louis XV, whom he addresses as "my very dear and very beloved cousin."[37] Carlos III attributes Louis XV's offer of Louisiana to "the pure effect of the nobility of his heart and of the love and friendship in which we live."[38] But neither king would offer such affectionate words to his subjects.

When Louis XV has an official letter sent to Governor D'Abbadie on April 21, 1764, to announce the transfer to his subjects, "love" still glows between the two kings, while the subjects remain in a colder emotional territory. The French king explains to the Louisiana governor that "my very dear and very beloved cousin"[39] accepted the colony in a treaty and that he hopes the "friendship and affection of his Catholic Majesty" will mean that he does not make changes to its religious institutions.[40] As for the people, there is a lesser concern for their property: "May the residents be guarded and maintained in their possessions."[41] The king adds, "Hoping, furthermore, that His Majesty will be willing to give to his new subjects in Louisiana the same marks of protection and benevolence that they have experienced under my domination."[42] Not only does the French king mention protecting the interests of the colonists at the end of the letter but also, as if it were something extra ("au surplus"), as an afterthought, he merely expresses the hope that the Spanish king will do this, but without any real force to back up this hope.

Undaunted by this coldness, the authors of the *Mémoire des habitans* make a plea for the king's love. In fact, they cite the letter to the French governor D'Abbadie at length and, either deliberately or naïvely, read much more paternal love into it than is warranted by the text itself: "Our great

King, in his letter that announces it to us, seemed to foresee our alarms. He [...] caused us to hope from him the same marks of kindness and protection that one enjoys under his cherished domination. Those august sentiments must embolden our love."[43] Surely, they presume, a "natural" sovereign and/or father would not reject its child; they are "well persuaded that the compassionate look of their natural sovereign would rest upon such devoted subjects."[44] The expression "natural sovereign" (Souverain naturel) suggests, in the newly Rousseau-infused mentalities of the 1760s, at once a metaphorically biological tie and the emotions that presumably emerge from this relationship. In an older sense, the expression refers to an acceptance of monarchy as a natural form of government, as apologists for monarchy had tried to establish.

The writers then apostrophize the people, the metaphorical baby I mentioned earlier, and try to calm its fears, presuming that their "natural" sovereign will offer the "protection" of "his cherished domination" (sa *chère* domination), which will strengthen "our love."[45] Once again, on the same page, they mention the oxymoron: "this cherished domination under which we wish to live and to die."[46] The concept of a cherished domination, suggestive of masochism, can perhaps be explained by a passage in the manifesto "Louis, par la grâce de Dieu": "The wishes of the public have always matched the prince's choice, those of giving him chief command of Louisiana."[47] The idea implied is that the desires of the people and the desires of a good king will always coincide, though there is no provision for discrepancies or for the choices made by a bad king. The handwritten version of the first manifesto contains the phrase "The Frenchman is born free and submissive," another version of the "dear domination," as if the French citizen had, paradoxically, freely chosen his state of submission.[48]

During the rest of the *Mémoire*, the authors continue to refer to the natural, paternal aspect of the relationship between king and subjects. For example, they cite the precedent of cities and regions like Quercy, Gascogne, and Cahors, which refused English rule even when the French king had ceded them. In this instance, they are probably referring to an episode of the Hundred Years' War in which King Jean II of France ceded these southwestern areas in the 1360 Treaty of Brétigny but they refused to obey. The Louisiana magistrates treat this refusal as a show of loyalty, which ultimately is rewarded by indulgence: "That noble resistance to the will of the natural sovereigns, far from exciting their anger, has awakened their tenderness."[49] They evoke the scenario of the wayward youth, a prodigal son, who disobeys his father but ultimately finds paternal forgiveness.

A "natural" rapport between a king and his subjects implies both certain emotions and, more challenging for Louis XV, a tie that cannot be legitimately broken. In other words, if the connection between king and people is *natural*, as biological ties are, then how can they be changed? Is it possible to transfer fatherhood? Is the king acting against nature? The situation could be judged according to John Locke's *Two Treatises of Government*,[50] in which he maintained that if the king is like a father, then he cannot alienate his subjects to another king, any more than a father has the right to sell his children into slavery.[51] Furthermore, following Locke's analysis of the father-king analogy, if the people are a child, will they one day grow into adulthood and consequently deserve independence?[52]

Even while declaring their desire for submission, then, the New Orleans magistrates hint at more daring thoughts. As Vidal remarks, "All the statements, petitions, and letters sent to the metropole by the insurgents appeared to demonstrate a great attachment to Louis XV, from whom they seemed to expect a great deal, while at the same time, some of their remonstrances questioned his absolutist ambitions."[53] For example, they offer the possibility that other people can also act as father figures, in particular themselves: "Our governors and magistrates have always been regarded by us as our fathers."[54] Similarly, the manifesto "Louis, par la grâce de Dieu" referred to "a people whose Council is the father."[55]

In fact, the idea that intermediary powers between the king and the people could be regarded as fathers was hardly a new one. In particular, it had reemerged a few decades earlier in France, when the parlements were struggling to maintain their traditional powers against encroachments by the absolutist king. The members of the parlements called themselves the "fathers of the people," and they considered the different parlements, including the colonial ones, part of a whole entity that represented the French nation.[56] Vidal asserts that the Louisiana Superior Council made strategic use of the word *père* in their letters addressed to the parlements of various French cities, including Port-au-Prince, in order to signal their support of the anti-absolutist cause.[57] These two referents of the word *père*, the king and the members of the parlements, in two sets of documents, expose a certain duplicity in the council's rhetorical strategy. On the one hand, they called for Louis XV's paternal care; on the other, they appealed to those legislative bodies, the parlements, with whom the king was in a constant power struggle.

If both powers ignored the insurgents' appeals, there was a third option: the council could take one step further in its opposition to absolutism by acquiring full independence and establishing a republic. In fact, one 1769 news report suggests as much. An article from the *Gazette d'Amsterdam* claims that the Louisiana rebels are going to "go native." If they are forced to live under the Spanish regime, the article states, "the residents are determined to go join the savages, who live in liberty."[58] It is uncertain whether the journalist invented this or simply recorded the statements of the Louisiana delegation. Vidal also sees this possibility of independence: "Well aware of the feeble interest they offered and of the strong possibility that their request would not be heard, they warned the duc d'Orléans in veiled terms that their only recourse in case of refusal would be to 'live independently.'"[59] In this case, the rebellion would be better described as a revolution, according to our present-day definition.[60]

Meanwhile, the Louisianians considered seeking an alliance with another European power, Great Britain. In their letters to the king, for example, the authors make the claim that French Louisiana had acted as a buffer zone protecting the wealthy colony of Mexico from "S. M. B.," or Sa Majesté Britannique (His British Majesty). "The keeping of this colony by France protects better the possessions of Spain on this side than the cession made to that crown."[61] Now that France was withdrawing, they reasoned, there would be little to stand in the way of a British attack. While in the *Mémoire* they discussed Britain as the danger to be avoided, the Superior Council had secretly sent several delegations to the British officer in charge of West Florida, Brigadier Frederick Haldimand, to propose some sort of alliance or pact of protection. According to John P. Moore, Haldimand "flatly rejected" any such proposal,[62] but it is worth noting that the rebels were capable of double dealing in this matter.

In any case, in the *Mémoire* there is no open expression of desire for independence or alliances with Britain; instead, the authors ostensibly plead for a benevolent monarch who, out of affection, will take Louisiana back. They describe the contrast between the French king and the Spanish representative Ulloa in terms of the good father versus the bad father. In the manifestos, the paternalism represented by Ulloa connotes only the bad, punitive aspects of absolutist monarchy and none of the pleasant ones, such as love, indulgence, and protection.[63]

One area in which Ulloa allegedly fails is as a protector of his subjects' prosperity. As Cosandey and Descimon state, the king's role of "roi nourricier" (king and provider)[64] is one of his most important attributes during the ancien régime. And, these scholars remark, the economic theory that is most associated with French absolutism is mercantilism, or the state's promotion of its own citizens' commercial interests, usually as a monopoly within the empire: "The rapports between the absolutist and mercantilist doctrines seem to be at the heart of the political vision of the 'great king.'"[65] Accordingly, many pages of the *Mémoire* (we must not forget the *merchants* in the title) are devoted to complaints about the adverse effects that Spanish policy will have on the French citizens' economic activity. Even though they admit that the Spanish government has granted them ten years' reprieve before trading laws are changed in the colony, the rebels worry that old trading partnerships and routes will be severed by an imposition of Spanish laws, while French products will now have to compete with more abundant ones from Spanish colonies such as Guatemala.

Instead of nurturing their prosperity, hence their well-being, Ulloa represents the violent side of paternalist monarchy, according to the *Mémoire*. Even though he has not established his legitimate authority, "severe punishments, chastisements unknown under the French domination still existing, are inflicted already by his order for the lightest faults."[66] In the meantime, there is no love to offset the paternal punishments, so the inhabitants obey out of a formal duty, not out of loyalty: "No bond attaches us yet to his authority; nothing but a respectful deference for the character with which one sees him clothed promises to him our obedience."[67] Not explicitly rejecting the monarchical form of government, the *Mémoire* claims that perhaps the Spanish king himself would be a good leader, but this particular governor represents him badly. "The law of Spain may have its pleasing features and advantages that we do not know; but the antipathy to humanity and the natural disposition to do harm recognized in the person entrusted with presenting that law to us make us feel its hardest consequences."[68] For them, Ulloa represents only the "avenging sword"[69] of the law.

If, as the rebels claim, royal authority is being misused, the only conclusion to draw is that the situation will degenerate into tyranny. They are conscious that this is a daring word: "The term tyranny appears strong; let us add to it that of vexation, to correspond with the truth of the facts."[70] Although the rebels claim that they still respect the monarchy, one cannot avoid thinking that if they are capable of judging a king's representative to be inadequate and even tyrannical, what is to stop them from scrutinizing the king himself in the same way?

Already suspicious of backroom dealings that affected their own lives, the rebels are incensed at being forced into silence. They complain of an incident that involved the announcement of an *ordonnance;* they are angry at the manner of the announcement, with Spanish soldiers openly bearing their rifles and bayonets and a military drum playing, as if the citizens were enemies, not subjects. "Was it to insult us, or to impose silence upon our murmurs?"[71] ask the authors of the *Mémoire*. The people's "murmurs" are all the more justified, they claim, because the new Spanish regime "was diametrically opposed to our welfare, and capable at first sight of exciting our murmurs."[72] The authors' repetition of the word *murmur* is important because it evokes a kind of speech, specifically an oral expression of dissatisfaction. In this passage, the authors are describing a scenario of competing voices. The one "from above" is the Spanish decree that is imposed by its governor and loudly disseminated with a show of military force to back it up (however scarce and weak those troops may have been in reality). The one "from below" is the murmurs of the people, who can protest only under their breath. The authors express fear that even these weak expressions will be silenced by Ulloa.

The leitmotiv of rival voices appeared in the first passages of the *Mémoire*. If we return to the first sentences, we notice that expressions like "plaintive cries of an oppressed people" and "calming the anxieties of a groaning people" are aural, not visual, metaphors. These expressions of pain involve the human voice (as opposed to, for example, tears or scars), because one of the major stakes of the revolt was the right to speak out; it was a question of who could impose their words as the official truth—the government or its subjects.

It was almost as a parody of the kings of France and Spain that the rebellious Superior Council, granting itself special powers beyond its original function, also issued "official" statements. In Alcée Fortier's words, La Frénière demanded that decrees against Ulloa be "read, published, and registered" with "copies [. . .] sent to all the posts in the colony."[73] Accordingly, the new Spanish governor, O'Reilly, treated these decrees as challenges to the monarchical power he represented. When he arrived, he issued an official statement to the people of Louisiana, which was "published and posted throughout the city,"[74] announcing the establishment of the Spanish government in Louisiana. Meanwhile, he sought out the authors of the *Mémoire*, especially La Frénière, whom he presumed to be the principal author. One report to the Spanish government, which Fortier presents to us, mentions that before the authors were killed, the accusations and the sentences were "published in a loud voice by the public crier of this city."[75] Fortier mentions that a few days after the execution, all copies of the *Mémoire* were burned publicly. Not only does O'Reilly literally impose the voice of the new regime on the public space for all to submit to, he also destroys rival voices by burning manifestos and executing their authors.

The Rebels' Propaganda

The fear that governments were hiding information and lying to the people created a feeling of bitterness among the long-suffering colonists in Louisiana. In retaliation, I believe, the rebels of 1768 decided to act as they imagined their leaders did, by spreading disinformation.[76] They manipulated both oral and written language to try to achieve their ends. One example of what could be described as the Superior Council's paranoia can be seen in the *Mémoire,* specifically in its complaint that one Spanish official persuaded some inhabitants to give written statements in favor of Spanish rule: "We are not ignorant that the envoy from Spain took, before his departure, and is still gathering through emissaries certificates from some individuals who reside among us."[77] But, they claim, he only obtained these "hardly authentic certificates"[78] through deception. Furthermore, the Spanish government turned these inhabitants into "mercenary clients whom he attached to himself by brilliant promises, and who are here seeking to proselyte by persuading the simple and frightening the weak."[79] Nevertheless, "they will never belie the general voice and public notoriety."[80] This is how the rebels explain the existence of some Louisiana residents who agreed to Spanish rule. They portray these people as illegitimate exceptions to the popular will.

The Spanish contingent, in turn, blames the rebels for abusing the credulity of the public, as we will see in their accounts of the events. In one letter, a Spanish captain named Joseph Melchior de Acosta, who accompanied Ulloa, describes the *Mémoire* as a libel: "At this time, a slanderous libel appeared in public, entitled *Mémoire des habitants et négociants de la Louisiane* [. . .] which satirized and calumnied Mr. Antonio de Ulloa and the whole nation."[81] Even the acting governor Aubry, who tried to maintain a moderate stance toward both the rebels and the Spanish, declares, in a letter to the French government: "By the most audacious writings and most rebellious talk the conspirators had resorted to every means to excite the people and give them a horror of the Spanish government [with] decrees [. . .] memorials [. . . and] documents of iniquities."[82] O'Reilly also blames the rebels for their influence on the "public," claiming that they "abused its ignorance and its too great credulity."[83]

Exactly how, according to their opponents, did La Frénière, Villeré, Foucault, and the other conspirators manipulate their fellow Louisianians? The historian John P. Moore recounts that in one instance, in preparation for the October 28 insurgency, the rebel leaders won the favor of the Acadians and the German farmers by lying. He states that the rebels persuaded the first group "that the Spanish governor had a large amount of money in the treasury, some of which could be used to redeem the paper currency" they brought from Canada, and "they succumbed to the propaganda." As for the second group, "propaganda was also effective among the Germans living on the farms above the city. Rouget de Villeré, commandant of the district, convinced the farmers that the Spanish governor had no intention of paying for the fruits and vegetables purchased during the year. [. . .] the credulous colonists felt impelled to act."[84] Other sources, notably pro-Spanish ones, claim that after the events of October 28–29, the Germans realized they had been duped. Joseph Melchior de Acosta, mentioned earlier, reports that in the April after the rebellion one of the conspirators, named Caresse, returned to the German areas to persuade the inhabitants once again to take up arms to guard the port, but "these simple people" refused; "having been fooled for the first time, they did not want to experience being fooled a second time."[85]

Another type of propaganda campaign waged by the rebels was less about persuading people to participate in the uprising than about presenting Ulloa in a bad light. Several texts issued by the Superior Council took trivial or perhaps invented complaints and expressed indignation about them out of all reasonable proportion. One complaint involved tortillas; others had to do with Ulloa's private life and, remarkably, his overly humane treatment of the enslaved. Villiers du Terrage calls these complaints about Ulloa "exaggerations" and contrasts them to other complaints that are "a little more serious."[86] While these complaints sound absurdly petty in the context of international politics, they were designed to provoke a reaction from the inhabitants of Louisiana; at the same time, they were symbolic of the rebels' plight, as they perceived it.

It is remarkable that after making serious complaints about trade routes being severed and traders being arrested arbitrarily by Ulloa's forces, the Superior Council should turn to tortillas. In the open letter, "Louis, par la grâce de Dieu," the authors exclaim that the tyrannical trade policies will lead the colony to "humiliations" and extreme poverty: "to top off so many tribulations [. . .] eventually they will reduce the colonists of Louisiana to the simple nourishment of the tortilla, while they will never be subjected to the most sober foodstuffs."[87] This statement is an abbreviated version of a passage in the letter from the Superior Council that begins with "Très-humbles représentations": "The penury became so great that half of the colony was reduced to eating rice and corn, and without the wise precautions of Mr. Foucault, who had them delivered from the German coast, fathers and mothers would have had nothing but tears to offer to the plaintive cries of the starving child [...]. Sire, must your Superior Council tell you that your people are convinced that Mr. Ulloa [...] had decided to reduce your subjects to eating tortillas?"[88] The authors reproach the French king for allowing Ulloa to starve the inhabitants of Louisiana, and they insidiously point out that it was Foucault, one of their own fellow conspirators and *commis,* who managed to acquire food. The authors call for the king to play the role of father and provider since Ulloa has failed, notwithstanding the multiple occasions under French rule when the people of Louisiana had been reduced to eating only corn or very little else.

The specific choice of the tortilla as a symbol of penury may have to do with the perceived value of its principal ingredient, corn. It is necessary to distinguish what the people of Spain call a *tortilla,* a hearty quiche-like food that includes eggs and potatoes, and the Latin American *tortilla,* the thin disk of cornmeal cooked on a griddle. The richness of the Spanish tortilla and the simplicity of the Latin American tortilla lead us to presume that the colonists were complaining about the latter. The local grain, designated as *maïs, blé d'Inde,* and *blé de Turquie,* could have provided abundant food for the colonists, remarks Marcel Giraud. Yet they persisted in trying to grow what was familiar to them, wheat, with only disappointing results. "The colonists had difficulty detaching themselves from the habits of the French countryside. [...] they could not resign themselves to sacrifice wheat farming."[89] It is very possible that the persistence in eating bread made of wheat instead of corn had to do with the colonists' pride, specifically in their self-perception as free, White Europeans. Villiers notes that corn was actually considered "like the food of Blacks."[90] Steven L. Kaplan, in *The Bakers of Paris and the Bread Question, 1700–1775* remarks that a few thinkers had tried without success to persuade the French that their obsession with wheat bread was irrational, when other grains were easier to grow: "It was impossible for the French to conceive of their well-being [...] outside the confines imposed by the bread paradigm [...]. Even if there were other foods available, the *Encylopédie méthodique* reported, 'the bulk of the people believe that they are dying of hunger if they do not have bread.'"[91] In the later version of the manifesto, the *Mémoire,* the comment about the tortilla has disappeared. Did the council decide that the complaint was too trivial?

In any case, the point they made with the tortilla was that the new Spanish regime would threaten commerce; therefore, it would not only metaphorically starve the inhabitants but take away their bread, a cherished symbol of their French identity. Another important part of French identity, wine, also made an appearance in rebel propaganda. Ulloa reported in a letter that one of the conspirators, Noyan, had spread false news that Bordeaux wine would become unavailable and that it would be replaced by "the stinking wine of Catalonia."[92] Thus another element of Frenchness would be under threat.[93]

Related to the subject of nourishment and identity was another complaint, this time about Ulloa's choice of a nursemaid for his newborn child: "He rushed to characterize his antipathy by requesting a wet-nurse from Havana, so that his child would not suckle a single drop of French milk: what pernicious principles! What barbaric dispositions for governing French subjects!"[94] On a literal level, people of the early modern period believed that national character was the product of their environment, including air, earth, and food. Following ancients such as Hippocrates and Aristotle and early modernists such as Juan Huarte and the abbé Dubos, scientific theory held that each particular terrain produced certain substances that were passed on to plants, which in turn nourished the people nearby and gave them certain qualities native to the terrain; this process explained differences in national character.[95] If Ulloa decided that his child would consume milk from a Spanish Cuban rather than a Louisiana woman, he was denying his child the possibility of absorbing the local character. There would be no quasi-biological link between Ulloa's family and the people he would govern. Symbolically, this decision (whether it was true or merely alleged) was seen as just one more example of Ulloa's disdain for the local population, along with his worship in a private chapel and his general abstention from social events in New Orleans.

Even though the tortilla and the nursemaid comments do not make it into the printed *Mémoire,* one complaint remains in the latter version. The authors express great indignation that Ulloa has presided over the marriage between a free White man and an enslaved Black woman. "Furthermore, he has made his chaplain confer the sacrament of marriage upon two persons, of whom the woman was a negro slave and the man White, without the permission of the curate, without any publication of the banns, without any form or solemnity required by the church, contrary to the Council of Trent and contrary to the precise disposition of all ordinances, civil as well as canonical."[96] Why was the indignation so great? As I explain in the next section, the presence of the words *slave* and *Black* throughout the documents of the revolt tell us something about the colonists' own imagined status. We see that in the colonists' eyes, Ulloa's alleged elevation of the status of some enslaved people necessarily lowers their own: Ulloa "has most openly granted his protection to non-mutilated Blacks based on their simple complaints and without having ever heard their masters. What a dire reversal! Your subjects were threatened with enslavement, and their Blacks would acquire the status of free men."[97] They see this situation as a world upside down—the word they use is *bouleversement*. The concern over mixed marriages can be compared to the outrage over the report that Ulloa will not allow enslaved people to be whipped within the hearing distance of Madame Ulloa because it upsets her.[98] From our twenty-first-century perspective, it would seem that Ulloa angered the French colonists by treating enslaved people too fairly instead of treating the masters too despotically. However, while the council's sometimes petty accusations against Ulloa may appear unjust to us, they can explain how the colonists viewed, or wished to view, themselves.

Colonists or Colonized? Who "We" Are Not

To fight for the continued separation between White colonists and enslaved people was, for the former, a fight for subjectivity. In the Superior Council's documents, we see a constant insistence on distinguishing those of European descent from other types of people who, they suggest, deserve less of a political voice. They evidently feel the need to distinguish themselves even from animals, since a word that appears constantly in these manifestos is *joug* (yoke), as if the colonists accused the government of treating them like cattle.[99] Who were the people whose interests they claimed to represent? The insurgents were of French descent, some of them by way of Canada; one, Pierre Marquis, was of Swiss descent. They allied themselves with some Catholic immigrants from Germany, many of whom had settled in Louisiana in the time of John Law. Some of these did not even speak French, as we can see in the depositions they gave during the time of the revolt.[100] The insurgents also expressed solidarity with the Acadians, who had immigrated from the parts of Canada that were now in British hands.

The authors of the manifestos draw a line between this *peuple* and others they abhorred being mistaken for. Specifically, they mention the Natives previously colonized by the Spanish: when the council complains that Ulloa is trying to silence their "murmurs," they exclaim, "Did he take us for savages of Peru and Mexico?"[101] The *légende noire* (Black legend) of Spanish cruelty toward Indigenous peoples had surely raised the alarm of Louisiana colonists, but the implication in this passage is not that the

Spanish were generally unfair. The indignation seems to come from the idea that Ulloa could put the colonists of Louisiana in the same category as conquered people such as Incas and Aztecs.

The other people the council keeps at arm's length are the enslaved people of African descent. Colonists also had some Native American slaves, but in the manifestos they are referring to African ones and they also disregard free people of color. One of the major economic causes of discontent among the merchants of Louisiana was the limit that the Spanish would place on their importations of enslaved Africans. In calling for this restriction to be removed, the insurgents claim that colonists have a "natural" right to buy other humans. Since their prosperity depends on this source of labor, they see it as a metaphorical kind of nourishment for the Louisiana economy. In fact, in "Louis, par la grâce de Dieu" the authors compare enslaved people to food: "the importation of Blacks" is "the most appropriate nourishment for its growth"[102]; in another part of the text, "the introduction of Blacks" favors "the plumpness" of the colony.[103] The colonists refer to enslaved Africans as if their debasement somehow increased the colonists' own status as active human beings. Thus they might well have seen their ownership of enslaved people as proof that they themselves were not enslaved. This would explain their seemingly exaggerated indignation over Ulloa's marrying an enslaved woman and a White man. This case, I believe, reveals the White colonists' fear of being forced to share the condition of enslaved people.[104]

When the rebels accuse Ulloa of treating Acadians like enslaved people, they are blaming him for a confusion of categories: humans for things, or subjects for enemies. For example, when the governor angrily confronts these new immigrants for minor faults, the authors of the *Mémoire* reproach him: "Trembling at his threats, [the Acadians] believed the liberty of their families at stake and thought they saw themselves being sold at auction to pay for the rations of the king. Are we at Fez or Morocco?"[105] The reference to Morocco recalls the cases of hundreds of Europeans who were kidnapped at sea and held in cities such as Fez.[106] In other words, Ulloa treats the people he governs as if they were his captive enemies, or in Lockean terms, as if they were in a state of war. Fears of the enslavement of Acadians are also evoked in "Louis, par la grâce de Dieu": "This population, for so long the toys of fate, determined, through a patriotic spirit, to come and live under the happy laws of their former master."[107] Upon his arrival in Louisiana, however, Ulloa "threatened to chase them away from the colony and to have them sold as slaves."[108] In the first phrase, the Acadians begin as objects, or passive "toys" (jouets), then transform themselves into active humans who are capable of feeling emotions (patriotism) and making decisions (to move). In the second phrase, the tyrant threatens to transform them back into objects who can be sold.

As for the Indigenous people living within the borders of Louisiana, the authors of the manifestos give them slightly more respect than the enslaved Incas and Africans. The reason may be that the majority had not been subjugated by the Europeans; on the contrary, the Europeans had to maintain respectful diplomatic and commercial ties with them or risk the survival of the colony. The authors of the *Mémoire* refer to Natives' consent to trade agreements in terms of "the affection of the natives."[109] The reference to "Naturels" recalls Le Page du Pratz's friendly relationship to the Natchez. However, we see that on the very same page of the *Mémoire,* the same appear as "Savage Nations" (Nations Sauvages) and "Barbaric Nations" (Nations Barbares). We can assume that when the authors need the Natives to be cooperative trading partners, they call them by the more respectful "Naturels," but they do not always see them this way. In any case, the "affection" the colonists attribute to the Natives may have resided only in the colonists' minds; perhaps at times they saw the Natives as the "human pets" that Srinivas Aravamudan describes, the domesticated foreigners who were treated with indulgence by Europeans.[110] By speaking for the Natives and boasting of their love, they are manipulating readers' credulity and making the colony seem more idyllic, just as earlier authors did in the *Mercure*'s propaganda for the John Law scheme during the second decade of the eighteenth century.[111]

In *Sentimental Figures of Empire,* Lynn Festa states that sentimentality (as opposed to sensibility) is a force that "seeks to master" emotion and define who will be acknowledged as human. These sentiments can be found in narrations written by European travelers who describe their encounters with the people of other continents. The authors of the *Mémoire* do seek to use emotion for their own ends, but they fall into neither the category of European traveler nor that of Indigenous people. In the texts I have examined, there are four levels of population, which I list according to the way their status is mentioned: (1) metropolitans (including the king and the rest of the French readers, who are invited to sympathize with the texts); (2) White colonists, who complain of mistreatment by the metropolitans but also claim to deserve more rights than the next two groups; (3) Native Americans; and (4) enslaved Africans.

The second group, the colonists who seek to make their voices heard for the first time through these documents, are the ones who will soon call themselves Creoles. As Vidal remarks, "In the settlement colonies of the

'New World,' the colonists of European origin found themselves in the particular position of being at the same time colonizers in relation to the Amerindians and the Africans, and colonized vis-à-vis the metropole."[112] A pertinent discussion of the plight of Creoles can be found in Benedict Anderson's *Imagined Communities*. The circumstances in Louisiana recall his idea that independence movements occurred in the New World when Creole elites were socially on the rise but still felt disregarded by the metropolitan elites.[113] Festa's concept of sentimentality also helps to explain the emergence of the Louisianians' consciousness of themselves as men of feeling and as citizens with a political voice, even if that voice was disregarded by the king.

As I mentioned, all the clever rhetoric of the insurgents could not prevent the Spanish governor O'Reilly from summarily ending the revolt, but we are left with many questions. For instance, was the Louisiana revolt an unusual event in French history? To glance at an example from the same era, we might notice that the end of the Seven Years' War determined not only the contested transfer of Louisiana but also the cession of Corsica from Genovese domination to French. The latter event also stirred up a rebellion that was violently suppressed. The tumult in Louisiana and in Corsica could perhaps be usefully compared to the provincial insurrections that France experienced from time to time. Perhaps the uniqueness of the Louisiana revolt was owing to the fact that it was verbalized by the insurgents themselves in a collective manner and in print. The revolt in Corsica was more about actions and less about words than the Louisiana revolt of 1768, though. The Corsican cause (and its earlier independence struggle, before 1768) was taken up by influential writers like Jean-Jacques Rousseau and James Boswell. The people of Louisiana strategically verbalized their identity and their demands so that they could have the maximum effect on the king and other metropolitan readers. Srinivas Aravamudan warns us that we should not equate literacy with subjectivity. Admittedly, the residents of Louisiana could have developed a sense of self and a set of political demands without writing manifestos; for example, they could have resisted exclusively through violence. Nevertheless, Aravamudan does call on us to examine the ways in which subjected peoples consciously wielded literacy as an instrument for their particular purposes.[114] It is hard to imagine how the people of Louisiana could have made their case to the French without their printed manifestos. By using rhetorical tropes familiar to metropolitan readers, they were able at least to reach a wider audience and to move some readers, as we will see. One could say that they wrote themselves into existence in the eyes of the metropolitan public.

According to a letter written by the Spanish captain de Acosta, La Frénière compared himself to the leader of a revolt in Brittany. In the letter, the author recounts that La Frénière, at a party during the lull after the insurrection and before the crackdown, exclaimed "that he saw in himself the history of the marquis de Pontcallec in the uprising of Brittany, in France."[115] The reference is to the failed Pontcallec Conspiracy of 1718–20, when the États de Bretagne, the provincial assembly of Brittany, refused to pay taxes to the French regent. The marquis de Pontcallec was executed for his acts, just as La Frénière would be, yet both men's legends lived on for many years.

While Breton resistance was definitively suppressed militarily and almost forgotten by history, it lives on in the realm of folk music. There is still a Breton song that keeps alive the memory of this homegrown insurgent, "Maro Pontkalek" (The Death of Pontcallec), which indulges in nostalgia and regional sentiment.[116] The legend of the revolt of 1768 is not as long-lived, but in the decades following the revolt the manifestos did not fall of deaf ears. One important writer who heard the call was abbé Raynal, who included the story of Louisiana's transfer to Spain in his bestselling *Histoire des deux Indes*. Lesser-known writers, mostly writers of memoirs, also kept the legend of the revolt alive and particularly expanded the myth of La Frénière as hero.

In the following few decades, imperial officials were increasingly aware of the dangerous spread of the spirit of revolt. Specifically, Vidal points out how the 1768 event played a role in "the debate then taking place on both sides of the Atlantic about the foundations and limits of royal authority, the institution more suitable to represent the nation—the king or the Parlement—and the sharing of executive and legislative power."[117] Would discourse about the rights of the people spread to the English colonies next door? to other colonies like Saint-Domingue? or to the imperial metropoles themselves? It would be inaccurate to claim that there was a single line of cause and effect from Enlightenment thought to the Louisiana revolt to the American War of Independence, which would begin soon afterwards. Mutual influences would be more complex and diffuse, but different parts of the Western world were spurring one another toward revolution. Even just the fears of one revolt sparking another would influence imperial policy toward the Americas.[118] Meanwhile, the words and sentiments that emerged in New Orleans in 1768–69 would spread to the French metropole and arouse indignation against the Bourbon monarchy.

4

The Sentimental Aftermath of the Revolt

On Sensibility

Even though Louis XV ultimately took no notice of the manifestos from the New Orleans revolt of 1768, they made waves that reached progressive thinkers in Europe several years later. The Enlightenment *philosophe* Guillaume-Thomas Raynal and lesser-known writers such as the chevalier de Champigny took the voices of the insurgents and amplified them for a much wider readership, using language that would stir up outrage against absolutist rule among readers. They told the story of the revolt based partly on facts and partly on their own imagination, with the goal of highlighting the abuses of absolutist monarchy. They cast the events in the mode of tragedy—not as plays to be staged but as prose narratives that displayed situations and speeches typical of tragedy.[1] This mode allowed them to depict the Creole rebels as self-sacrificing national heroes in protracted death scenes in which they pronounced eloquent (though futile) harangues.

Aside from transferring tragic tropes into narrative prose, these retellings of the revolt of 1768 made lavish use of the language of *sensibilité*, a literary trend that peaked in the second half of the eighteenth century. This way of expressing oneself was on display in many novels in which innocence was persecuted, families were torn apart and then reunited, and lovers shed tears over precious keepsakes. It is a vision of human nature based on emotion, which explains much of the success of novels such as *Manon Lescaut*, by the abbé Prévost, and *Julie, ou la Nouvelle Héloïse*, by Jean-Jacques Rousseau. *Sensibilité* permeated not only the world of novels but also the paintings of Jean-Baptiste Greuze and the plays of Denis Diderot. It was a pan-European sensation, as we can see in the influential novels of the English writer Samuel Richardson and in the Sturm und Drang movement in Germany. According to memoirs and correspondence of the epoch, the trend even manifested itself in people's actual behavior: "Men are not afraid to weep with admiration, tenderness, or joy and they often like to make it known—an attitude that had no feminine connotation at the time," as

Anne Vincent-Buffault tells us of this era in her *Histoire des larmes* (*History of Tears*).[2]

Many see Jean-Jacques Rousseau as spearheading this trend, but he was far from the first author to write in this manner. In Vincent-Buffault's words, people "were crying while reading before Rousseau appeared. Rousseau did, however, set off among anonymous readers a process of identification that had no real precedent."[3] Although he inspired a veritable cult of tears and sighs, most of the major Enlightenment thinkers offered a vision of human nature that included emotion, as much as reason, as a means of discovering certain moral truths: "The pleasure of crying allowed one to receive a moral lesson in a pleasant way, without the intervention of reason."[4] They saw the feeling of pity, for a smaller animal being attacked by a larger animal, for example, as pointing one toward the path of virtue, because pity could reveal one's inner sense of justice. In this way, one supposedly could gain access to the "natural law" that was hidden inside one's heart.[5]

At some point, this taste for tears permeated the world of politics as a form of resistance to the ancien régime. Sentimental rhetoric often swayed public opinion in favor of the underdog—that is, the weaker person within a rigid power structure. It is a well-known feature of French revolutionary oratory, but historians such as Sarah Maza have also discovered examples of it in pre-revolutionary legal *mémoires* that made appeals to the public concerning cases between private citizens. In her article "Le Tribunal de la nation," Maza demonstrates how lawyers defended their clients in printed emotional harangues that were widely circulated. And she emphasizes that it was not the facts that made these writings popular but their style, which was meant to draw tears: "It is literary form that especially guarantees the success of a *mémoire judiciaire* [legal brief]. On that point, contemporaries agree unanimously: a good *mémoire* has the qualities of a literary work. It touches you, it moves you, it makes you tremble and cry."[6] While Maza concentrates on the popularity of these legal *mémoires* in the 1770s and 1780s, we can already see a mixture of *sensibilité* and politics in the manifestos of the New Orleans revolt of 1768. Apparently, La Frénière and his fellow insurgents were at the forefront of this literary-political aesthetic.

Scholars note that one important feature of *sensibilité*, in fiction and in politics, is the "Manichean" vision of a conflict between a virtuous underdog and a villain who is more highly placed on the social hierarchy, and this opposition increasingly tended toward a critique of the monarchy. In the case that Maza cites, a count owed money to some commoners, so the latter's lawyers portrayed the count as a corrupt courtier. Maza claims that this case between individuals became a more generalized opposition between "the people" and a small clique of powerful aristocrats: "Through social critique, a political critique emerges that pits the law, expression of the general will, against the court, domain of individual interests."[7] The lawyers in question also instrumentalized the fictional trope of "innocence persecuted"[8] to attack other aspects of the monarchical system, for example the *lettres de cachet,* mentioned above in my discussion of forced exiles to Louisiana. To uphold the principle of the law for all against the arbitrary will of the monarch and his entourage tended toward the "desacralization of the central institutions of the Ancien Régime, beginning with the monarchy itself."[9] I believe that the writings inspired by the 1768 revolt in New Orleans also fall in line with this questioning of the monarchical system itself, via a form of writing that combined legal argumentation with the *sensibilité* of fiction.

Several observations about *sensibilité* are relevant for both these legal *mémoires* and the 1768 manifestos: They were written by newly empowered upwardly mobile commoners with legal training, anticipating the tear-jerking speeches by revolutionary leaders. They used techniques and themes from fictional literature to achieve their effects; for instance, the metaphors of the abandoned child crying out to his parent, which echo the frequent theme in melodrama of the family that has been torn apart. Also as in melodrama, the 1768 manifestos create a "Manichean" schema, in which there are innocent victims (the French colonists) and dastardly villains who wield power (the Spanish governor Ulloa).

These manifestos, which I analyzed in the previous chapter, elicited responses from writers in France that imitated and exaggerated their tone when retelling the events. Sophie Wahnich describes the importance of recounting events in revolutionary France in order to inscribe them into the public memory: "To describe a regime of emotion, one must put on display some forms of emotional expression and the ways in which they were socially regulated: public or private inscription, inscription in the political or literary field, in the series of events or in the writing of narratives *a posteriori*, the management of emotions at the center of public space or the denial of emotions that inhabit the public space."[10] This revolutionary "writing of narratives *a posteriori*" involved mixing fact and fiction, as did the texts inspired by the revolt of 1768. The retellings that I analyze below, like the legal rhetoric of the same pre-revolutionary period, would also tend dangerously toward a critique of "the cruelty of absolutism."[11]

Raynal's Voice of America

As I mentioned earlier, Raynal includes a diatribe against the transfer of Louisiana to Spanish rule in his *Histoire des deux Indes*. He uses this event as ammunition against absolutist monarchy and what he saw as the irresponsible policies of imperialism. The whole book 16 of the *Histoire des deux Indes* excoriates the French government for every phase of the colonization of Louisiana. Raynal begins with the initial greed and delusion that motivated the exploration of the Mississippi River valley, then continues to its disastrous immigration policies, which excluded Protestants, until it culminates in the revolt of 1768. While he acknowledges that the people of Louisiana did not want to liberate themselves from the French king, he shows the cruelty of the arbitrary power of an absolutist monarch who disregards the pleas of his subjects. In his narrative, Raynal seeks to show that the feelings of loyalty among the people count for nothing; they are treated like things that can be sold from one owner to another.

As is typical for the whole *Histoire des deux Indes*, the style of the Louisiana section alternates between a detached statement of facts (geographical features of a landscape, for example, or latitude and longitude) and exceedingly histrionic harangues. The emotion rises and falls until it eventually reaches a crescendo, when the author plays the role of a personified Louisiana tearfully reproaching France for having abandoned her. The variety of tone can be partly explained by the fact that the text has two authors, Raynal and Denis Diderot. We can guess that the latter may have been the one who added the passages full of pathos or rage, since many of his own writings played a major role in the trend of *sensibilité*, including his plays, his novels, such as *La Religieuse*, his descriptions of Greuze's works, and his praise of the sentimental novels of Samuel Richardson. However, scholars have not been able to determine for certain who wrote which section of the *Histoire des deux Indes*.[12] For the sake of convenience, I will refer to the two authors using only the name Raynal.

The books of the *Histoire des deux Indes* describe different parts of the world, and each works as if it were a musical piece, beginning with quiet moments such as "Louisiana is a vast area, which borders on the sea to the south, on Florida and Carolina to the east, on New Mexico to the west, and, to the north, on Canada and unknown lands that must extend as far as Hudson Bay."[13] After explaining its location, he presents a pessimistic view of the Gulf Coast that echoes Lamothe-Cadillac's or Vallette de Laudun's descriptions of an infertile landscape.[14] In describing the area between the

Mississippi delta and Pensacola, Raynal states: "Its soil is sandy and its climate is scorching. You only see a few cedars, some sparse pines [...]. This position—the saddest, the most sterile of these lands—is the one they chose for settling the small number of men that Iberville had brought, lured by the greatest hopes [...]. A colony that was built on such bad foundations could not prosper."[15] After discussing the foolishness of the Law scandal, the frustrated greed of the French, and the wasted agricultural potential of upper Louisiana, Raynal softly broaches the topic of the transfer of Louisiana to Spain. "The court at Versailles announced, on the 21st of April 1764, to the inhabitants of Louisiana, that by a secret convention of November 3, 1762, it had abandoned to Madrid the possession of their territory."[16] It is a factual statement with precise details, but his critical judgment pierces through in words like *secret* and *abandoned*. The secrecy of the proceedings, which implied the use of Machiavellian *arcana imperii* to keep the residents in ignorance of this transfer for several years, was in fact one of the reproaches that the insurgents made to the French authorities. Also, the author erases from this sentence the human role of the kings or ministers who made these decisions, referring instead metonymically to the cities where they resided, making the whole transaction even more impersonal. And the choice of the word *abandoned* is the first note that announces the harangue that is to follow.

But first Raynal launches into an abstract argument about political philosophy, namely, the legitimacy of monarchical power. He combines logical argumentation and an escalating emotional tone: "But in whatever political way one can see this event, at the moral tribunal it will always be a crime to have sold or given away citizens to a foreign power. By what right, indeed, does a prince dispose of a people who does not consent to change masters? Do nations owe everything to kings, while kings owe nothing to nations? What is the meaning of *droit des gens* [*jus gentium,* or law of nations]? Is it not only the law of princes?"[17] He refers to a "moral tribunal" and then to a "tribunal of conscience"[18] as if it were a court case, anticipating revolutionary and pre-revolutionary speeches.

As he does frequently in the *Histoire des deux Indes,* Raynal asks a question and then pretends to represent both sides to make his point. In this case, he presents an argument from the point of view of a monarchist: he claims that kings "hold their power, they say, from God alone."[19] He then makes various counterarguments: One is that religious authorities invented this idea of divine right of kings in order to increase their own power: "This maxim, imagined by the clergy, [...] puts kings above people, only to command these same kings in the name of the divinity."[20] (This theory about conniving priests should be familiar to anyone who has read the more controversial articles in Diderot and d'Alembert's *Encyclopédie*.) The other is that kings and the clergy do not even work in harmony, since they, and in particular the pope, have often been at odds. In fact, they keep each other in check, "religion being the only rein to despotism."[21] In any case, Raynal is no fan of the clergy (in spite of his own religious profession), so he ultimately claims that monarchs do not receive their authority from God but from the people's hearts: "But why would authority want to disguise the fact that it comes from men? Nature, experience, history, inner sentiment, all sufficiently teach kings that they receive everything they possess from the people."[22] The idea that rulers derive their authority from the consent of the governed is one we presume today, but the particular French Enlightenment twist is the emphasis on the people's hearts, "inner sentiment," as the true origin of moral righteousness. Consequently, Raynal states that when a king abuses his power, the people's hearts cry out in protest. "It is thus in vain that princes have recourse to Heaven to recall their rights when they fail in their duties. The law they invoke rises against them. It thunders and strikes them down through the mouths of pontiffs. It cries out from the bottom of the hearts of a people that groans."[23] Human sentiment is therefore an important building block of Raynal's progressive idea of government.

Raynal calls for an authority that comes from reciprocal consent, echoing Locke's and Rousseau's ideas about the social contract. "Since one receives from the people all the fruits of obedience, why not accept from them alone all the rights of authority? What does one have to fear from wills that give of themselves, and what does one win from the abuse of the power one usurps? Should not one restrain this power with violence when someone seizes it by surprise? And what is the happiness of a prince who commands only by force and who is obeyed only out of fear?"[24] The lack of consent evokes the rapport between slave and master. Raynal asks, is monarchy not "merely an iron chain that keeps an entire nation under the feet of a single man? It is then no longer a reciprocal connection of love and virtue, of interest and faithfulness."[25] Literal and metaphorical descriptions of the plight of enslaved people, designed to elicit readers' empathy and consequently make them conscious of the ethical and political judgment to be made, were present in many abolitionist texts of the epoch, not least in the *Histoire des deux Indes* itself.

Finally, after evoking these power relations between ravisher and victim, slaver and enslaved, Raynal reaches the emotional climax of the section on

Louisiana with a metaphor we recognize from the manifestos of the revolt. To illustrate how much he empathizes with the colonists' plight when put into Spanish hands, he presents Louisiana speaking as if it were a child to its mother, France.[26] He introduces this part by claiming to hear "a voice that cries out from the depths of America; it is the voice of a populous colony." With this echo of Isaiah's "A voice cries out in the desert," Raynal puts the narrator in the position of a biblical prophet, warning worldly kings that divine justice is nigh.[27]

The voice that he claims to hear cries to her "métropole" in the following words:

> What have I done to you that you would give me up to a foreigner? Did I not come out of your womb? Have I not sown, planted, cultivated, harvested just for you? [...] But no, you have abandoned me. You involved me, without my knowledge, in a negotiation whose secrecy itself was a betrayal. Unfeeling mother, ingrate, were you able to cut, against natural vows, the ties that connected me to you by my very birth? [...] You tore me from my family. [...] Return my father to me, cruel one. [...] I will languish, I will perish from pain and weakness.[28]

The purpose of this passage is obviously to persuade readers that the transfer of Louisiana to Spain was wrong.[29] But by the time Raynal first publishes this work in 1770,[30] it is too late to remedy the situation specific to Louisiana, so the *Histoire des deux Indes* makes use of this episode as an example of suffering caused by absolutist monarchy and by colonialism in general.

Raynal takes the metaphor of the child, which was already present in the *Mémoire,* and transforms the king as father figure into a France as mother figure. He adds "return my father to me" at the end of the passage above, suggesting that a good king can make everything right again. The family was a typical trope of *sensibilité,* both in fictional plots and in the way people spoke about their relationships in real life. As Vincent-Buffault tells us, a "collective effusion is born from the image of the family (conjugal or filial love) that some public figures present and which makes the whole audience melt into tears: it resembles a *comédie larmoyante.*"[31] It is significant that Diderot was at the same time one of the authors of the *Histoire des deux Indes* and the very creator of the *comédie larmoyante* genre, in which children and fathers are separated and then tearfully reunited.

We can judge Raynal's representation of Louisiana as a baby crying out to its parent as either an absurd fictionalization of a political situation or a powerful literary choice that will move the audience. The term for this particular rhetorical device is *prosopopeia,* originally meaning to put a mask on someone's face, but it is used when an author pretends that an absent person, thing, or abstraction is speaking or acting. When Quintilian describes "*impersonation,* or προσωποποιΐα [prosopopeia]" in *Institutio Oratoria* as putting "words of advice, reproach, complaint, praise or pity into the mouths of appropriate persons,"[32] he muses that it is basically a fiction that could go in two different ways: for "things which are false and incredible by nature there are but two alternatives: either they will move our hearers with exceptional force because they are beyond the truth, or they will be regarded as empty nothings because they are not the truth."[33] These "appropriate persons" who are being impersonated by the speaker or author can include dead persons, abstractions, or, notably, cities or states.[34] The "bold" example he gives involves a place accusing a person of wrongdoing: "Your country, Catiline, pleads with you thus, and though she utters never a word, cries to you, 'For not a few years past no crime has come to pass save through your doing!'"[35] We can see the similarity with Raynal's prosopopeia of a colony reproaching its monarch.

This magical transformation of a thing into a speaking subject is an apt choice for Raynal's political purposes. Prosopopeia, Michael Riffaterre argues, differs from personification in that the latter grants an object the qualities of a person, but it can remain an object in the sense on being acted upon, while prosopopeia imagines that the object has agency and a voice: "Their [the objects'] depiction shifts from objective descriptive to subjectivizing prosopopeia."[36] Furthermore, Riffaterre remarks, "prosopopeia in most cases merely lends a voice to a voiceless always, or now silent, entity."[37] He gives an example from Proust, of the narrator imagining that furniture is gazing upon the protagonist Marcel and provoking him. This example has no political import. However, when we think of Raynal's use of it in this Louisiana section or in the famous passages on the Caribbean in the *Histoire des deux Indes* that represent enslaved people's laments, we can see how this rhetorical device that grants subjectivity to an object, place, or fictional person does become political, because the author is giving the voiceless a voice.

If Raynal is being presumptuous in assuming he can put words into the mouths of the oppressed, at least he is thinking about how these people—enslaved people, for example—could argue to protect their own interests, and he is forcing his readers to empathize with them. It is a reversal of the silencing by the powerful entity (monarchs, officials, slave masters) of the weaker party, by granting the latter an opportunity to plead their case, even if it is fictional. It is also a commentary upon the objectification of colonies and people in the first place. Accordingly, Raynal compares the Louisiana colonists to mere property, specifically furniture or farm animals: "Does one see that they have the right to buy, sell, and exchange peoples without consulting them? What, princes will seize the barbaric right to alienate or mortgage their provinces and their subjects like possessions and real estate? [...] against natural law, against the law of nations, you dispose of your colonists like a herd of animals, you give them up without their consent."[38] While these humans have been turned into objects by their governments, Raynal grants them a voice once again with his imagination.

Raynal ratchets up the emotion by layering on another literary form, that of the genre "adieux," mentioned above in regard to the Quoniam songs. Poems from the point of view of someone who has been abandoned, usually by a lover, were hugely popular in the eighteenth century. We see countless poems in the archives from Dido to Aeneas or Circe to Ulysses, for example. Thus we see that Raynal (or Diderot) makes use of several literary devices, previously apolitical, to judge the ethics of imperial policy.

As was typical of the fiction and the oratory of *sensibilité*, Raynal creates heroes and villains. While the New Orleans insurgents were "generous men, whose only crime was to have an attachment without limits for their metropole,"[39] their opponents were "barbarian, bloodthirsty, perfidious Spaniards."[40] Following the melodramatic paradigm, the heroes are cruelly victimized by the more powerful oppressors. Indeed, *victim* is the word Raynal chooses to describe La Frénière and his fellows once the Spanish decide to execute the leaders of the revolt: "They wanted victims," he writes,[41] and, addressing the Spanish, "Your eyes designated in the crowd the first victims of your authority."[42] He then judges those who contemplate these events according to the degree of emotion they feel. He states not only that the "inhuman masters" from Spain "ordered this horrible tragedy!" but also that "the French ministry did not feel any indignation!"[43] Raynal's exclamation points give us an idea of how the volume and the emotion would escalate at these points in the text if they were to be spoken out loud.

Raynal turns to the Louisiana residents who stood by passively as their leaders were executed:

> They lead to the gallows, they throw into dark common graves your friends, your relatives, your leaders, your defenders, the objects of your tenderness, of your veneration: and you are immobile! When and why would you expose yourself to death?[44]

A few pages later he writes:

> But can one really pity very strongly the sad situation of the colonists who allowed their compatriots to be slaughtered [...]? Conscience, the severe judge of our duties, did not cry out to them, without interruption: "[...] It was your father, your brother, your child, and you calmly saw them led to the gallows or weighed down with chains! And you bow coldly to the stone that they stained with their blood!"[45]

Once again, the emotion is heightened by the mention of family ties, as well as by the metaphors of blood and chains, and with exclamation points. As we will see, writers would sentimentalize the events of the 1768 revolt in New Orleans even more after reading the manifestos and Raynal's text. They would also add more details from their imaginations, in order to heighten the tragic mood and to eventually persuade readers of the cruelty of absolutist monarchy.

The Bitter Tears of Jean Bochart de Champigny

One of Raynal's many admirers was the chevalier de Champigny, author of a text published under two titles, the more histrionic *La Louisiane ensanglantée* (Louisiana bloodied) (London, 1773) and the more sober *État présent de la Louisiane* (The present state of Louisiana) (La Haye, 1776). The complete title of the latter refers explicitly to Raynal: *État présent de la Louisiane, avec toutes les particularités de cette province d'Amérique, pour servir de Suite à l'Histoire des Etablissemens des Européens dans les Deux Indes* (Present state of Louisiana, with all the particularities of this province of America, to serve as a sequel to the History of the European Establishments in the Two Indies),[46] although it is unclear whether Raynal was ever aware of his book. The author of this text was named Colonel Jean Bochart, chevalier de Champigny. If his name was legitimate, it indicates that he came from a family of *noblesse de robe* of whom several members had distinguished themselves in the Bourbon administration, including one intendant of Nouvelle France from 1686 to 1702 who was also named Jean Bochart de Champigny.[47] There is a great deal of documentation about this intendant but very little about the author in question, who may be his descendant or may have fraudulently taken his name.

We do not know whether the author of *Louisiane ensanglantée* had firsthand experience in Nouvelle France, but we do know a little about his publications. The titles of books under his name give us an impression of his political and his novelistic tendencies. Copies of these books are present in the libraries of Germany, Sweden, and the English-speaking world. Many of them are labeled as self-published (*au dépens de l'auteur*). His works, all written in French, include translations of a history of Denmark; an account of William Pitt's recent actions; Champigny's own histories of England and Sweden; and novels such as *Mémoires de Miss Fanny Palmer, Lettres angloises ou les époux à la mode* (Memoirs of Miss Fanny Palmer, English letters, or the fashionable spouses), and a pseudo translation obviously modeled on Jonathan Swift: *Supplément aux rêveries d'un habitant de Lillyput. Traduit du lillyputien en françois* (Supplement to the reveries of an inhabitant of Lilliput. Translated from the Lilliputian to French).

The few traces that have remained in the archives about Champigny are not exactly favorable. One biography of the Irish writer Oliver Goldsmith reports that the latter would give money to any "swindler," such as the one "who called himself the Chevalier de Champigny, who was obtaining subscriptions for a projected *History of England* in fifteen volumes, to be written in French."[48] Another biography of Goldsmith refers to "deceptions" by "persons professing the cultivation of letters": "Among these was a foreigner at this time in London, countenanced by the Bavarian Ambassador and others, under the name of Colonel Chevalier de Champigny."[49] This biographer adds that Champigny had already claimed to have as subscribers "crowned heads" and other prominent people, whose names were meant to give confidence to new subscribers.[50] Goldsmith's biographers refer to Champigny as a swindler, but he did actually write books. Admittedly, the history of England that he finally published was in only one volume, when he had promised fifteen. Contemporary reviews of his books are also largely negative, accusing him of repeating what had already been written in other histories.

In short, he made a negative impression in England, and it was no less negative in France, specifically in regard to one of the American Founding Fathers. Specifically, we see that he pressured Benjamin Franklin to subscribe to his books during the latter's diplomatic mission to France in 1777–78.[51] Champigny had his *Histoire d'Angleterre* delivered to Franklin at his house in the Parisian suburb of Passy and subsequently sent him multiple letters demanding payment for it and asking for his patronage. Finally, Franklin responded to him in the following terms on July 24, 1778, writing, "A Gentleman of your Name, to whom I was entirely a Stranger, apply'd to me for a Subscription to a History of England which he propos'd to write. I consider'd the Affair as one of those genteel Methods by which

Men of Letters are assisted when their Circumstances require Assistance, without being put to the Blush in being oblig'd to ask it as a Benevolence"[52] and then returned the books to their author. In short, Franklin treated him as a penniless gentleman who needed a handout rather than as an author or fellow man of the Enlightenment.

Why should we pay attention to the works of this possible charlatan? Is his account of the Louisiana revolt worth reading? I believe his account is indeed worth reading as one of the many sentimental narratives of the revolt that authors embellished to increase their emotional effect. These narratives begin with Raynal and continue to the Napoleonic era. Among these authors, Champigny is the one who exaggerates the most, adding details from his imagination and reaching emotional heights that would be matched only by Chateaubriand. For these reasons, I believe he provides a worthy example of fictionalizing history to make a political point.

From the very beginning of *État présent de la Louisiane*, which is in substance the same text as *La Louisiane ensanglantée*, the chevalier de Champigny presents a paratext that blurs the lines between fact and fiction, between news and romance. He first undercuts his own trustworthiness by declaring that he is the author of both history books and "a few bad novels,"[53] which makes the reader ask herself which of these genres she is about to read. He adds to the uncertainty of his text's genre by presenting contradictory claims about his status as an eyewitness. First, the "editor's preamble" states that he will describe "facts that are purely historical and that happened, so to speak, before my eyes; they are even so recent that the tears that they provoked, in America as much as in Europe, have still not dried. I advance nothing but what is true; all that remains for me to communicate to the reader is by what means this manuscript came to me."[54] Note how he qualifies his eyewitness status with "so to speak" (pour ainsi dire), which actually puts it into question. The mention of tears prepares us for the omnipresence of sentiment throughout the story. He then proceeds to tell us that the main text that follows is his transcription of someone else's words. The narrator creates a brief prefatory fiction that is as implausible as it is clichéd: he meets an English officer, and within a few days they become close friends; the Englishman suddenly falls mortally ill, and with his last breath he tells the story of the revolt in Louisiana, which he witnessed.[55] When we read the body of the text, we see that telling the story from this Englishman's point of view can serve as a pretext for the author's praise of English liberties in opposition to supposed French and Spanish cruelty.

With this beginning, as ambiguous as any eighteenth-century novel, Champigny proceeds with a brief history of Louisiana.

The historical-novelistic text by Champigny is definitely a work of its time, since it participates zealously in the trend of sensibility with political implications. In his "preamble," for example, he establishes his ideal readership: "I write for the sensible souls."[56] He also explains his desire to inspire future generations "by transmitting to posterity these heroic and sublime traits that will be the object of this work," words that signal to us that he is going to cast his story in a tragic mold.[57] In his text, Champigny's imagination embellishes characters from both sides of the revolt in order to make them fit the Manichean paradigm. For instance, he depicts the "villains," that is, the Spanish governor Ulloa and the French official who cedes the colony to him, Aubry, as physically unattractive. He describes Ulloa as small and shifty-looking, thus revealing his bad character: "Without dignity, without generosity [. . .] there is the man in regard to his soul. As for his body. . . . . . . it would be hard to be smaller and thinner than Don Antonio de Ulloa was; a weak and shrill voice announced his character. His physiognomy, although regular enough, had nevertheless something fake about it: large eyes, always lowered to the ground, only threw out furtive glances [. . .]. A mouth whose forced laugh announced some trickery, duplicity, and hypocrisy finishes off the portrait of Don Antonio de Ulloa."[58] The mention of *physiognomy* in this description reminds us that in this era people took seriously the idea that facial features were an outward manifestation of the character within. Likewise, as pre-modern literary convention would have it, fictional heroes were beautiful and villains were ugly. When it comes to Aubry, the French governor who is complicitous with the Spanish, the narrator tells us that he is not just obsequious but unattractive: "Mr. Aubry was a small, dried-up, scrawny, ugly man, without nobility, without dignity, without poise."[59] At the end of these descriptions, Champigny announces: "There you have the portrait of two men who were responsible for the loss of Louisiana, the first out of malice, the second out of weakness,"[60] as if the cession of Louisiana happened because of these men's defects rather than because they were duty-bound to carry out their governments' decision.

Meanwhile, Champigny selects La Frénière out of all the rebel leaders and turns him into the type of hero that audiences would be familiar with: handsome, with a noble bearing, and morally good. He describes La Frénière in quasi-aristocratic terms, claiming that the rebel leader had a "noble face" and a "majestic bearing,"[61] in contrast to Aubry, whose appearance was "without nobility." In spite of La Frénière's prosaic legal profession, an exultant Champigny declares him to be "a warrior" and a "gallant man."[62] If he was aware of the humble beginnings of the Chauvin family, Champigny simply chose to ignore them in order to insert him into the mold of a classical epic or tragic hero, who traditionally had to be of the princely class. Even though the author is socially progressive, we see that he still attaches prestige to his protagonist's social status, just as he uses his (possibly fraudulent) noble title of *chevalier* in his own authorial identity and just as, according to the Oliver Goldsmith biography, he boasted of his royal connections.

Although the real La Frénière had already expressed himself in published writings and in speeches, some of which are quoted in letters and reports, Champigny invents more speeches for him. Ironically, the longest speech he puts in his hero's mouth actually urges the people *not* to revolt. After the arrival of O'Reilly to put down the rebellion, the residents are ready to take up arms: "Already the white cockades were on display, already people were getting ready to march on the enemies, when Monsieur de la Frénière [. . .] dampened this ardor with a speech whose substance is as follows."[63] He presents a speech of several pages that ends with an exhortation to "obey the orders of the king" and continues: "Let us expect everything from a benevolent king, from a king of the same blood as ours, let us listen to the promises of the one who represents him, and let us try to earn their fulfillment by a submissive and respectful conduct."[64] In this attempt to show La Frénière as a morally perfect character, the author strangely betrays the real man's efforts to defy the government. In fact, Champigny neglects to say anything about the main event of the revolt, namely, the march on New Orleans that drove Ulloa out. Like a novelist, Champigny omits and adds facts of the revolt of 1768 to shape a narrative that will draw the maximum emotional reaction from the readers. The unfeeling villains are on the side of absolutist monarchy, and the tearful, attractive heroes are on the side that tends toward subverting the old regime.

One truly unique feature of Champigny's narrative, compared with other accounts of the revolt, is the scene in which the narrator, surely inspired by Rousseau, describes the interval between the march on New Orleans and the arrival of O'Reilly as a sort of pastoral utopia. After Champigny tells us of the failure of the diplomatic mission of the insurgents to the courts at Madrid and Versailles, he turns his attention back to New Orleans. In cinematic terms, it would be a sudden change of scene that brings with it a radical change in location, sound, and mood.

> We are approaching the terrible moment that will decide forever the fate of the colony. Before turning our glances to the scenes of horror that I have yet to trace, let us transport ourselves to Louisiana and let us see how the residents are occupying themselves since the departure of Monsieur de Ulloa.
>
> I am admiring, along the river, the happy products of liberty and contentment. Each person has doubled his effort: the crops are in the best condition, the revenues are more considerable than they had been before the time of stagnation marked by Ulloa's term. Every place I see breathes joy and tranquility.[65]

Whereas the previous section, which takes place in France, is recounted in the past tense and in the third person, this new section becomes suddenly personal, since the narrator says "I admire" and "I see," and it is in the present tense. These narrative choices would presumably make the reader feel as if he were there himself, seeing through the point of view of a narrator who is a human individual, not simply a disembodied all-knowing voice.

The reader then follows the narrator, who chances upon two buildings, which he proceeds to describe. He presents the first one thus: "What is this edifice that I see rising in the middle of the city? It is the temple of the Lord."[66] His choice of the word *temple* rather than *church* (*église*) suggests a general spiritual practice that could potentially include ancient Greek rites, rather than the Catholicism that was officially practiced in Louisiana. This strategic vagueness is typical of Enlightenment writers, most of whom were deist, and it also hints at future attempts by the French revolutionary government to replace Catholicism with the Cult of the Supreme Being and to establish Temples of Reason.

After a few reflections on this temple, the narrator leads us along:

> Farther, I discover another building, curiosity takes me there; one reads above the entryway this beautiful inscription:
>
> **ASYLUM**
> **FOR THE POOR AND THE ORPHANED**[67]

The typography Champigny chooses, centered and in all capital letters, gives dramatic emphasis and almost re-creates the building's inscription on the page. Once he enters, he realizes that it houses orphans, women in labor, and poor and sick people "without tumult or confusion,"[68] thus representing the community's self-sustaining altruism.

This emphasis on tranquility recalls the beginning of this section, in which the narrator describes the "joy and tranquility" that reigns over the colony during the interval between French and Spanish rule. The reference to calmness also appears a few pages earlier, where the narrator ad insisted on the nonviolence of the revolt: when Ulloa retreats to his ship, "all of this happened without the slightest attack on the Spanish banner or on the Spaniards who remained in the colony. [...] he unanimous report from all foreigners makes this event out as the most extraordinary and the most surprising for its good order, its decency, and its moderation [...]. These shows of attachment to the King of France were the only cries that troubled the calmness and the silence during the three days that the inhabitants were assembled in New Orleans. Immediately after the departure of Monsieur de Ulloa, calm and tranquility *reigned*" (emphasis added).[69] Champigny insists on this tranquility in order to give credit to the insurgents, whom he makes great efforts to depict not as wild rioters but as virtuous, self-abnegating sages. It is certainly a manipulation of the facts, since many eyewitness accounts tell us that there was chanting against the Spanish and arms were wielded, though not used. The verb used in the last phrase of this passage, "calm and tranquility *reigned*," suggests that this colony can be ruled by personified calmness, in the absence of a king or governor.

Indeed, these non-persons, calm and tranquility, that "reign" over the colony are reflected in the description of the temple and the asylum, in a vision of a leaderless yet virtuous society. Who decided to establish this asylum? asks the narrator, as full of wonder as Candide when he visits the utopia of El Dorado. Someone answers, "A unanimous accord created these foundations: the general cry proposed them";[70] no one individual emerged as a leader, but the people spoke as one, as in Rousseau's ideal of universal consent in his *Social Contract*. It is significant that it is "someone" (quelqu'un)—no description is given, no gender or class is specified—who responds to the narrator, because that faceless person represents the undifferentiated multitudes. This person further explains that the construction and provisioning of the building was also a spontaneous communal effort, without regard for self-interest but inspired instead by "pity" (the preeminent human emotion for Rousseau), by patriotism, and by "the love that we have for one another."[71] "Each person has provided according to their faculties, without taxes. One gave the wood necessary for the frame, another the materials for the masonry; this one beds, that one other furniture. Each one took part as they wished, and they contributed to the necessary funds for the expenses incurred in this hospital."[72] This society that functions peacefully and successfully without a leader, without the constraints of laws or punishments, was envisaged by Montesquieu in his famous parable of the Troglodytes in the *Lettres persanes*. In their perfect society before the advent of government, everyone acts altruistically to make one another happy and to make the society flourish. This is how Montesquieu's virtuous Troglodytes live: "Nature provided for their desires as abundantly as for their needs. In this happy land, cupidity was alien. They would give each other presents, and the giver always thought that the advantage was his. The Troglodyte nation regarded themselves as a single family; the herds were almost always mixed up together, and the only task that was usually neglected was that of sorting them out."[73] So we see that Champigny's vision of a perfect society, whether in the past or future, or in a distant colony, was aligned with the utopias of the major Enlightenment writers.

In Champigny's text, the vision of an idealized Louisiana makes the narrator metaphorically burn with intense emotions, among which he counts patriotism: "'O virtue!' I exclaimed, full of enthusiasm, 'O divine patriotism! Of what are we not capable when your sacred fire sets us ablaze? Among what men have I been transported?'"[74] The emotions such as pity and love for their compatriots, which lead to virtuous action, spark enthusiasm in the observer. The observer's account, in turn, should inspire the same admiration and perhaps sympathy for the people of Louisiana in the reader.

Why does Champigny invent this scene? If Louisianians can live happily without a leader, why does he try to persuade the French king to take them back? Perhaps autonomy—peaceful anarchy or democracy—was too daring for Champigny to propose for Louisianians in 1776, in spite of the events happening in the nearby thirteen British colonies. Even when Champigny apostrophizes the French king to rule over Louisiana again, it is unclear why these colonists would need the king: "O happy monarch who reigns over the French, how these subjects are worthy of your support! [...] Their fate must always be to see growing, under your domination, the sentiments of religion, humanity, charity, and generosity that I see shining in them at a moment when their will has no other guide than the movement of their hearts and no other rein than the desire to prove to the whole universe how much they cherish you."[75] The words he chooses to describe his idealized view of the relationship between king and subjects are "support" (appui) and "growing, under your domination" (croître sous ta domination); thus the king does not so much lead them as look kindly upon their own spontaneous, benevolent actions. These actions are motivated by "the movement of their hearts" and their love for the king. This is a political vision that is entirely built on emotion.

Just as positive feelings lead to a happy society without a leader or under a benevolent and somewhat hands-off king, bad feelings signal the dangers of tyranny. After the enthusiastic description of an ideal society, the narrator alters his tone when he describes a new change of mood among the colonists: "But where is this general murmur coming from that is all over the city? Each person whispers to the other, they are afraid to raise their voices [...] a pallor is on everyone's faces, soon I see tears streaming. Sobs suppress cries of pain; I take part in the public dread."[76] This is the beginning of the end for the insurgents, since the ominous mood announces the arrival of the villainous Spanish governor Alejandro O'Reilly and foreshadows the ultimate execution of the heroes.

These executions represent the high point of the narrative, which Champigny sets up like the end of a theatrical tragedy, with a short dying speech by Pierre Marquis (an officer of Swiss origin) and a longer one by La Frénière. "'Death has nothing frightening for us,' said Monsieur le Marquis [sic], asking for a pinch of snuff, with peerless sang-froid. 'Know that although I am a foreigner, my heart is French; it has always been for LOUIS THE WELL-BELOVED [Louis XV, "le Bien-Aimé"], at whose service I sacrificed thirty-odd years of my life, so I am proud that my love for him is the cause of my death.'"[77] Then his co-conspirator La Frénière exclaims, in front of the firing squad, "May our Well-beloved King learn how dear he was to us, how much we exult in dying as his faithful subjects. [...] To die for the king..... to die French..... what is more glorious! This idea elevates my soul so much that in this terrible moment when I am ready to appear before the Eternal, if the Spaniards offered to spare my life in return for no longer being French, I would tell them with the same firmness that I say to them at this very moment ... *Shoot*."[78] When the first shot fails to kill La Frénière, the author draws out the scene to make it even more touching: "Still beating, he placed his hand over his heart; someone thought they heard him say, 'It is French.'"[79] The narrator then tells us how we are to react: "Let us give free rein to our tears."[80] Our correct reaction, according to the narrator, brings us into this world of *sensibilité*—and if we empathize, it is implied, we must agree with the political message.

How does Champigny justify adding this speech to a supposedly factual history? In the note to La Frénière's dying speech above, Champigny adds that a certain Mr. Bradley "swore to me that he had been present at this cruel execution and has permitted me to make use of his name to render this fact even more authentic."[81] This claim to truth emphasizes the oral transmission of this story, typical for much of Louisiana's colonial history, which depends so much on rumor and oral reports, as we have seen in this study. The orality of the information transmitted in and about Louisiana can be explained by the facts that the majority of the residents were illiterate and that subversive writings were subject to censorship. The footnote in question also exemplifies, more specifically, the way in which legends surrounding the revolt have been preserved (or amplified) by word of mouth.

Why is the dying speech so important in *La Louisiane ensanglantée* and in later retellings of the revolt? The speech slows down the narration and momentarily transforms the narration into something akin to a theatrical scene. The "zooming in" to one man's gestures and speech is far more likely to make readers cry than a sentence that simply declares that the rebel leaders were executed or imprisoned. If indeed the events were perceived as tragic by the witnesses or by the writers of these histories, the dying monologue fits the expectations for the culmination of a heroic drama. Even the frequent ellipses that Champigny includes in his characters' speeches suggest that there are moments when emotions are so strong that words fail. Through the ellipses he is also inserting pauses, thus establishing a rhythm to the speeches, to create a dramatic effect, as if he were directing a theatrical performance. The heroes' eloquence, their stoicism before death, and their willing self-sacrifice for an ideal is typical of the tragedies of Corneille, for example. The very sangfroid of these men only heightens the emotions felt by the onlookers in the scene and supposedly by the public reading the account.

However, Champigny's tragic death scene differs from classical French drama in two significant ways. First, in most of Corneille's tragedies, as in the ancient Greek model, there is no clear villain: all the characters act honorably even though their goals may clash. Champigny, by contrast, depicts the Spanish governors as ugly, malevolent characters, more like the moustache-twirling villains of the popular drama of the nineteenth century. After the executions, Champigny's narrator angrily apostrophizes O'Reilly as a "bloodthirsty tiger" whose "savage and barbaric soul"[82] is insensible to the tears of the rebels' widows and children. He continues, "Satiate your rage and your greed . . . do more evil in one day than the Caligulas and the Neros would have done . . . even more: dare to say that the order that issued from your odious mouth had been dictated by your king . . . this horrible blasphemy was the only thing left for you to commit."[83] The Manichean division of characters into heroes and villains is less like classical seventeenth-century French drama and closer to the coming trends in theater: the melodramas of the nineteenth century.

In the passage above, Champigny goes as far as to accuse the royal governor of being worse than Caligula and Nero, but he restrains himself when it comes to blaming the king of Spain for the executions. Champigny creates the fiction that O'Reilly acts dishonestly, without the approval of his king. This brings us to the second difference between this tragic moment and the works of Corneille and Racine. Classical French drama, often commissioned by the king himself, always steered clear of criticizing him. But Champigny, while he hesitates to apostrophize the kings directly as Raynal had done, questions the government policies and ministers that created the tragic event. At first he denies that any Bourbon king would order such a cruel action as the punishment of the rebels: "It is completely impossible that a council as enlightened and as equitable as the one in Madrid, over which a just and clement king presides, would have passed a bloodthirsty judgment against the accused."[84] He then cites a proverb that he claims we should not believe, yet the very mention of it makes us reflect on it: "Let us brush aside from a work dictated by truth that political maxim that we have seen spread [even] in a century of philosophy and Enlightenment, a barbarous maxim that the least civilized nations have rejected with the greatest care but that the Spanish adopt with an unpardonable blindness. 'Whatever happens,' someone said, 'a leader must never be in the wrong, and it is dangerous to let him believe it.'"[85] So who is to blame for the violent crackdown? Champigny is ambivalent. He implies that the French ministers are certainly complicit through their inaction: "The universe was surprised to see the French ministry remain in silence about the conduct of Monsieur O'Reilly, not demand any reparation for his inhumanity, remain quiet about his infraction against the law of nations."[86] But he also hints at excusing ministers: "Let us say that until now one had not known the truth, let us say that the French ministry had itself been deceived."[87] This is what he suggests we say, but whether this is what Champigny believes, he refrains from stating. These final judgments are ambiguous enough to leave readers the possibility of believing that not only the ministers but also the kings were responsible for the tragedy. This tragic account, then, is unlike the classical tragedies that simply recount an episode from ancient history. This one has villains who are still in power and who, if readers take this accusation to its natural conclusion, must be deposed.

Bossu, Berquin-Duvallon, Vergennes, Baudry de Lozières

After Champigny, other writers who claimed to write factual histories of Louisiana included briefer accounts of the events of 1768–69, but they maintained the same sentimental rhetoric. In 1777, an officer sent to Louisiana named Jean-Bernard Bossu published a series of nine letters addressed to a friend, M. Douin. They record Bossu's observations during his tour of Louisiana and Cuba, some in a neutral tone, others in a more melodramatic one. In regard to the New Orleans revolt, he begins: "I am trembling, dear friend, as I give to you the details of this bloody tragedy, for the pain that penetrates me makes me shed tears of regret as I visualize the fatal posts, stained with the blood of the victims and pierced with the murderous bullets that brought death to our illustrious fellows, more unfortunate than criminals, who displayed in this terrible instance the most courageous virtue and the most heroic firmness."[88] He lets the reader know how he or she should feel about "this bloody tragedy" (cette sanglante tragédie), which he bases on the physical manifestations of his own emotions, which he describes with the words *trembling, pain,* and *tears*. Additionally, he provides a strong visual element on which the emotions can focus and which prepares us for the story that is to follow: the image of the blood-covered posts on which the rebels were executed by firing squad.

Bossu chooses to focus on Pierre Marquis rather than La Frénière. To Marquis he attributes a heroic speech that partly confirms Champigny's account:

> He never wanted to have his eyes blindfolded, saying that having braved death so many times in the service of his master the King of France, he had never closed them or turned them away before his enemies. [He says:] "let us die as men" [...].
>
> "Spanish gentlemen," he continued, "bear witness that we are dying for having always wanted to be French; yes, know that although I am a foreigner, my heart is French; it has always been for Louis the Well-Beloved, in whose service I sacrificed thirty-odd years, and I am proud that my love for him is the cause of my death."[89]

In this case, the words are supplemented by theatrical gestures: "After these words, this brave officer tore open his shirt and showed his stomach scarred with wounds received in war, as he said, 'Shoot, executioners.'"[90] The visual aspects of this scene—the defiant baring of the scarred body and the eyes not covered by any blindfold—heighten the sublimity of this death scene. In these ways, Bossu turns this man into a tragic hero: a warrior and leader, courageous before death and willing to sacrifice himself for an ideal.

The rest of Bossu's narrative, in the remaining letters, turns to other lands and other issues, but we see a similar type of short, emotional narration of the revolt of 1768 in a number of histories from the French revolutionary era to the Napoleonic era. I deal with the revolutionary writings about Louisiana in the following chapter, but for now I will address some Napoleonic-era texts because they focus so closely on La Frénière as a tragic hero. Whether the surge of interest was motivated by *sensibilité*, by economic or military strategy, or by a new conception of the French empire, French people continued to express regret over the loss of this colony. Pierre-Louis Berquin-Duvallon, a planter exiled from Saint-Domingue who settled in Louisiana, notes in 1802 how powerful the memories of the revolt still are among the residents. "I do not exaggerate at all the impression of pain and fear that spread, in these unhappy times, through all the colony—an impression so strong in itself that I have seen, and see on a daily basis, former colonists, witnesses to these tragic scenes, so struck by them that after an interval of thirty years and more they cannot recount the tale without visible signs of sadness, fear, and horror, with which they were filled in this era that was so frightful for them and which engraved itself so indelibly in their memory."[91] These "tragic scenes" from 1769 still cause "pain," "sadness," and "horror" among the colonists. In keeping with the reigning *sensibilité* of the era, Berquin-Duvallon describes the emotions of the colonists to express his own sense of the injustice of France's decision to cede Louisiana.

This observation is averred by another writer of the same period who traveled to Louisiana, Louis-Narcisse Baudry de Lozières. Like Berquin-Duvallon, Baudry de Lozières was a wealthy planter from Saint-Domingue and coincidentally the son-in-law of Jean Milhet, one of the Louisiana insurgents.[92] His 1802 *Voyage à la Louisiane* covers the period from 1794 to 1798, nearly thirty years after La Frénière's execution, so he never met La Frénière. Nevertheless, he demonstrates how the image of the charismatic leader of the rebellion lived on, since he must have gathered this information partly from other memoirs and partly from oral accounts he heard while in Louisiana.[93] Like Champigny, Baudry de Lozières focuses on La Frénière to elevate him into the role of the tragic hero. In his description, he emphasizes his beauty and his royal bearing: "Monsieur Chauvin de La Frénière, attorney general of the Superior Council, a Creole whose bravery was remarkable even among Louisianians [. . .]. M. de la Frénière was one of the most beautiful men that nature had ever been pleased to shape. Tall, well-built, with a noble, imposing, and brave air about him [. . .]. His physique was so remarkable that since it was not knowing to whom to compare him, he was popularly called 'Louis XIV' because he really had that majesty that one sees in sovereigns."[94] He also depicts the rebel leader as sophisticated and eloquent: "He knew how to agreeably make persuasive speeches [. . .]. He had done his studies in France, and he had brought back its charms and the good taste that he lent to everything he said and everything he wrote. [...] nothing, so to speak, could resist the torrent of his eloquence."[95] The author often refers to him as "De la Freynière," emphasizing the *de*, which would suggest that his name was an aristocratic title (which the French call a *nom à particule*), when it was not so at all.[96] This choice perhaps highlights the importance that Baudry de Lozières gave to the old social hierarchy in general, which would make him imagine an aristocratic version of La Frénière who could fit the mold of a classical tragic hero. This idea corresponds to the prestige Baudry de Lozières gives to the memory of Louis XIV: even though he was writing in the post-revolutionary era, he remained an admirer of the Bourbon monarchy. It is important to note that these two writers who published histories of Louisiana in 1802, Baudry de Lozières and Berquin-Duvallon, while progressive enough to question the decisions of Bourbon ministers, are still nostalgic for the ancien régime. Rather than championing the Revolution, they favored Napoleon's empire, as well as the slavery he reinstated, because his régime supported these two writers' social role as planters and slave owners.

Later in the text, Baudry de Lozières takes a stand similar to Champigny's in refusing to blame the king for the New Orleans revolt of 1768, but making this choice after the French Revolution has different implications. Much less subject to persecution and much less able to gain from royal patronage, Baudry de Lozières nevertheless chooses to leave Louis XV untouched and focus instead on the royal entourage and their bad decisions: "One must admit that the name of a sovereign is often merely the obvious pretext that covers a lot of foolishness. [...] Monsieur de Choiseul took advantage of the name of the king just as one takes advantage of a talisman elsewhere, and Louisiana really was sold. [...] Monsieur de Choiseul [...] came, by force of intrigue, to deceive the prince on this matter. The king did not suspect the wrong that he inflicted on Louisianians or the attachment of these brave Frenchmen."[97] He also puts the burden of tyrannical behavior on the Spanish authorities' shoulders, claiming that Ulloa exercised "the most revolting tyranny."[98] His fellow planter Berquin-Duvallon had referred to Spanish rule as "tyrannical" and the experiences of the French colonists as "inquisitorial investigations" and "general terror."[99]

Baudry de Lozières's narration, like Champigny's and Bossu's, reaches an emotional climax with the execution of the rebels. He provides a very similar speech on the part of Pierre Marquis as Bossu does, but there are also small differences that make me believe that he did not simply copy Bossu.[100]

The similarity between the speeches and the documentation that confirms that both Bossu and Baudry de Lozières spent time in Louisiana suggests that this speech was likely based on fact. Such evidence does not exist for the speech Champigny attributes to La Frénière. Baudry de Lozières's readers are meant to react with pity and terror to the execution of Marquis; he calls forth our *sensibilité* when he describes the reactions of the onlookers. Baudry de Lozières writes in regard to O'Reilly, "The tears of the wives, mothers, and children, only irritated his ferocious soul" and "nothing softened the tiger,"[101] an animal metaphor also used by Champigny. He shows O'Reilly as the opposite of a man of feeling: insensible, therefore on the side of tyranny, just like a novelistic villain.

Yet another anecdote that elicits pity and terror in regard to the execution of the rebels appears in the *Mémoire historique et politique sur la Louisiane,* purportedly by Charles Gravier, comte de Vergennes, who was Louis XVI's foreign minister from 1774 to 1787 and held other prestigious positions during the ancien régime. Vergennes died in 1787, and this work was published in 1802. Its authorship is questioned by Baudry de Lozières, who published his own work in the same year. The latter remarks that "whoever it is who hides behind the imposing name of Monsieur de Vergennes, he is no less useful," for he provides good information about the colony.[102]

In any case, it is in the unnamed editor's "Summary of the life of Monsieur de Vergennes" that we find the most interesting allusions to the 1768 revolt. Recounting the executions according to a certain M. de Saintelette, who was purportedly a member of the Louisiana delegation sent to France to address Choiseul, the editor remarks that several rebels "who did not want to submit to the Spanish yoke"[103] were ordered to be executed. A new detail appears that we had not encountered in other accounts: "Since there was no executioner in the colony, they addressed a negro, who refused. They threatened to hang him if he did not obey. After fifteen minutes of absence, this negro, atrociously sublime, returned and threw into the middle of the council the fist and the axe with which he had just cut it off. 'Now,' he told them, 'you can no longer make an executioner out of me.' They had the Frenchmen shot."[104] The "atrociously sublime" man who cuts off his own hand provokes strong emotions, including fear and awe, that ancient Greek and early modern French literary critics associated with tragedy.[105] Did this grisly event occur, was it a false rumor, or did Vergennes's editor invent it? All we know is that the editor assures us in a note, "I have these facts from a friend of Monsieur de Saintelette."[106] This anecdote is missing in the body of the text presumably by Vergennes, although he does present the revolt in the usual terms of O'Reilly's perfidy and cruelty.

In the main text, the purported Vergennes addresses Louis XVI and tells him how he should mourn the rebel leaders: "Ah! sire, maybe the names of the five unfortunate Frenchmen who were executed never reached Your Majesty; deign to scatter some flowers on their tombs, while deigning to say: 'La Frénière, Noyant, Caresse, Villeret, Marquis, and Millet were massacred by the orders of the barbaric O'Reilly, for having missed serving me and for having upheld the laws that a monster wanted to annihilate.'"[107] Because Vergennes (whether the real or the invented one) served as ambassador under Louis XVI and died before the Revolution, it is clear that his loyalties would lie with the Bourbon monarchy, even though he was progressive enough as foreign minister to aid the American Revolution. We see in this passage that he is sympathetic enough to the king to try to imagine him saying respectful words in favor of the rebels rather than blaming him for the situation.

The very specific era in which these last three texts were published, 1802–3, was significant because Napoleon, who was in power then, was attempting to rebuild the French empire after the loss of Saint-Domingue. This was the moment when the Spanish returned Louisiana to France. We know that the colony would remain in French hands for less than a year, but before the Louisiana Purchase the idea of returning the colony to the French fold still provoked strong emotions, especially nostalgia, among certain French royalists and revolutionaries alike.

For revolutionary orators, *sensibilité* was the moral compass that pointed to the right thing to do. In contrast to the eighteenth-century French public, modern-day Americans are suspicious about policy being based principally on feelings. We can look askance at the idea that "emotions were deemed to be as important as reason in the foundation of states and the conduct of politics," as William Reddy puts it.[108] Although mourning a death or expressing outrage in public appear acceptable in a political context today, opponents also see these emotions as potentially manipulative.

Were eighteenth-century orators and writers being manipulative or sincere when they expressed heightened emotions? Reddy addresses this issue of sincerity in eighteenth-century mentalities from his point of view as an anthropologist. For instance, he compares ostentatiously sentimental revolutionary oratory to various socially expected shows of emotion, such as the mourning practices of the Paxtun people of Pakistan; both "encouraged the pursuit of excess."[109] It is not important whether those involved truly feel what they are expressing; what matters is that they are conforming to the unspoken rules of their culture. Reddy provides a useful concept, the speech acts that he calls *emotives,* inspired by J. L. Austin's performative speech acts. Emotives may or may not be truly felt, but in either case they engage with the expectations of society and by doing so have certain effects on their audience: "Sincerity should not be considered the natural, best, or most obvious state toward which individuals strive. On the contrary, probably the most obvious orientation toward the power of emotives is a kind of fugitive instrumentalism."[110] Without taking a stance on whether political decisions should be made on the basis of sentiment, we can still observe how orators and writers surrounding the 1768 revolt used the literary mode of *sensibilité* to persuade readers to agree with their demands or opinions. Whether they truly felt what they wrote is impossible to gauge, but we can see the connection between their sentimental style and the political changes they tried to effect.

After the Louisiana Purchase, the revolt of 1768 continued to be commemorated, but by different people and for different purposes. One researcher, Mathé Allain, has discovered three different plays about the revolt written by Louisiana residents during the course of the nineteenth century. It was perhaps the next logical step to transform the events that had been told in prose into actual theatrical tragedies. As Allain remarks, these authors were inspired by Raynal and Champigny: "Very quickly, the leaders became, in the Louisiana imagination, patriots who thirsted for liberty and independence, precursors to American independence, veritable George Washingtons. And very quickly, the Louisianians found the interpretation they needed in a pamphlet published in London in 1773, *La Louisiane ensanglantée* [. . .]. In this pamphlet destined to serve as the sequel to the *Histoire des deux Indes,* as Champigny explains, the author praises the 'patriotic virtues of these generous Frenchmen that the Spanish sacrificed to their resentment.'"[111]

Nowadays, the revolt has been largely forgotten, except among specialists of Louisiana's colonial history. Few New Orleanians remember that Frenchmen Street, now a corridor of live music on the edge of the French Quarter, was named after the French rebel leaders who were executed there. Just after the fall of the French monarchy, however, it was important to keep their memory alive in order to influence the French public to feel enough indignation to call for the return of Louisiana to the French empire. In the next chapter, we will see how revolutionaries on both sides of the Atlantic also evoked sentimental and blood ties between France and Louisiana to call for their reunion.

5

In the Age of Revolutions

The New Orleans revolt of 1768 and the subversive writings it inspired were rumblings before the larger movements in the Western world that completely cast off the old monarchies. Soon, Louisiana's neighboring English colonies would wage war for independence; then France would be transformed by its own revolution, while its former colony Saint-Domingue rose up against its metropole. While these three major world events were taking place, Louisiana residents remained staidly in the hands of the Spanish Bourbon monarchs Carlos III and then Carlos IV. There was evidence that the colonists passionately supported the American Revolution and strained against their own government, but they never overthrew their leaders. On the other side of the Atlantic, however, what French citizens wrote about Louisiana and what the Spanish governors did to tamp down any potential subversion tell us how these imperial powers perceived the strategic—and sentimental—importance of controlling Louisiana in the Age of Revolutions.

The American Revolution as Seen from Spanish Louisiana

Let us return to Spanish Louisiana after it was subdued by O'Reilly. While interest in the revolt of 1768 was secretly fermenting in metropolitan France, the situation in the colony itself took a turn that the insurgents surely could not have predicted. One would expect the colonists of French descent to harbor a deep resentment against their Spanish rulers from the moment when O'Reilly ordered the execution of La Frénière and his fellows. They had enough reasons to maintain a hostile distance from the Spanish: not only the same economic concerns that remained from the revolt and the memory of the violent crackdown but also fear of the "Black legend," about the depraved cruelty of the Spaniards in the New World. Instead, the Spanish and French populations coexisted and intermarried under the relatively rational and effective policies of Carlos III (r. 1759–88), whose reign could be described as enlightened despotism.[1]

In 1777, eight years after O'Reilly's term in New Orleans, a remarkable new governor, Bernardo de Gálvez, arrived. While French texts had depicted Ulloa and O'Reilly as the villains of sentimental novels, this 30-year-old gentleman was perfectly suited to be a pre-Romantic hero. Within months of arriving at his post, he married a woman from a prominent French Creole family, Marie Félicité de Saint-Maxent, in contrast to Ulloa, who had offended locals by seeking a bride outside the colony. Scholars have treated Gálvez as a perfect example of the new Spanish Enlightenment, though little is known of his actual education or whether he was directly influenced by the *philosophes*.[2] Gonzalo Quintero Saravia tells us that Gálvez adhered to the new military reforms of the day and that he was involved in scientific research.[3] And David J. Weber informs us that the uncle who oversaw his whole career, José de Gálvez, was typical of the rising elite in Bourbon Spain, who were thoroughly versed in Enlightenment literature: "[José de] Gálvez possessed an impressive library for his day. It included titles in history, geography, and science. Gálvez's command of French allowed him to read the works of René Descartes and the French encyclopedists in the original and gave him access to works translated into that language, like William Robertson's *History of America* (1777)."[4] Perhaps because of this influence, his nephew Bernardo de Gálvez reportedly governed with mildness and efficiency. We can see from the laudatory poems that the planter and later politician Julien Poydras wrote about him that Gálvez also won the hearts of the population by waging war against the British during the American Revolution.[5] Gálvez was responsible for protecting New Orleans from British attacks by establishing control of Pensacola, Natchez, Mobile, and Baton Rouge. One could point out that he merely carried out Spain's policies, which were hostile to Britain at the moment, but Americans considered him as a valuable ally nevertheless.[6] He died of typhus at the age of 40, after his term in New Orleans, when he was governor of Mexico. He was remembered for instances of generosity and clemency, as well as for advancing the sciences when he commissioned a comprehensive catalogue of Mexican botanical specimens. Since then, North Americans have hailed him as a hero and commemorated him in a number of place names, such as Galveston, Texas; in 2014 the United States Congress named him an honorary citizen.

Admittedly, Gálvez's military victories during his term as governor of Louisiana were a matter of Spanish strategy against Britain. Gonzalo Quintero Saravia remarks that "the Spanish government considered the independence of the United States as a by-product of the war that could set a dangerous example for the Spanish possessions in the Americas [...]. In this context, it is not surprising that the Spanish government never considered the United States an ally. For Spain, the American Revolutionary War was just another imperial war between France and Spain against Britain."[7] The situation recalls the way the French Bourbons also supported the American Revolution, unaware that the sparks of revolution might catch fire in France itself. In this sense, Gálvez can be compared to Lafayette: both were young, Enlightenment-educated leaders who inspired enthusiasm among the masses when they participated in the American War of Independence. Lafayette returned to France to act as a moderate revolutionary, while Gálvez did not engage in any anti-monarchical activity as far as we know. In any case, both advanced the creation of the American republic. Were Louisiana residents encouraged by this "dangerous example" of a neighboring revolutionary government that fulfilled the promises of Enlightenment political ideas? Some French officials, after the Revolution, certainly hoped so.

French Attempts to Get Louisiana Back

Back in Europe, once the French monarchy had fallen, emotions toward Louisiana could finally come out from behind the cover of censorship to express themselves at full volume. The government that emerged from the tumult after the fall of the Bastille, the Convention (1792–95), led at first by the moderate Girondins, sent a diplomat named Edmond-Charles Genêt to represent his country in Philadelphia.[8] A fervent revolutionary, Citizen Genêt arrived on American shores in 1793. His mission was to instigate a takeover of Louisiana, supposedly with American cooperation: he went as far as to recruit allies such as General George Rogers Clark to lead the military operation. As a number of scholars have documented, the plan ultimately failed when President George Washington would not endorse a Franco-American attack on a Spanish property but instead insisted on neutrality. By 1794 the Girondin government had been replaced by the more radical Jacobin government, which recalled Genêt. Fearing for his life, Genêt requested asylum in the United States, where he remained for the rest of his life.[9]

The "Genêt Affair" involved not only military maneuvers but also propaganda. Genêt was an erudite man fluent in many languages, and he poured his eloquence into a pamphlet titled *Les Français libres à leurs frères de la Louisiane* (The Free French to their brothers in Louisiana), whose purpose was to rouse enthusiasm among the residents of Louisiana to join the French Convention—in other words, to start their own revolution. Published anonymously in Philadelphia in 1793, the six-page pamphlet takes the form of a written speech from an anonymous Frenchman to his overseas brethren. In the soaring oratorical style typical of French revolutionaries, the author begins, "The moment has arrived when despotism must disappear from the earth," and then he declares that his country is ready to help others liberate themselves as well: "France, which is now free [. . .], announces to all peoples that it is ready to facilitate, with its powerful support, the efforts of those who will want to follow its virtuous example."[10] He turns to address Louisiana in particular: "Your hour has finally arrived," the author exclaims. "Show yourselves, inhabitants of Louisiana."[11] And he commands them to undertake their own revolution. He states that this colony, once transformed into a new republic, can accept France's offer of temporary protection until it decides to remain independent or to join France or the United States.

Citizen Genêt, born in 1763, was too young to have followed the events in Louisiana as they happened, but he was surely moved by secondhand accounts by Raynal or Champigny, because his text echoes the words of the 1768 insurgents. (It is very probable that he had read Raynal, since *Histoire des deux Indes* was a massive success.) For instance, he indicates that he knows how the colonists feel, as if they had told him: "The French nation knows your sentiments."[12] He also reflects some of the same imagery as the manifestos of 1768, such as the comparison with farm animals: "It is time that you no longer be led like a herd."[13] This image of a herd reflects the multiple references in the manifestos to metaphorical "yokes" that the colonists say the government places on them.[14] The colonists also frequently compared themselves to enslaved people, and this image appears in the 1793 pamphlet: the author refers to their "heavy [. . .] chains" and exhorts them, "It is time that you stop being the slaves of a government to whom you were disgracefully sold."[15] At the end of the pamphlet, he evokes the image of Louisiana as a child, the most prominent figure in Raynal's harangue. In this passage, however, Genêt tells Louisianians that once they have overthrown the Spanish rulers, they can decide who to ally themselves with, "supported by France as long as your weakness does not allow you to defend yourselves."[16] This Enlightened sort of parenthood recalls John Locke's idea of a child being a temporary responsibility of the parent until the child can be independent,[17] an idea he offered as an analogy for government.

Another family relationship more frequently mentioned in Genêt's text is that of brothers. Like La Frénière and his co-conspirators in the 1760s, Genêt refers to an essential French identity based on sentiment and blood, in spite of time and distance. The word *frères* in the title of the pamphlet could refer to the brotherhood of man celebrated by the Revolution, but in this case it becomes evident that the author is evoking a family connection between the Frenchmen of the metropole and those of the Louisiana colony, linked by blood. Not only should this inborn sense of Frenchness, this "titre de Français" (title of Frenchman),[18] motivate their revolt against the Spanish, it should also give Louisianians the strength to fight. He encourages them to "prove [...] that you have preserved in your heart French valor, courage, and intrepidity,"[19] as if courage were a trait specific to their nationality.

Typical of this era of *sensibilité,* emotions are front and center in Genêt's call for political change. He does make a brief foray into economic issues when he explains that Louisiana should give the United States access to shipping channels at the mouth of the Mississippi, one of the major sources of tension in this period. But the rest of the pamphlet makes emotional appeals to familial love, stirs up outrage over Spanish cruelty, and tries to soothe fears that may make the colonists reluctant to revolt. He tells the colonists, "Frenchmen of Louisiana, you still love your former fatherland; this attachment is innate in your hearts,"[20] presuming that the "love" in their "hearts" will motivate them to action. In this passage he addresses the colonists as if he had heard their pleas, and he refers to Frenchness as if it were an essential substance born, "innate," in every person of French descent.

As in a novel with a victim and a villain, the 1768 insurgents' experiences have "carved into your souls the profound sentiment of an honorable vengeance."[21] He then describes to colonists their own feelings—"you tremble with indignation"—but tells them that they have not acted yet because "the fear of failure, the fear of not being supported, weakens your zeal."[22] He reassures them of military support from France and offers an idealized vision of a state run by brotherly love, without a villainous king to prevent their happiness: "Men were born to love one another, unite, and be happy, and they would be so if those who claim to be the images of God on earth, if the kings did not seek to divide them and to oppose their felicity."[23] His rhetoric makes it seem as if achieving independence were an affair of the heart.

In the family drama imagined in this pamphlet, the ties between brothers on either side of the Atlantic can finally be expressed openly, now that the villain—the monarch—can no longer keep them apart. In line with revolutionary ideology, Genêt refers to the French king himself and his court as "a perjurious king, neglectful ministers, vile and proud courtiers who fattened themselves on the sweat and the blood of the people."[24] While Enlightenment philosophers and critics of colonial policy in general had carefully blamed problems on the king's entourage, after 1789 a writer could finally point the finger at the "anciens tyrans" (ancient tyrants),[25] the kings themselves. In this case, Genêt may be referring to any of the Bourbon kings who had approved the bad decisions in Louisiana: Louis XIV, the regent Philippe d'Orléans, Louis XV, or Louis XVI.

Genêt pillories the other Bourbon kings, the ones ruling Spain, based on the *légende noire* that French people circulated about Spanish cruelty in the Americas, while turning a blind eye to their own depredations: "Spanish despotism surpassed in atrocity, in stupidity, all known despotisms. Did not this government, which rendered the name *Spaniard* detestable across the American continent, mark all its steps with brutality? Was it not under the hypocritical mask of religion that it ordered or permitted the massacre of more than twenty million men? Was it not to quench its insatiable greed that it depopulated, impoverished, degraded entire nations?"[26] He also warns them against the "abominable intentions" of Spain, which is threatened by the prosperity of the neighboring Kentucky territory.

More generally, Genêt creates an opposition between the nefarious despots of the world and the French nation, which has defeated its own monarch. By giving people their rights, France has provoked "the hatred of all the kings and their accomplices."[27] To condemn despotism, he cites a famous passage that we have seen before: "When the savages want to pick fruit, they cut the tree at the base: that is the picture of despotism."[28] As I discussed in chapter 2, this quotation appears in Montesquieu's *De l'esprit des lois*, specifically as the enigmatic definition of *despotisme*, which matches the quote from the Jaucourt article "Despotisme" in the *Encyclopédie*. In turn, the source of this anecdote is a description of the Natchez by the père Marest (which, I argue, does not refer to despotism). Like Montesquieu and Jaucourt, Genêt uses this anecdote to explain that despots act against the nation's economic interests. In Genêt's interpretation, the flourishing American economy contrasts with Spanish policies that inhibit growth specifically by blocking free access to the Mississippi. Immediately after saying that the "savages," coincidentally of Louisiana, cut down the tree just to get the fruit, he remarks: "In fact, to tyranny the fate of nations matters little; everything must be sacrificed to passing enjoyments, everything must bend to its will."[29] It is not clear whether free association makes him think of this purported Natchez practice when addressing people in Louisiana or whether there is really a lesson to be drawn about despotism.[30] In any case, he closes the argument by taking the first sentence of the pamphlet, in which he had declared that it was time that "despotism disappear from the earth"[31] and transforms it into a call to action, specifically commanding Louisianians to fight—"prove that despotism has not turned you into brutes"[32]—and ending with "ça ira," the title of a revolutionary song.

In his *Histoire de la Louisiane* (1829), Barbé-Marbois, who later negotiated the Louisiana Purchase, frowns on Genêt's imprudence: "He persuaded himself that he would find, not only in the western regions but in New Orleans itself a large party ready to assist him. He had been assured that all of Louisiana desired to return to French domination, and he applied himself seriously to its conquest."[33] As a diplomat himself, Barbé-Marbois judges that Genêt was too impetuous by nature (perhaps an excess of *sensibilité?*), so he garnered President Washington's disapproval.

We do not know how Louisianians reacted to Genêt's call to action, but we do have proof that some residents expressed themselves publicly in favor of the French Revolution and of the unrest in Saint-Domingue, which began in 1791. One Spanish official, Manuel Gayoso de Lemos, muses in a 1792 report that residents of French extraction tended to be peaceful but were "fond of novelty" (a common stereotype about the French, even perpetuated by French writers themselves) and "hear with the greatest pleasure of the revolution in that kingdom. Especially do the inhabitants of New Orleans and its vicinity conceal but little their mode of thinking."[34] He ventures to guess that most would choose to side with the French if a conflict broke out.

Another source we can look at is the first newspaper published in Louisiana, *Le Moniteur de la Louisiane,* founded by the Haitian immigré Louis Duclot. Although the Spanish officials approved its publication, the few existing copies from the 1790s offer us a glimpse of how Louisianians got news about the Convention, the Directoire, and future forms of government in France. In one issue from 1798, for example, among information about boats entering and leaving New Orleans, advertisements for the sale of slaves, and a government decree about shipping, we see a detailed description of a social event in London: specifically, a Bastille Day celebration. More than 650 people gathered "to celebrate the anniversary of the Liberty recovered by the French." A stone from the Bastille was placed on display, and Lord Stanhope (British peer and chairman of the Revolution Society) "certified that this stone had really been taken from the frightful lair in which despotism had made its unfortunate victims groan."[35] Other news of plays and celebrations of Bastille Day in other European cities, using laudatory words such as *patriot* and *liberty*, suggest that the journal favored the Revolution and that it aimed to encourage its readers to favor it as well. Other types of sources also show us how people felt about the political situation.

Researchers have discovered the cases of specific people in this era who were charged with seditious language. For instance, Kimberly Hanger presents us with the example of a free man of color, Pierre Bailly, a lieutenant and businessman who allegedly "urged his fellow militiamen to take up arms against white Louisianians. Bailly had announced that he and his colleagues were only awaiting word from Saint-Domingue to 'strike a blow like at the Cap,'" one of the sites of revolt.[36] Authorities accused him of conspiracy and insurrection, but the Spanish governor Esteban Miró, in office from 1785 to 1791, acquitted him. However, witnesses came forward, and in 1794 the new governor, the Baron de Carondelet, judged Bailly as guilty of "having professed ideas suggestive of revolution" and had him imprisoned in Cuba for two years.[37] Other examples of pro-revolutionary pronouncements include incidents in 1793 when New Orleans "theatergoers insisted that orchestras play 'La Marseillaise' and French partisans boldly sang the Jacobin song 'Ça ira'" in the streets.[38] Bailly's and these other residents' words were precisely the types of murmurs, rumors, or *bruits* that ancien régime authorities considered seditious.

We can also see how Spanish officials, especially Carondelet, acted based on the fears of revolution. A Spanish translation of Genêt's pamphlet, *Alocución de los franceses libres a sus hermanos de Luisiana*, appears among official documents in the Biblioteca Nacional in Madrid, so we see that the Spanish administration was well aware of the dangers of insurrection.[39] Genêt's pamphlet, along with rumors and localized instances of seditious speech, led the Spanish governor, Carondelet, to respond in kind. His correspondence tells us about his strategies to defend the colony against any military attacks and propaganda. For instance, he attempted to contain the spread of the French Revolution on the rhetorical front with a "Circulaire, adressée par le gouvernement à tous les habitans de la Louisiane" (Memorandum, addressed by the government to all the inhabitants of Louisiana), printed on February 12, 1794. He evokes violence and destruction brought by revolts around the world and names Genêt as a schemer who will bring "the same scenes of horror among you."[40] As in the novelistic scenario that many orators borrowed at the time, Carondelet warns innocent

Louisiana of these "scoundrels" and "vile seductors scattered among you."[41] He asks, "Would you let yourself be dazzled by the false hopes of a liberty, an equality that could not be established in France or in its colonies? [...] The [French] liberty of the press, fundamental law of the constitution, has been disgracefully violated and pitilessly bloodied by the massacre of those who wrote against the operations of the members of the Convention."[42] Like a naïve young woman, Louisiana might be dazzled by false promises, such as Richardson's novelistic heroine Clarissa, who is later raped by the villain, one of the most famous examples of literary *sensibilité*. Carondelet mentions that the freedom of the press was *violée*, a word that can mean "raped" or, more abstract, "violated." One might also note here the choice of the word *ensanglantée* (bloodied) applied to the personified colony: could Carondelet be referring to the title of Champigny's *La Louisiane ensanglantée*? He also uses that trope typical of *sensibilité*, the separation of families: "Every Frenchman without exception has been torn from his family, under threat of death."[43]

Carondelet counters Genêt's emotions with other emotions, namely, horror, as if to evoke the genre of gothic literature.[44] Elsewhere in his "Circulaire," he evokes a deceitful "phantom of liberty" that will only lead to people's loss of property. To scare the residents, he evokes the violence— "the murders, the fires, the devastation," "the torrents of blood that have been flowing for four years"[45]—caused by the revolutions in France and Saint-Domingue. He describes the former as a "theater of massacres and horrors."[46] He tells Louisianians (supposedly those with property): "Pillage, the loss of your properties; the massacre of your families; the renewal of all the calamities that devastated Saint-Domingue—that is what the monsters escaped from the Cap, and who are gathering on the Ohio, prepare for you."[47] The revolts in Saint-Domingue were the big "bang" felt all over the Gulf Coast, as Sarah E. Johnson writes in *The Fear of French Negroes*.[48] It reverberated in the sense that slaves had heard of the successes in Haiti and the French metropolitan government's debate about abolishing slavery in the colonies, so they were inspired to revolt, and fears of these movements often spurred officials to act.

The Spanish authorities in Louisiana had cracked down on the White, elite revolt of 1768, and they would have even fewer qualms about doing the same in future revolts by enslaved Black Louisianians and their sympathizers. In his *Circulaire*, Carondelet specifically addresses the free and enslaved Black people of Louisiana in a seemingly conciliatory tone, giving some residents of Saint-Domingue the noble epithet of "braves." This is how he refers to them: "Blacks themselves, [. . .] tossed around alternatingly by opposing parties, victims of the mad hope for liberty they had been lulled with, and which was only cemented by the massacre of a large portion of the bravest among them."[49] Carondelet does not go as far as to offer paternal love to the Louisiana residents, but he does remind them "of a sovereign who has constantly lavished his beneficences on you during the twenty-three years that you have lived under his laws," and he offers his own "lively interest that I take in your felicity."[50] Whether or not he persuaded them was a moot point, since Washington forced Genêt to abandon his plans. Still, Carondelet's fears would be realized in the 1795 slave revolt at Pointe Coupée, upriver from New Orleans; the conspirators were eventually executed by the Spanish officials.

Meanwhile, other French people under the Convention and later serving Napoleon continued to publicly call for the return of the colony, using tropes of sensibility. While officials on diplomatic missions, like Genêt, had their own opinions about taking back Louisiana, other French citizens expressed some of the same strong feelings. Let us examine the letter from a Société populaire de la Rochelle to the Comité de Marine et des Colonies dated "30ᵉ frimaire, l'an 3 de la République" (December 20, 1794). When this letter was written, France was in the third phase of the Convention, the Convention thermidorienne, after the fall of Robespierre. Why La Rochelle? It is possible that political clubs in other cities wrote letters like this one, but this city had particular reasons to argue for a closer connection to North America. First of all, it had been the port with the highest volume of trade with the Louisiana colony, including trafficking in slaves.[51] Second, the Louisiana rebels of 1768 sent missions to several chambers of commerce, including the one in La Rochelle.[52] This city had historically been at odds with the monarchy because its large Protestant population had been oppressed for centuries, so it may have been more sympathetic toward dissidents. After many Protestants had gone into exile, the remaining citizens depended largely on commerce. The majority approved of the Revolution, avoiding the extremes of both the Montagnards and the royalist insurgency of the neighboring Vendée.[53]

This letter about Louisiana does mention concerns about the commercial advantages of reclaiming the colony, yet it couches these concerns in terms of *sensibilité:* anger at past monarchs, longing for the writers' long-lost brothers, lament at the death of the rebels. The authors use the tropes and style of revolutionary speeches to specifically blame "the venality of the former government" for "the great interests of the nation sacrificed in Louisiana."⁵⁴ More specifically about Louisiana: "If it were necessary to awaken resentments about this disastrous cession and through painful memories animate vengeance against Spain, we would evoke the spirits of the ancestors of six heroes, massacred in cold blood at the heart of the Mississippi for having committed, along with all their fellow citizens, an act of loyal attachment to a fatherland that was abandoning them; we would present these illustrious victims given up by the odious vizier Choiseul."⁵⁵ It is worth noting that by calling Choiseul, minister of the marine under Louis XV, a "vizier," they refer to the vision of "Oriental despotism" that originated in ancient Greece and appeared prominently in the works of Montesquieu and other early modern philosophers. Further in the text, they accuse Spain of "trafficking at the boudoir of a courtesan, as in the time of despotism, in the honor and the property of France."⁵⁶ This is clearly a reference to the marquise de Pompadour, who persuaded her royal lover Louis XV to appoint Choiseul in the first place.

The writers of the letter from La Rochelle make use of typical revolutionary catchwords, such as *concitoyens* (fellow citizens) and *patrie* (fatherland), and they also use a very elevated register, with words such as *mânes,* a term used in ancient Rome to refer to a family's ancestors. Even before the Revolution, the word was not commonly used but reserved instead for the high oratorical style: in a 1694 dictionary it is noted under "mânes" that "one still uses it sometimes in poetry and in the sublime style."⁵⁷ The letter from La Rochelle thus points out that these ancestors are shared by the letter writers and the colonists; it also recalls the classical French tragedies of Corneille and Racine so that readers understand that they should react to the 1768 revolt as a sublime, theatrical, and sad event.

The sublime that the authors are trying to evoke, akin to the one we see in literature, continues as we read the letter: "Console yourselves, generous phantoms, of having preceded us in the fight against tyrants! Soon the appearance of the dazzling sign of their destruction will delight these riverbanks that are still covered with mourning crepe that your demise made them put on!"⁵⁸ Once again, terms from the elevated register, such as *ombres généreuses* (generous phantoms, a reference to the afterlife in the ancient Greek tradition) and *trépas* (demise) signal to readers that they are witnessing a classical tragedy and that their heroes are the Louisiana rebels of 1768. The apostrophe or direct address to these imaginary phantoms/shades and the metaphorical image of the banks of the Mississippi being covered in funerary crepe fabric further maintain the elevated register.

There is no doubt that this letter is informed by the narratives of the 1768 revolt and its crackdown. One note provides a summary of the events: "It was an Irishman named O'Reilly who came to Louisiana one year after the expulsion of Ulloa to wreak Spanish vengeance on the unfortunate inhabitants."[59] We then see an account of the execution of one of the rebels, the Swiss military man Pierre Marquis, that is similar to one that appears in the 1777 *Nouveaux voyages dans l'Amérique septentrionale*, by Jean-Bernard Bossu, but with variations. The letter from La Rochelle states: "One of the victims, the immortal Marquis, an old man past sixty years of age, uncovered his scarred chest and cried out, 'Your cowardly lead [bullets] can tear through this chest, which for forty years has withstood Prussian and Austrian bullets, but they will not destroy the hatred that I have sworn against your odious nation.'"[60] Although the speech varies from the one quoted in the previous chapter, both are worthy of a scene to be performed on a stage, and both present the rebels of 1768 as heroes whose dignity in their self-sacrifice will make the public feel what spectators of tragedies are supposed to feel: terror and pity.[61]

The letter from La Rochelle appeals to yet more emotions, specifically love between family members. Like Raynal's *Histoire des deux Indes,* it evokes the trope of abandoned children in reference to the Louisiana colonists: "They are still affectionate children who must return to the heart of a mother who ignored them for too long."[62] The authors of this letter appeal to the Convention to set things right vis-à-vis the abandoned heirs to their common ancestors, as if they were the long-lost descendants of a family in a novel or a play: "Legislators, it is the special responsibility of the inhabitants of this city, long united by commercial relations and forever by the ties of blood and fraternity with the colonists of Louisiana, to act as executors of the will of these magnanimous, unfortunate men who in their last cry still called to their fatherland amid their torments."[63] After all, the members of the Société de la Rochelle see themselves reflected in the people across the Atlantic: "Everything there is French: the inhabitants, their customs, their language, the very iron that plows their fields. They are our friends, our brothers, our children, whose hearts aspire to be readopted into the greater republican family from which no power can separate them for long. Their titles? Legislators, if they may have been forgotten or ignored, they could still find them at the bottom of the Mississippi, sealed with their purest blood."[64] The authors create an expectation of a touching family reunion in the end, as if French colonial history had a plot that resembled Diderot's *comédies larmoyantes*.

Perhaps as a response to calls such as the one from La Rochelle, perhaps out of its own self-interests, the French Convention sent a number of adventurers and officials swarming across North America in the 1790s with the goal of "repossession of Louisiana."⁶⁵ Genêt was not the only one. Another agent was Captain La Gautrais, who addressed a letter to "Citoyens Représentants" (Citizen Representatives) on 2 Germinal, An III (March 22, 1795), claiming to speak in the name of the French people of Louisiana: "The inhabitants of Louisiana offer you their wishes through my voice. They groan under the yoke of despotism: they are French and want to be part of the Republic. They see with horror the inquisition that is wrought upon them. They secretly groan over their sad situation and ask to be liberated."⁶⁶ La Gautrais also penned a letter in which he gives more details about the commercial advantages of Louisiana, including lumber, minerals, and shipping access to the Mississippi. In trying to persuade his readers (he addresses "citoyens représentants" and "vos comités" [your committees]) to desire the return of Louisiana, he emphasizes the common bond of Frenchness between "frères de la République": "All the inhabitants are French: they desire to be part of the Republic. They can take their complaints only to the French: it is from them that they must expect their liberty."⁶⁷ He enjoins his government to take action: "The time is favorable and the moment is precious. Let us take advantage of it and bring liberty to this people, this victim of despotism. Let us pursue our enemies beyond the ocean. You will possess this advantage by establishing liberty, by this means you will make the Republic known to this unfortunate people and you will bring it out of the state of slavery to which it has been reduced for twenty-five years."⁶⁸ In these two letters we can recognize some of the revolutionary keywords that surely tended to elicit certain emotional reactions among his readers: *frères, liberté, despotisme, esclavage* (brothers, liberty, despotism, slavery). By repeating words like *gémir* (groan), he creates a certain pathos that is typical for these reports on Louisiana. In any other era, we would expect a report on military or commercial strategy to be in a neutral, bureaucratic tone, but this was the era of *sensibilité*.

Once the Convention gave way to the Directoire in November of 1795, this government sent the diplomat Pierre-Auguste Adet to represent France in the United States. Like his predecessor Genêt, he plotted to undermine Spanish control of Louisiana, this time by sending General Victor Collot, who had fought in the American Revolution under General Rochambeau. Collot had also been governor of the island of Guadeloupe from 1792 to 1794. In a document found in the archives of the French Ministry of War in

Vincennes, presented by Durand Echeverria, Collot states his objectives in his 1796 trip through Louisiana. Collot asks about the United States in the form of a questionnaire to himself: "What is the attitude of the people of the southern states toward the federal government and toward France? Are they truly republicans? Do they wish to be free and independent?"[69] About Louisiana in particular, he notes: "Examine from every angle what support we may draw from the French element that still exists there. Have they degenerated? Are they still proud to bear the name of Frenchmen? In this case, make them understand that Africans too have been included among the subjects of France. And that we have left courageous Frenchmen in slavery."[70] In spite of his plans, Collot's trip was cut short when he was arrested by Carondelet's troops.[71] The Spanish governor interrogated him and then sent him back to the United States, which in turn deported him back to France.[72]

During his fact-finding trip in 1796, Victor Collot wrote to the diplomat Adet, who in turn was to present these findings to the Ministries of the Exterior and of the Marine, outlining the advantages of taking back Louisiana. Aside from mentioning commercial interests, such as the lumber trade, Collot puts heavy emphasis on the sentiment of Frenchness binding the residents of both continents. Much of the language he uses in this report echoes the very language of Raynal, and as in the writings of Raynal and Genêt discussed earlier, *sensibilité* is allied with a condemnation of the ancien régime. In this report, "Extract of a Memorandum on the Necessity for the French Republic to Have Louisiana, Seen through Different Political, Commercial, and Maritime Rapports,"[73] Collot hews very closely to Raynal's prosopopeia that baby-Louisiana addresses to parent-France. Before suggesting a course of action, Collot insists that France acknowledge its fault in giving up the colony in the first place, referring to "the loss that France suffered by the cession of Louisiana [. . .], the injustice that it committed by abandoning its own children."[74] He then presents a legal question: "whether kings had the right to cede Louisiana." And in his immediate response he grows lyrical, borrowing words familiar to those who have read the Raynal passage:

> I will ask the Convention if it hears me through *a voice that cries out from the depths of its vast forests:* "what?" "*you have abandoned the children born from your womb* who, in spite of their justified desperation, have not stopped seeding and cultivating their fields, in the hope of being claimed by you; who, having fertilized the soil with their sweat, again irrigated it with their blood

to preserve it; and who, glorifying in your name, sought by good deeds and benefactions to win renown for it among the most savage nations, who have remained your faithful friends through their care?"[75] (emphasis added)

"Voice that cries out" is the same biblical phrasing Raynal uses at the beginning of his harangue. What follows is a long question that reproaches France for abandoning its children "born from your womb," just as in Raynal's reproachful question in the voice of the child. Both passages also emphasize the blood and sweat the residents have put into cultivating the soil for the sake of France; Raynal's text reads, "After having fertilized it with my sweat, have I not irrigated it with my blood to preserve it?"[76] And like Raynal and other defenders of Louisiana's role as a French colony, Collot evokes the "yoke" that makes beasts of burden out of the colonists: "Men, who have always looked with horror upon the yoke under which they live; who have put all their effort into shaking it off and whose weakness alone could constrain them to bear chains. Burning for liberty, for their fatherland, in spite of its ingratitude and its insensibility, forgetting our rights, forgetting your duties, you have not deigned to claim these children by breaking the chains that they detest and by granting them the only consolation that they have aspired to—that of living under your laws."[77] Unlike Raynal, Collot can try to offer them the rights and liberties of republican France, but both Frenchmen claim to speak for the colonists, whose aspiration they presume is still to belong to the mother country.

Aside from metaphors of children and cattle, complaints about Louisiana automatically brought up critiques of the Bourbons and of monarchy in general. These critiques make use of words like *tyranny* and *despotism*. Collot exclaims, in the voice of the Louisianians: "In the time of tyranny, a perfidious government sold us against the law of nations to oppressive, intolerant, and superstitious foreigners."[78] Collot has recourse to the trope of the corrupt royal entourage: "Unfortunately, France under the ancien régime, deceived by ignorant or greedy people, oppressed by presumptuous viziers, ignored all its advantages, and Spain its weakness."[79] As we saw in the letter from La Rochelle, Collot specifically calls the duc de Choiseul a "vizier," the word used for the ministers of Oriental despots, and accuses him of not appreciating the value of Louisiana: "If M. de Choiseul, or the minister at the time, had known Louisiana better, enlightened men would have been in charge of managing it; they would have glorified in making known to France all of its importance. This colony, previously so misunderstood and scorned, would today be a great compensation for the momentary loss of its islands that the Republic has just suffered."[80] Since this letter is from 1796, he writes perhaps strategically, perhaps earnestly, with revolutionary fervor against the Bourbon administration. By the time he writes his *Voyage dans l'Amérique septentrionale* (published in 1826, after his death in 1805), Collot has softened his views on Choiseul. He reflects that after the Louisiana Purchase in 1803, Louis XV's minister actually had "real reasons of state" for giving up the colony and that unfair judgments of him came from the revolutionary era, in which "calumny called itself 'history' and persecution, 'republicanism.'"[81]

A Digression about a Song

Even though French people often expressed their feelings about Louisiana in a tone of tragedy or melodrama, Louisiana residents themselves, even those who were sympathetic to the French Revolution, sometimes expressed themselves in the comic mode instead, as we can see in Carondelet's correspondence. These archival materials give us information about ephemera that would otherwise have been lost, since residents communicated orally and presumably in secret, to avoid arrest. Carondelet sent detailed reports to his local officers and his superiors in Spain, and he exchanged information with diplomats and military men from other nations: Great Britain, Native tribes such as the Osage and the Creek, and the leaders of the newly established United States. So we get an idea of what the restive French residents were up to when we read the official reports about their potentially subversive actions and words.

One series of letters from 1795–96 concerns rumors of a possible revolt in the town of Pointe Coupée. Specifically, Carondelet and his local officers heard about certain songs being sung at parties: "During these entertainments, they sing revolutionary songs that are capable of inciting the most loyal subjects to rebellion."[82] One of these songs has come down to us; entitled "Cochon de lait" (Suckling pig), it can be found in the Spanish colonial archives. The historian Ernest Liljegren assumes that the "cochon de lait" in question is Carondelet. I believe that this is very probable, since both start with a *C* and have four syllables, the last of which rhyme. Nowadays New Orleanians pronounce the final *t* in the name (it remains a street name), presumably the way his Spanish contemporaries did, but it is highly possible that the French colonists pronounced it in the original French way, since he was of French descent. If the final *t* is not pronounced, then "Carondelet" and "Cochon de lait" rhyme.

This is the text of the song, which is labeled "Chanson patriotique" (Patriotic song). I include it here in full, since I believe it has not been published until now.[83]

When we're Republicans (repeat x 2)

We will punish all the rascals (repeat x 2)
Suckling pig will be guillotined first
Let's dance the Carmagnole, long live the sounds, long live the sounds,
Let's dance the Carmagnole, long live the rounds, long live the sounds of our songs.

The contador [accountant] will have his share (x 2)
He will be hanged on the rampart (x 2)
The auditor will take part, the public will laugh
Let's dance the Carmagnole...

Fat Hevia the master thief (x 2)
Let's carefully follow his good boss (x 2)
He'll be on a hook, he will dance in the wind
Let's dance the Carmagnole...

Our intendant will fear nothing (x 2)
If he remains a good man (x 2)
We will never forget
His generous deeds
Let's dance the Carmagnole...

The great Mestaignier lends a hand
Just like Admiral Cuen, cuen
To applaud the plans of the famous suckling pig
Let's dance the Carmagnole...

The suckling pig's intention
Was divulged by Asseret
But his strike failed thanks to M. Brognier
Let's dance the Carmagnole...

I'll be hanged by Pontalba
Then he will be whipped

And we will keep him and use him as a spy
Let's dance the Carmagnole...

This type of song is defined as a "Table *ronde,* or simply *ronde,* a song with a refrain that each person sings in turn."⁸⁴ It is also a kind of dance, as in "a village *ronde,*" a folk dance that involves people holding hands in a circle and dancing round and round. The melody of the song is cheerful and enjoins the listeners to dance. The joyful spirit of the melody contrasts ironically with the violent lyrics, both of the Louisiana version and of the original "Carmagnole." To this day, New Orleanians follow a tradition of adapting popular songs (e.g., Christmas carols) to reflect local experience, to comic effect.

When Carondelet heard about this song, he ordered a criminal investigation in July of 1795, the purpose of which was to find out which residents were singing these songs, how the songs passed from one to another, and whether they were plotting an uprising. A number of witnesses were interviewed, and the transcriptions remain in the archives. Several pages are devoted to each interview, but first I will quote a few parts from the prefatory remarks that explain the context. A recent slave revolt in Pointe Coupée had led the Spanish officials to be extremely vigilant against other unrest. The writer of this preface to the interrogations names the possible reasons for the uprisings: "Twenty thousand Blacks who were inspired by the desire for liberty and the thought of acquiring it through the death of Whites, a natural restlessness, their fanaticism about the new French constitution, the inclination that men generally conserve for their original homeland, poverty or the disorder of the fortunes of many who hope to find in the insurrection the means of concealing their bad faith: everything conspires in Lower Louisiana for a revolution."⁸⁵ In fact, the statement is somewhat muddled: the writer mentions that the slave revolts aimed to kill White landowners, but Spanish authorities also suspected many of these White landowners of being revolutionary sympathizers. In the above quotation, the writer clearly designates enslaved people first as desiring liberty, inspired by the Revolution. However, when he refers to "el fanatismo de estos" (their fanaticism), it is not clear whether he is referring to the Black or the White people. When he claims that "los hombres [...] generalmente" (men [...] generally) have an inclination toward their homeland and that everything in Louisiana conspires toward Revolution, it is unclear whether he means enslaved people, colonists of French descent, or everyone. And the aspirations of Blacks and Whites, including some Whites who supported slavery, also vary in the potential spread of the Revolution to Louisiana.

In any case, the clerk notes some behavior among the residents of unspecified race that threatens the Spanish authorities: "The patriotic song, whose copy I submitted to you, spread artfully throughout the province [...] the danger that the colony is in, since many are arming themselves in their homes, others have tried to overpower me and the auditor [judge], another tried to assassinate me during some confusion that was provoked [...] and the tricolor flag was hanging in the trees."[86] Songs, hoarding of arms, violence, and the French revolutionary flag—in the governor's eyes, all these signs point to a coming revolution, so he has to take action.

The two *regidores* (councilors) who led the investigation set up a "legal inquiry against various principal inhabitants who were suspected of being the authors of the patriotic song or of allowing it to be sung in their homes."[87] They interviewed a number of subjects in French and in Spanish, including the *nègre libre* (free Black) François de Lande, who guesses his own age as 55 but is not sure, a 21-year-old so-called *griffe libre* (3/4 Black, 1/4 White, free)[88] named Charles Joseph l'Ange, and Commander Santiago Manicot. A few incidents emerge from these interviews, which are examined from several different angles.

One, that a certain Monsieur Penn (we can presume anyone given the title "Monsieur" is a member of the White elite) had visited the household of the *griffe libre* Charles Joseph l'Ange (possibly, as they mentioned, because it was raining), while other people of color of both sexes—some free, some enslaved—were present. While there, this M. Penn began ranting in favor of the French Revolution, specifically "that they had done very well to kill the king, because he was a rascal and a man like any other."[89] As for the Louisiana residents of French descent, "when the time comes, they would take up arms, but afterwards they would turn them against the Spaniards and cut off their heads during the night."[90] Several witnesses recount the same episode involving M. Penn, some of them adding that a man named M. D'Arembourg passed by and overheard the conversation and that he asked M. Penn about it at a dinner party afterwards. Others report that M. Penn tried to persuade his own enslaved men Jupiter and Jaco, as well as several Natives, that a French takeover of Louisiana was imminent. M. Penn was also rumored to have made his pro-revolutionary views known very loudly at his own dinner parties, which were attended by other prominent local residents and witnessed by his enslaved servants, who passed on the gossip to the free Blacks of their acquaintance.

The free people of color interviewed also recount that other gentlemen, the brothers Trépagnier, instead of trying to win the people of color over to their side, were reported to be boasting that when the French took over, they would re-enslave these free Blacks. The Trépagniers and their co-conspirator Alexandre Labranche gathered under a pecan tree, according to witnesses, and discussed the Revolution. In regard to the "Cochon de lait" song, the Spanish commander Santiago Manicot is asked whether he knows the song and whether he heard it at Trépagnier's house. He denies having heard it there. Of course none of the people interviewed admit any guilt in singing or distributing the song, or more generally in defending pro-revolutionary views—why would they incriminate themselves? Aside from a rumor that a Black man named Louis Benoît was heard singing the song (and unfortunately the file that records his testimony is illegible), little information seems to have been extracted from these interviews. The *regidores* did not uncover the author of this song, and as far as I can tell, no one was prosecuted as a result of this investigation.

Why does an episode like this deserve our attention? Why should we look at the history of unfounded fears and might-have-beens? To a certain extent, the "Cochon de lait" episode was less about an insurrection that didn't happen and more about Carondelet's fears. The possibility that Louisiana's residents could collectively decide to seek independence or to re-join the French empire was enough to alarm the governor, who in turn expressed to the Spanish government his fears that they were on the brink of losing control of the colony.

In terms of networks of communication, the "Cochon de lait" case gives us a peek at the paths taken by revolutionary words that spread throughout the Spanish Americas in the 1790s and following decades. In some cases they resulted in independence movements, in other cases not. But as Arlette Farge and Jacques Revel demonstrate in their study of rumors that became riots in 1750 Paris, these inquiries end up revealing how these communication networks functioned, especially in a time of royal censorship. People had no legitimate, sanctioned way to express certain political opinions or desires; they rightly feared being arrested, exiled, and even executed for expressing views in opposition to the government. So they turned to ephemeral, elusive modes of communication, including rumors and satirical songs.

In the case of "Cochon de lait," we see how Louisiana residents of various colors, sexes, national origins, and social ranks interacted socially (sometimes in a collaborative, sometimes in a hostile way) to transmit information about, for example, an impending invasion. The attempted revolution in Louisiana was less a series of actions and more a war of words—or of hearts and minds, as we say now. Accordingly, singing the "Cochon de lait" song was a way for some Louisianians to signal, if not that they were ready for a French takeover, at least that they were dissatisfied with Spanish monarchical rule. In New Orleans, humor and sociability are still vehicles for political satire. Coincidentally, in one 2010 Mardi Gras parade, specifically by the satirical Krewe du Vieux, we see the motif of the roast pig applied to the former mayor, Ray Nagin, who had recently been arrested for corruption. Marchers carried a banner bearing the words "Cochon de Ray" ahead of the float that featured a large effigy of Nagin naked, roasting over a fire with an apple in his mouth. This play on the term *cochon de lait* and the mayor's name unintentionally recalls the satire of Governor Carondelet and shows an uncanny continuity in the satirical tradition that plays on French words and symbolic violence. In 2006, after the US government failed to protect the population during Hurricane Katrina, the Krewe du Vieux featured a float that carried members disguised as distressed-looking mimes (referring to the alleged French love of pantomimes like Marcel Marceau) bearing large signs with the words "Buy us back, Chirac." While appeal to France was a joke, it still demonstrates a certain nostalgia for reunion with the colony's original empire that happens to reflect the feelings expressed by French politicians and writers in the nineteenth century.

In the 1790s, people on the ground in Louisiana also behaved subversively by singing other songs, spreading rumors, and in some cases pledging their loyalty to France not with words but through symbolic gestures like wearing the cocarde. These other expressions of rebellious feelings toward the Spanish monarchy appear in a very thoroughly researched article from 1939 by Ernest Liljegren. He cites official correspondence from Spanish officials who report seditious behavior, specifically the formation of Jacobin clubs, in which people sang "La Marseillaise" and "Ça ira" (but "Cochon de lait" has special significance because the words are adapted to local circumstances). He also recounts the slapstick story of a French priest named Delvaux who was exiled on a boat for his pro-revolutionary harangues in Natchitoches and other parts of lower Louisiana. Tracing the pathways of communication networks, written or spoken, reveals how sociability works in this era as an alternative to official hierarchies, the former being a Deleuzian rhizome, while the latter is a top-down imposition of laws. These comic expressions of adherence to French revolutionary principles coexisted with the sentimental ones discussed in this chapter. We could note, however, that the satire remained an underground, ephemeral form of expression among residents, while the expressions of *sensibilité* became, in this era, the official, publicly accepted mode for metropolitans to discuss the relationship between France and Louisiana.

The Napoleonic Interlude

After the Directoire era in France, Napoleon took control as head of the Consulat in 1799, but amid all the changes in regime and ideology the expressions of yearning from the metropole for Louisiana remained constant. With the Third Treaty of San Ildefonso in 1800, Spain finally ceded the colony, along with other territories, back to France. Saint-Domingue had been ever present in the minds of Spanish officials in the 1790s, as we see in their published announcements to Louisiana residents. It could be argued that fears (whether well founded or not) that Louisiana would become another Haiti led the Spanish to find Louisiana too troublesome, so they welcomed the chance to return it to France. And perhaps for the same reasons, Napoleon ultimately decided that it was too hot to handle, since his army was overextended and that it would be better to sell it to the United States while he still owned it.

In the brief period in which Louisiana was French, Napoleon sent Pierre-Clément Laussat as the new *préfet colonial* of Louisiana in December 1802. As we see in the latter's personal journal, he was a man of the Enlightenment, full of *sensibilité*, who expressed his high ideals for the colony. On April 1, 1803, he notes to himself: "I promise selflessness and purity everywhere, support during good times and suppression during the bad. I expect a great deal from the colonists, because they are a good race of men."[91] Upon settling among the prominent citizens in New Orleans, he writes optimistically on March 27, 1803, "All Louisianians have a French heart."[92] He then states, "It was time for the French government to show itself and to announce here its rights and its intentions."[93] It is as if he has come to fulfill the desires of so many Frenchmen to reunite with their brothers across the Atlantic and to right the wrongs of the 1760s, when the French monarchy disdained its own subjects.

In his inaugural address, which after he delivered it was then issued in print, Laussat touches upon all the tropes I have marked out in the speeches and letters mentioned in this chapter, and he presents this as the culminating moment in the joint history of Louisiana and France. As a "man of feeling" of his era, Laussat first acknowledges the pain the colonists must have felt upon being separated from their mother country.

> Your separation from France marks one of the most shameful epochs in its chronicles, under an already weak and corrupt government, after an ignominious war and as a consequence of a withering peace.
>
> Next to a cowardly and unnatural abandonment, you offered the contrast of a heroic love, faithfulness, and courage.
>
> All the French hearts were touched and have never lost the memory: they cried out then, with pride, and they have since then never ceased to repeat that *their blood flowed in your veins* (author's emphasis).[94]

These opening lines of his speech cover the corruption of the ancien régime, the emotional tale of the unnatural parent who abandoned his or her child, and the common essential Frenchness that binds both populations, all common tropes we have seen before.

Laussat then tells his public that as soon as the Revolution occurred, the French "turned their gaze back upon you" and "they wanted your retrocession to signal their first peace [agreement]."[95] However, these missions having failed, they had to wait: "one Man needed to appear"—as if Napoleon were a Messiah.[96] He praises his leader to the skies and claims that Napoleon is receptive to their needs: "This Man presides today over our Destinies, and from this moment on, LOUISIANIANS, he is responsible for yours."[97] Among the missions of the military men and administrators Napoleon sends, he includes protecting the property and commerce of Louisiana residents, maintaining order, and respecting the Catholic religion. At the end, Laussat responds to what he imagines are the emotional needs of the colonists: he promises to "strengthen every day the ties that one single origin, the same customs, the same inclinations establish between this colony and the Mother Country."[98] To emphasize the blood ties between colonial and metropolitan French people, he further states: "You will thus congratulate yourselves, on every account, for being French again: with each passing day, you will feel the value of this beautiful title, an object of envy around the globe."[99] This Frenchness he evokes transcends location.

As for Spain, which appeared as the villain in the family drama created by other officials who wrote about Louisiana, Laussat has to be more careful, since the two European powers are allies at this moment. In his speech, he seems to have spoken harshly of Spain in regard to O'Reilly's crackdown, as he mentions in his personal journal: "A proclamation in which I made some allusion to the atrocities of O'Reilly against the French when he took possession of the colony for Spain displeased Governor Salcedo, but it encourages the national devotion of the colonists. The enemies of the French name, whether out of fear or jealousy, sought to embitter spirits, to worry them and even to irritate them."[100] This entry is from March 27, 1803, the day after his speech. So he may have changed the text of the speech before it was printed in this document, which states, more favorably: "Nevertheless, we know, LOUISIANIANS, and we do not want to dissimulate that for thirty years Spain, through the gentleness of a reformist and generous government, made efforts to make you forget the bloody fault of one agent of this noble nation. It is the close and faithful friend of ours: we are not the ones who will inspire you to pay it back with ingratitude."[101] These concessions to Spain are an early inkling of how political self-interest would ultimately be more important than *sensibilité* in policies concerning Louisiana.

In spite of all these effusions of emotion, the tender reunion of melodrama would turn out to be anticlimactic. First of all, how did Laussat's listeners react to this speech? The diplomat Barbé-Marbois remarks that businessmen were skeptical about how the change in regime would affect commerce. "They did not exhibit those signs of contentment that the return of the French would have produced in other times."[102] He then quotes an unnamed witness who further describes people of French descent receiving Laussat's speech "without emotion"—a succinct expression for the end of the era of sensibility between the colony and metropole.

Another writer confirms the waning of emotion: Berquin-Duvallon, the exiled planter from Saint-Domingue we encountered in chapter 4, observes the people of New Orleans reacting (or rather, not reacting) to the rumor that they will soon return to the French empire. This is a piece of news that is "made to transport all the sensible hearts with joy and contentment, and especially the good and true French ones."[103] Notice that he sarcastically refers to the "sensible hearts" (cœurs sensibles) and the patriotism that appeared so often in calls for the return of Louisiana. In this instance, however, the local residents' "personal interest" creates a feeling not of joy but of "inquiétude" (worry). Everything is "morne, froid" (gloomy, cold), and there is "no rejoicing, neither public nor private parties consecrated to this happy event, even though they are in the time of balls and performances (Carnival)."[104] The silence contrasts singularly with the emotion of the French administrators' writings of the previous years.

Berquin-Duvallon's bitter outlook surely has to do with his personal situation or with his sullen character, but in any case, he provides an interesting counternarrative to the novelistic plot of Louisiana and France as a separated family. First, he questions the supposed heroism of the colonists in general, saying that "the Creoles in this place are, for the most part, without moral energy"[105] and motivated only by personal gain. He then asks, "What can be the measure of their supposed patriotism and of the attachment they affect for France, their former fatherland"[106] if they submitted so quickly to O'Reilly's crackdown after making a show of rebellion? He then judges their gestures toward joining in the revolutionary movement to be useless. "Weren't they seen, a few years ago, after they agitated themselves without thinking [...] and after they threw parties where, in front of their slaves, the imbeciles sang at the top of their voices and with an inconceivable imprudence the French hymns that celebrated the Rights of Man?"[107] As a slave owner, he is especially troubled by the possibility that this insurrection could put ideas of freedom and rights in the minds of enslaved people. In his view, their calls for revolution were a "vain display and noisy racket," after which the residents chose to "go back into their shells and settle down under the control of the Spanish government, like a herd of sheep under the shepherd's crook."[108]

> One may tell me: "But these same inhabitants asked several times to be reunited with their former government, to become French again. What is more, since the era of the Revolution, there appeared, in their collective name and to this same end, a petition drafted and signed by a member of the Society of the Friends of the Constitution, Des Odouarts-Fantin, in the name of the colonists." That is true. But let us go back in spirit to the dates of these divisive demands and even to this petition, made in 1790, and moreover let us attentively examine the principal object, the essential point of all these demands.[109]

He puts less emphasis on the emotions expressed and more on the issues of commercial self-interest. In this case, he claims, the Louisiana residents called for a return to the French empire because a free-trade agreement was going to expire in 1791. In short, "We will see [...] that the claims of the Louisianians, in this matter, had as a base and as a direct motive not strictly speaking their innate attachment to France but their fear of the prohibitive regime of the Spanish colonies."[110] Although Berquin-Duvallon was a biased and embittered observer, some of his views anticipate those of modern historians who study this period. These historians speculate whether the Louisiana rebels were motivated by patriotic emotions or by commercial interests: were the emotions part of a performance? Ultimately, we cannot know how sincerely the colonists and the metropole felt the emotions that they expressed. They may have been exploiting the trend in *sensibilité* to persuade the public or other officials to accomplish something that was in their economic interest. Or they may simply have been speaking in the style and tropes that were common currency at the time: it may have been the only way that people could consider communicating.

This final reunion of France with its North American colony was short-lived. Just a month after Laussat's speech, Napoleon signed the treaty that sold Louisiana to the United States, and French troops withdrew five months later, in November 1803. In his memoirs, Laussat reflects on what might have been: "France loses a colony to whom the most beautiful destinies have been promised. While waiting for its natural emancipation, by the lapse of time, we could plant the seed of an immense French population. [. . .] A new France would have been formed. [. . .] Everything vanishes; all that remains to me is the regret over one year of idleness, over a useless transmigration of my family toward a new world, over many expenses and bother and fruitless disruption."[111] The residents of Louisiana, disdained by the Bourbon kings, transformed into tragic heroes by the partisans of the Enlightenment and of the Revolution, were ready to move on to the next troubled stage of their history, as Americans. Sentimental attachment to Louisiana would live on in the French imagination, even as the political connection was severed forever.

CONCLUSION

The Protest Tradition in New Orleans

In 2005, after Hurricane Katrina caused untold damage to the city of New Orleans and the surrounding areas, people around the world reacted in manifold ways. One notable reaction was by the Québécoise singer Céline Dion, who appeared on a CNN interview crying and indignantly denouncing the inaction of federal authorities vis-à-vis the city's poorest residents, who remained trapped inside the Superdome under horrific conditions. Like Raynal, Champigny, Laussat, and others whom I have discussed, Céline Dion at that moment made herself the spokesperson of the suffering Louisianians and attempted to move the political authorities to save them. She channeled her tears, her poignant voice, and her impassioned words to persuade her audience. She did not evoke a common French identity, but we could see her as a member of the French diaspora who was speaking on behalf of her brethren. The emotional high point of her harangue was when she claimed that babies were being assaulted in the refugee centers (a widespread rumor at the time, which was later proven to be baseless). These babies recall the metaphor of Louisiana as a child abandoned by his parent, France, evoked by Raynal and by the people who echoed his words. In all cases, the image of a suffering child, even an imaginary one, is the ultimate means for eliciting an emotional response from an audience. I find it fascinating that Louisiana, now as in the eighteenth century, evokes so much emotion among those who are not residents. Do they believe they must act as spokespersons because Louisianians themselves lack a voice? Is Louisiana so underdeveloped that its people lack the eloquence and the access to media outlets to make their voices heard? Do outsiders feel a shared brotherhood with Louisianians?

Prominent locals did express themselves at the time of Katrina: political commentator James Carville, New Orleans mayor Ray Nagin, and Louisiana governor Kathleen Babineaux Blanco all spoke on national television, the latter in tears. But the most attention was garnered by nationally known figures like Céline Dion; Kanye West whose pithy phrase "George Bush doesn't care about Black people" went viral; or Spike Lee, who created an excellent documentary, *When the Levees Broke,* in which he pieced together interviews with residents. The thoughtful and well-researched television series *Tremé,* created by David Simon and Eric Overmyer, also showed the residents' struggles after Katrina.[1] Meanwhile, how did local individuals express their reactions to Katrina? Much was expressed through satire, for their mutual consumption rather than for the national or international public.

New Orleanians, after experiencing their collective trauma, found solace in humor. Discarded refrigerators became improvised billboards for *bons mots:* the city obliged people to put their irretrievably rotten refrigerators out for trash collection, so many people spray-painted them with bitterly comic messages to the government or to a personified Katrina. This ephemera was captured in quickly published volumes and on websites. The ultimate satirical event, however, was the first Mardi Gras celebration after Katrina, especially in the very first parade that rolled out, that of the Krewe du Vieux, which I witnessed personally. Floats featured papier-mâché effigies of Hurricanes Katrina and Camille (the latter had hit the city in 1969) in the form of female mud wrestlers. Bystanders mockingly took pieces of the blue tarp given out by FEMA and wore them as capes. Mardi Gras and especially the Krewe du Vieux parade are occasions for New Orleans residents to express their anger toward corrupt or ineffective political figures through satire, often in ways that others may judge to be vulgar or obscene. These expressions are not created in a Hollywood studio, by national news outlets, or by political PR teams; they come from local residents who make their own costumes at their own initiative, dictated only by whim.

Whether such creative displays of resistance have an effect is a matter discussed by historians of carnival like Natalie Zemon Davis.[2] Perhaps New Orleanians feel powerless before their eternally corrupt local officials and neglected by the federal government. For these reasons, true political reform seems impossible, as it probably did for royal subjects during the ancien régime, so the only way to protest is to turn to the absurd. Joseph Roach has laid the groundwork for study of satiric performances in New Orleans as expressions of creative resistance against the status quo of political power relations.[3]

From its beginnings as a colony to its current status as one of the fifty states, Louisiana has always played a double role. On the one hand, it is a poor relation to be pitied, an economically less developed and politically chaotic part of its successive empires—French, Spanish, and American. On the other hand, it is a place that fascinates, a place onto which outsiders project their fears and desires. Just as the state is suffering under the environmental threat of coastal erosion, more and more frequent hurricanes, political corruption, a high crime rate, health crises, and more, it continues to excite the American imagination, as we can see in the number of films and television shows that are set in New Orleans and its environs. We locals know that Louisiana is neither the hellscape nor the eternal party that outsiders imagine it to be. It is a place where families live, where people work and achieve things, and whose residents are proud of their unique culture. While it is firmly an American state, it still preserves the tradition of calling out in imaginative ways local and federal authorities when they behave badly. The revolution I evoke in the title of this book never happened in Louisiana. The 1768 revolt of New Orleans failed, as did many other slave and Native uprisings. The French Revolution never managed to export itself to its former colony. However, the culture of New Orleans, though it has yet to bring political reform, still acts as mirror to the failings of a central power with its own unique sense of revolutionary spirit.

Notes

Introduction

1. The definitions of *Creole* relevant to Louisiana are (1) in colonial times, a person of European descent born in the Americas; (2) a person of any race who claims French or Spanish, rather than Anglo-American, ancestry; and (3) the version of the French language spoken in Louisiana. See Tregle, "Creoles and Americans." By contrast, *Cajuns* (a derivation of *Acadians*) are people of mostly French descent who first settled Acadie, or present-day Nova Scotia, but emigrated en masse to southern Louisiana in the mid-eighteenth century. There is a lot of mixture between the two populations (and their two types of cuisine), but the distinct words *Creole* and *Cajun* remain, along with various stereotypes associated with each.
2. For a comprehensive look at this suppression of French in Louisiana public schools, see Nathan Rabalais's 2019 documentary *Finding Cajun*. I have also encountered people whose parents lived through this experience.
3. Coronado, *A World Not to Come*, 28.
4. Coronado, *A World Not to Come*, 8. He is also referring to Benjamin Anderson's classic work on Creole revolutions around the world, *Imagined Communities*.
5. Armitage and Subrahmanyam, *Age of Revolutions in Global Context*, xv.
6. Armitage and Subrahmanyam, *Age of Revolutions in Global Context*, xii.
7. Paul Mapp documents the search for this mythical Mer de l'Ouest in *The Elusive West and the Contest for Empire*. The government pushed for the discovery of this mythical sea, and the Delisle family of mapmakers promoted the myth that it existed.
8. The official names *Louisiane* and *Mississippi* had variant spellings such as *Loüysiane* and *Miscissipy*.
9. Antoine-Simon Le Page du Pratz remarks, "Il est nommé par quelques Sauvages du Nord *Meact-Chassipi*, qui signifie à la lettre *vieux père des rivières*" (It is named by some northern savages *Meact-Chassipi*, which literally means "old father of rivers"). *Histoire de la Louisiane*, 1:141. He does not specify the tribe, but modern historians have established that it was the Ojibwe who named it *Misiziibi*, or "long river." Dean Klinkenberg, "The 70-Million-Year-Old History of the Mississippi River," *Smithsonian Magazine*, September 2020. https://www.smithsonianmag.com/science-nature/geological-history-mississippi-river-180975509/.
10. See Spang, "Ghost of Law."

11. In *The Queen's Embroiderer*, Joan DeJean recounts the case of a woman who was arrested and sent to Louisiana after her own father falsely accused her of prostitution.
12. See Farge and Revel, *Vanishing Children of Paris*.
13. Hunt, "French Revolution in Global Context," 20.
14. Geggus, "Caribbean in the Age of Revolution," 91.
15. Hunt, "French Revolution in Global Context," 31.
16. Hunt, "French Revolution in Global Context," 29.
17. The trope of Louisiana as a place of punishment continued in later centuries, such as in the novel *Uncle Tom's Cabin,* by Harriet Beecher Stowe (1852), and the nonfiction account *Twelve Years a Slave,* by Solomon Northup (1853). In these narratives, Louisiana represents a place more brutal and lawless than states farther north. Of course, the consequences for White and for Black people who were sent to Louisiana were vastly different: Whites could languish from disease, indigence, or other misfortunes but eventually flourish, while generations of enslaved people faced a lifetime of forced labor and dehumanizing conditions that often led to death.
18. Louisiana and Canada also assimilated a number of Catholic immigrants from other parts of Europe, such as Switzerland and Germany.
19. Not all readers were in France. People in other colonies and other European countries bought these books too, as evidenced by Thomas Jefferson's library, for example.
20. It was only toward the end of the eighteenth century that writers began to distinguish between Frenchmen and Louisiana Creoles, the latter being a category that now included residents of Spanish and African descent. In spite of this distinction, and while there was no question of Louisiana and France reuniting after the Louisiana Purchase, many Louisiana Creoles spoke French well into the twentieth century, and many wealthy families continued to send their children to France for their education.
21. France had abolished serfdom/slavery in the fourteenth century, but this rule only applied to the metropole, so slavery was still legal in the colonies. It was briefly abolished in 1792, reinstated in 1804, and then definitively abolished in 1848.
22. Several historians, such as Keith M. Baker and Dena Goodman, have broken down the concept of "public opinion" that Habermas established in writings such as *The Structural Transformation of the Public Sphere* (1991). Mona Ozouf points out that even eighteenth-century revolutionaries found it impossible to reach any kind of consensus. Ozouf, "Le concept d'opinion publique au XVIIIe siècle."
23. For example, Olivier Ferret mentions evidence of the "l'origine parlementaire" of many songs against the regent. Henri Duranton studies the poems entitled the *Philippiques,* which were written by the scholarly Lagrange-Chancel, who was protected by "la faction des légitimés." See Ferret, "Philippe d'Orléans dans

les pièces manuscrites," 79; and Duranton, "Les Philippiques," 90. The duchesse du Maine in particular was motivated by the reduction of privileges of the illegitimate children of Louis XIV to order her "plumitifs" to write songs satirizing the regent. Petitfils, *Le régent*, 481–92.
24. Farge, *Subversive Words*, 3–4. Throughout, bracketed ellipsis points represent an omissions by me, while unbracketed ellipsis points are present in the original text.
25. Foucault, "Discourse of Language," 216–17.
26. Roger Chartier discovered a rapid rise in literacy in eighteenth-century France at various levels of the social hierarchy, among both men and women, even among artisans and servants. *Lectures et lecteurs dans la France*.
27. Meanwhile, lower-class women were extremely active in commerce and played major roles in street protests and even street violence.
28. As Sara E. Johnson states, "Performative culture provides an excellent medium to study the dialogues that took place between members of mobile black communities. [. . .] In a multilingual era when reading and writing were proscribed for the enslaved, any investigation of circum-Caribbean contact and collaboration must take into account interactions that did not exclusively use written or spoken language as the dominant criteria of meaning and belonging. I am interested in how nontextual, embodied practices highlight the importance of intellectual publics." These practices include rhythms, dances, and rituals. Johnson, *Fear of French Negroes*, 164–65.
29. Sara E. Johnson approaches Louisiana history from a literary standpoint, but she mostly deals with the nineteenth century. Christopher L. Miller and Marlene Daut are also literary scholars who have studied French colonialism in the eighteenth century, but their main focus is the Caribbean.

1. The Regent's Seduction

1. "Si vous m'avez refusé cent fois le plaisir de vous entretenir de choses très intéressantes, écouteriez-vous avez patience ce qu'il y a de plus ennuyeux?" "Lettre touchant la Loüisiane, autrement le Mississippi," *Nouveau Mercure*, February 1718, 107. The English translation is from Waggoner, *Le Plus Beau Païs du Monde*, 51 (hereafter cited simply as Waggoner).
2. Dawdy, *Building the Devil's Empire*, 43.
3. See Viala, *La France galante*, 31–37.
4. "En proposant comme destinataire idéal un lecteur *féminin*, le texte galant fondait la *lectrice* en paradigme non seulement de la juste réception, ni même en archétype socioculturel du lectorat mondain, à former et à conquérir—tout cela ne fait aucun doute—, mais encore engageait une approche spécifique de l'échange littéraire, conçu comme véritable stratégie de séduction." Denis, *Le Parnasse galant*, 305.

5. "Se mêle quelquefois aux choses les plus sérieuses et [...] donne un charme inexplicable à tout ce qu'on dit et tout ce qu'on fait." Quoted in Viala, *La France galante*, 129.
6. "La séduction est inséparable des stratégies politiques pour capter les faveurs du peuple, pour s'en faire aimer, pour conquérir le pouvoir et s'y maintenir." Delporte, *Une histoire de la séduction politique*, 12.
7. "L'opinion comme une femme à conquérir." Delporte, *Une histoire de la séduction politique*, 15.
8. In an extensive biography of Philippe d'Orléans, Jean-Christian Petitfils convincingly argues that the regent was not just a man of pleasure but in fact a highly effective leader who dutifully handled matters of state with great intelligence. Petitfils, *Le régent*.
9. Faure, *La banqueroute de Law*; Murphy, *John Law*.
10. Mathieu Marais mentioned in 1721 that the regent had given him his copy of Bayle's *Dictionnaire* because it contained this supposedly flattering image by Picart, which the regent could no longer bear to look at after the Bubble had burst. *Journal et mémoires sur la Régence et le règne de Louis XV*, 2:82. Aside from French prints, a wealth of prints satirizing the Mississippi Bubble emerged from the Netherlands, most notably the ones collected in *The Great Mirror of Folly*, or *Het Groote Tafereel Der Dwaasheid*. See Labio, "Staging Folly"; and Leemans, "Verse Weavers and Paper Traders."
11. "Law, voyant bien qu'il fallait donner aux actions un fondement du moins *fictif*, le fit porter sur les prétendues richesses qui reviendraient du Mississipi." Duclos, *Mémoires secrets sur le règne de Louis XIV*, 277.
12. Poovey, *Genres of the Credit Economy*.
13. "Une pratique financière [...] qui joue continuellement sur la *promesse*, donc sur l'incertitude même de l'avenir; pratique doublée d'une politique basée sur le caractère 'fictif' de la monnaie." Rey, *Le temps du crédit*, 16–17.
14. "C'était, disait-il, *une terre de promission*, abondante en denrées de toutes espèces, en mines d'or et d'argent." Duclos, *Mémoires secrets sur le règne de Louis XIV*, 277.
15. The disappointment of these early hopes of Louisiana as a paradise surely led to the creation in the public imagination of Louisiana as a hell, a popular image that lives on to this day. Dawdy remarks on this polarization in *Building the Devil's Empire*, 42.
16. "Pays fortuné après lequel je soupire comme après la Terre de promission." Hachard, *Relation du voyage des dames religieuses ursulines*, 5.
17. "La Banque promet payer au porteur à vue, dix livres tournois en espèces d'argent" (The Bank promises to pay the bearer, on sight, ten pounds of silver in cash). See http://www.papier-monnaie.com/galerie.php.
18. Giraud, *Histoire de la Louisiane française*, 3:138–47. Arnaud Orain traces many of these texts to an original manuscript source from 1717, "Mémoire sur la

Compagnie du Mississipi et les établissements qu'elle se propose de fonder en Louisiane," found in the Archives Nationales d'Outre-Mer (hereafter ANOM), C13A 15. Orain, *La politique du merveilleux*, 181n12.

19. Sgard, *Dictionnaire des journaux, 1600–1789*.
20. In regard to critiques of the disorder of the *Mercure*, see Tsien, *Bad Taste of Others*, 173–81.
21. Letts, "Responsive Readers of the *Mercure Galant*."
22. "Ancien Conseiller et Secrétaire du Roi." http://dictionnaire-journaux.gazettes18e.fr/journal/0922-le-nouveau-mercure.
23. Waggoner, 19.
24. Giraud, *Histoire de la Louisiane française*, 3:139.
25. The editor of the March 1719 article prefaces it by mentioning that it is written by a husband to his wife, so the plain tone of this one contrasts with the flirtatious tone of the others.
26. "Franche duperie." Giraud, *Histoire de la Louisiane française*, 3:147.
27. "Un heureux hasard." *Nouveau Mercure*, February 1718, 105; Waggoner, 49.
28. "Il est à présumer que ne comptant pas qu'elle dût paraître imprimée, il n'a eu aucun intérêt d'en déguiser la vérité." *Nouveau Mercure*, February 1718, 105; Waggoner, 49.
29. "J'entre dans la description générale de la Louisiane: que l'étendue que je lui donne ne vous épouvante pas, Madame." *Nouveau Mercure*, February 1718, 115; Waggoner, 55.
30. "Ces monstres ne vous effraient, et que la promenade dans un pays qui n'est pas encore trop frayé ne vous ennuie." *Nouveau Mercure*, February 1718, 150; Waggoner, 79.
31. "Cela ne fut pas si loin, Madame. Je vous vois déjà révoltée contre l'hyperbole." *Nouveau Mercure*, February 1718, 109; Waggoner, 51.
32. "Représentez-vous, Madame, un Jésuite, comme un héros de roman." *Nouveau Mercure*, February 1718, 140–41; Waggoner, 73. Several decades later, Chateaubriand would take up this suggestion in *Atala*.
33. "Du même œil que les Israëlites regardèrent Josué & Caleb, à leur retour de la Terre de Canaan," *Nouveau Mercure*, February 1718, 106; Waggoner, 49.
34. "Tout le mérite que j'espère auprès de vous de ma relation, n'est fondé que sur ma soumission, et non pas sur ses agréments." *Nouveau Mercure*, February 1718, 152; Waggoner, 81.
35. "Permettez-moi, Madame, de vous faire faire une promenade de cinq ou six lieues dans un terrein charmant: là tantôt dans un bois, où nous marcherons sur la vigne et l'indigo sauvage qui ne demandent qu'à être cultivés, tantôt sur un coteau, ou dans une plaine vaste et agréable par sa verdure et la variété des fleurs." *Nouveau Mercure*, February 1718, 147; Waggoner, 77.
36. The *Oxford Classical Dictionary*, 4th ed., defines *locus amoenus* as a "charming place, pleasance," and states that it is "a phrase [...] used by modern scholars to

refer to the literary topos of the set description of an idyllic landscape, typically containing trees and shade, a grassy meadow, running water, song-birds, and cool breezes. [...] In Theocritus and Virgil's Eclogues such landscapes form the backdrop for the songs and loves of shepherds. [...] This perfect nature is also the setting for the innocence of the golden age."

37. Viala, *La France galante*, 50.
38. "J'accepte avec plaisir la commission de vous conduire dans un pays qui mérite toute votre curiosité." *Nouveau Mercure*, February 1718, 105; Waggoner, 49.
39. *Nouveau Mercure*, February 1718, 147; Waggoner, 77.
40. Kenny, *Uses of Curiosity*, 130.
41. Kenny, *Uses of Curiosity*, 399.
42. "Si vous m'avez refusé cent fois le plaisir de vous entretenir de choses très intéressantes, écouteriez-vous avez patience ce qu'il y a de plus ennuyeux?" *Nouveau Mercure*, February 1718, 107; Waggoner, 51.
43. Lamb, *Preserving the Self in the South Seas*, 24–25.
44. "Nous pourrons parcourir le pays des Natchtoches [sic] [...] nous visiterons les montagnes situées sur cette rivière qui vient du Nouveau Mexique; nous en tirerons à coup sûr des morceaux des mines d'argent [...] je vous ferai remarquer que ces montagnes étant dans la même chaîne que celles du nouveau Mexique, où les Espagnols puisent des richesses immenses, il est impossible qu'elles ne soient pas aussi fécondes." *Nouveau Mercure*, February 1718, 147; Waggoner, 77.
45. "Les sauvages... *font entendre* qu'il y a des mines d'or et d'argent et qu'il s'y trouve une roche fort précieuse, de laquelle ils sont contraints à détacher à coup de flèches de certaines pierres vertes, fort dures et fort belles, *semblable* à l'émeraude dont ils ornent leur lèvre supérieure qu'ils percent à cet effet." *Nouveau Mercure*, September 1717, 130; Waggoner, 37.
46. This image of the reputed emerald boulder appears in other travelers' accounts, notably those of Le Page du Pratz and Bénard de la Harpe.
47. Women were active as authors and readers of fairy tales; Antoine Galland, who brought the *1001 Nights* to France, dedicated his translation to a patroness, the marquise d'O, which in a way makes her the ideal reader. Voltaire parodies Galland's dedication to her and mocks women's taste for so-called Oriental tales in *Zadig* (1747).
48. Sayre, "How to Succeed in Exploration," 53.
49. On attempts at producing silk in the British colonies of North America, see Bigelow, "Gendered Language and the Science of Colonial Silk."
50. On the importance of Asia in the exploration of the Americas, see Padrón, *Indies of the Setting Sun*.
51. "J'ai su par tous les voyageurs que j'ai consultés qu'on y trouvait des coques de vers-à-soie qui s'y perpétuaient naturellement." *Nouveau Mercure*, February 1718, 145; Waggoner, 73.

52. "Les mûriers y sont en abondance et ne demandent aucune culture [...] comme la soie n'exige aucuns soins pénibles et fatigants, quelques ennemis du travail que soient les sauvages, je suis convaincu qu'il ne sera pas difficile de les y habituer, surtout lorsqu'ils verront que par ce moyen ils auront tout ce qui peut contenter leurs besoins et leur curiosité. Alors, nous tirerons d'eux pour des bagatelles la plus précieuse des marchandises de l'Europe." *Nouveau Mercure,* February 1718, 146; Waggoner, 76–77.
53. "Nous n'aurons à craindre que quelques serpents [...] petites écailles emboîtées les unes dans les autres [...]. Sans cet avertissement, ils seraient fort dangereux." *Nouveau Mercure,* February 1718, 149; Waggoner, 79.
54. *Nouveau Mercure,* February 1718, 133; Waggoner, 67.
55. See "Tribal History" on the Chitimacha Tribe of Louisiana website, http://www.chitimacha.gov/history-culture/tribal-history.
56. "Comment se soutenir et se concilier une *infinité* de nations sauvages, dont l'amitié et la soumission ont toujours nos présents pour objet et qui étaient *incessamment* solicitées par les libéralités de nos voisins?" *Nouveau Mercure,* February 1718, 132; Waggoner, 67.
57. There is a great deal of overlap between what we know as *précieux* language, the style of *galanterie,* and trends like *parler roman*. As Esmein-Sarrazin states in "'Parler roman,'" "The hyperbole is the characteristic most often mentioned."
58. "Un sauvage s'amuse peu à soupirer, pour obtenir une fille qui lui plaît." *Nouveau Mercure,* February 1718, 129; Waggoner, 65.
59. "Le mariage chez les sauvages n'est pas, comme chez nous, l'affaire la plus sérieuse de leur vie." *Nouveau Mercure,* February 1718, 128; Waggoner, 63.
60. Claude Habib points out the inherent falseness of *galanterie:* "Idôlatrie générale, mais vénération feinte [...] peut-être même dès l'origine, la galanterie tourne au jeu. Il s'agit d'inventer des flatteries nouvelles, des hommages toujours plus ingénieux et dont personne n'est dupe" (General idolatry, but fake veneration [...] *galanterie* is a game, maybe from the beginning. It is all about inventing new forms of flattery, more ingenious compliments, which no one believes). *Galanterie française,* 214.
61. "Voilà, Madame, une étendue de terre habitables, dans laquelle l'imagination se perd." *Nouveau Mercure,* February 1718, 117; Waggoner, 57.
62. For example, A. L. Boimare, in "La Floride et l'ancienne Louisiane," 38, states that these three publications are merely different editions of the same text.
63. John Carpenter traces these publications' sources to earlier exploration journals in *Histoire de la littérature française sur la Louisiane* On plagiarism, see Edelstein, Morrissey, and Roe, "To Quote or not to Quote."
64. The second text was published in volume 5 of the 1724 edition of *Recueil de voyages au nord,* edited by Jean-Frédéric Bernard.
65. Carpenter, *Histoire de la littérature française sur la Louisiane,* 218.

66. "Que l'auteur de ce livre fût ou non aux gages de la Compagnie, son livre exploite des mensonges et des exagérations qui avaient été accumulées au cours de trente-huit ans. [...] l'auteur n'est plus qu'un membre d'un grand mouvement commercial, soutenu par le Roi et par l'État, et qui vise à détruire toute juste connaissance de la colonie." Carpenter, *Histoire de la littérature française sur la Louisiane,* 218.
67. "Une sorte de manuel sur la manière de parler de la Louisiane dans les salons ou dans la société," "simple, claire, et un peu puérile." Carpenter, *Histoire de la littérature française sur la Louisiane,* 213.
68. "L'entretien de tant de compagnies, dans l'espérance où ils sont des immenses profits que le royaume doit retirer de son commerce." Bonrepos, *Description du Mississipi,* 3.
69. "Les Français y sont si fort aimés, que pour s'en rendre les maîtres, ils n'ont qu'à vouloir s'établir en ce pays-là en suivant l'exemple de tant d'autres, je ne vous conseillerais pas de laisser échapper cette belle occasion." Bonrepos, *Description du Mississipi,* 43.
70. "Je finis ici ma lettre, en vous témoignant que j'aurais toujours un sensible plaisir de vous être utile à quelque chose et que personne n'est plus touché que moi des petites peines que vous ressentez de l'absence de votre amie, qui pourrait bien se dérober au monde pour passer le reste de ses jours dans le monastère où elle s'est retirée." Bonrepos, *Description du Mississipi,* 45.
71. "Depuis peu on a découvert deux mines d'or, qui sans doute vont rendre le royaume de France aussi riche que le Pérou." Bonrepos, *Description du Mississipi,* 43.
72. "Leur plus grand revenu se tire de la pêche des perles." Bonrepos, *Description du Mississipi,* 25.
73. "Ces vilains crocodiles qui sont si terribles et si dangereux aux pauvres humains." Bonrepos, *Description du Mississipi,* 16.
74. Bonrepos, *Description du Mississipi,* 30.
75. "FRIAND, [fri]ande. adj. Qui aime les bons morceaux. *Il n'est pas gourmand, mais il est friand.*

    On dit, qu'*Un homme est friand en vin,* pour dire, qu'il y est delicat, & qu'il se connoist en bon vin." *Dictionnaire de l'Académie française* (1694), https://www.dictionnaire-academie.fr/.
76. "M. de la Salle, pour fixer l'inconstance de ce peuple, qui est assez naturelle aux Américains, et pour affermir l'autorité du Roi, y fit bâtir un fort sur le bord de leur rivière." Bonrepos, *Description du Mississipi,* 24.
77. On the European perception that the Native American elite was similar to their own aristocracy, see Liebersohn, *Aristocratic Encounters.*
78. "Les tireront bientôt de leur oisiveté et de la paresse dans laquelle ils vivent, n'ayant presque d'autre exercice que la chasse, la pêche et la guerre, qui est toujours cruelle." Bonrepos, *Description du Mississipi,* 6–7. "La guerre, qui

est toujours cruelle" suggests perhaps a facetious allusion to a poem or song popular at the time.
79. "Vous donner le divertissement d'une chasse qu'ils font de temps en temps." Bonrepos, *Description du Mississipi,* 26.
80. "Recevant parfaitement bien les étrangers, et particulièrement les Français, à qui ils ont accordé de la meilleure grâce du monde d'y construire un fort pour leur servir d'entrepôt et d'habitation dans un pays si beau et si charmant." Bonrepos, *Description du Mississipi,* 17.
81. "Les sauvages ne croiraient pas avoir remporté la victoire, s'ils ne rapportaient à leur chef la peau de la tête de leurs ennemis avec leur chevelure." Bonrepos, *Description du Mississipi,* 33.
82. "Il faut cependant avouer que depuis que ces sauvages se sont mis sous la protection du roi, les Iroquois ont bien perdu de leur brutalité [...]. Ainsi les Français les ayant un peu humanisés, il y a à espérer que les colonies que l'on y envoie présentement en feront des peuples dociles." Bonrepos, *Description du Mississipi,* 33.
83. "Tout cela fait une étrange cassolette et on aurait bien besoin en ces lieux-là des parfums et des aromates de l'Arabie dont ces pauvres sauvages manquent aussi bien que moi." Bonrepos, *Description du Mississipi,* 42.
84. "M. de la Salle, voulant accoutumer ces différentes nations qu'il parcourait à connaître la cour de France, changea les noms de ces grands lacs dont nous avons parlé et les appela, l'un le lac d'Orléans, l'autre le lac de Condé, etc." Bonrepos, *Description du Mississipi,* 22.
85. "On ne saurait concevoir la richesse et la beauté de toutes ces terres habitées par tant de peuples qui sont déjà presque tous soumis à notre jeune monarque; l'abondance y règne tant en grains qu'en fruits et en bétail." Bonrepos, *Description du Mississipi,* 42.
86. "Près de huit cents maisons fort logeables et commodes." Bonrepos, *Description du Mississipi,* 43.
87. "Cette célèbre compagnie, à qui toutes les autres compagnies étrangères ne peuvent être comparées, ne prennent personne par force et ne veulent même engager que pour trois ans ceux qui se présentent." Bonrepos, *Description du Mississipi,* 43.
88. I use the term *disinterested* in the sense of not seeking any personal gain, just as aesthetic philosophers such as Kant asserted that only a disinterested viewer could make a reliable judgment about taste.
89. See "Buzz Marketing," *Business Week,* 30 July 2001. http://www.businessweek.com/stories/2001-07-29/buzz-marketing.
90. For an overview of the two reputations of Louisiana, see Berthiaume, "Louisiana, or the Shadow Cast by French Colonial Myth."
91. It was published in 1768 in La Haye, where many books banned in France were published. Did it receive permission to publish in France? The BNF

site notes that it was in fact published in France, with tacit approval: "L'adresse de La Haye est fausse: publié et impr. en France d'après les matériel et usages typogr. ainsi que le papier (Normandie).—Approbation censoriale du 17 mars 1768. Une permission tacite a été demandée pour une 'Relation du voyage de la Louisiane en forme de lettres écrites à M[a]d[am]e … en l'année 1720' par Jean-Baptiste-Paul Valleyre, qui a finalement obtenu un privilège (BnF, ms. fr. 21993, n° 137); le privilège, octroyé me le 1er juin 1768 à Valleyre, a été cédé par celui-ci à Jean-Baptiste-Guillaume Musier. L'ouvrage a toutefois une double adresse, caractéristique des permissions tacites; le privilège et l'approbation censoriale, absents de certains exemplaires, ont dû être ajoutés après." http://data.bnf.fr/15004022/vallette_de_laudun/.

92. "Sous la forme épistolaire qui lui est commune avec plusieurs autres relations." [Vallette de Laudun], *Journal d'un voyage à la Louisiane,* v. Choisy's letters are addressed to "un ami," not a lady, though that does not exclude the possibility that they are flirtatious, given Choisy's openly bisexual life.

93. "Pourrait amuser avec plus de fruit que tant de mauvais romans." [Vallette de Laudun], *Journal d'un voyage à la Louisiane,* vi–vii.

94. "L'officier qui pour son propre amusement écrivait chaque jour jusqu'aux plus petits incidents, comptait bien qu'elles seraient lues par la dame pour laquelle il s'était imposé cette tâche, dans le même esprit qu'on les présente au public." [Vallette de Laudun], *Journal d'un voyage à la Louisiane,* vii–viii.

95. "Ceci se passera entre vous et moi, et ne sera vu de personne." [Vallette de Laudun], *Journal d'un voyage à la Louisiane,* 3.

96. "Adieu Madame, je vous promets, foi de chevalier errant, de ne point parler de ce pays-ci, que je n'aie fait connaître votre nom chez les Illinois, les Hurons et les Iroquois." [Vallette de Laudun], *Journal d'un voyage à la Louisiane,* 248.

97. "De sorte que cette île est presque déserte." [Vallette de Laudun], *Journal d'un voyage à la Louisiane,* 241.

98. "Il est si fin et si brillant, qu'on le prendrait d'abord pour de la poudre d'or dans le pays de Quincampoix." [Vallette de Laudun], *Journal d'un voyage à la Louisiane,* 243.

99. "Les Chicachas, qui jusqu'ici avaient été de nos amis, se lassent d'être des gens de bien, et nous menacent de nous déclarer la guerre." [Vallette de Laudun], *Journal d'un voyage à la Louisiane,* 246.

100. "On dit au reste que les Européennes qu'on transplante dans ce pays-ci y deviennent stériles. [. . .] Je crois plutôt que les femmes qu'on envoie ici sont si malsaines et si usées par les galanteries qu'elles ont eues qu'elles étaient stériles même avant leur départ." [Vallette de Laudun], *Journal d'un voyage à la Louisiane,* 256.

101. The dubious virtue of the residents is also evoked by the Ursuline nun Marie-Madeleine Hachard, who writes, "Non seulement la débauche, la mauvaise foi et enfin toutes les autres vices règnent ici plus qu'ailleurs, mais encore en

abondance demesurée" (Not only debauchery, bad faith, and all the other vices reign here more than anywhere else, and in excessive abundance). She complains of the large numbery of "filles de mauvaise conduite" (loose women). Hachard, *Relation du voyage des dames religieuses ursulines,* 113.

102. "Déchu de toutes mes espérances. Je croyais, comme tout le monde, que les actions tiraient d'ici leur origine." [Vallette de Laudun], *Journal d'un voyage à la Louisiane,* 243.

103. "Plus triste voyage qu'on fera jamais." [Vallette de Laudun], *Journal d'un voyage à la Louisiane,* 315.

104. *Recueil Clairambault-Maurepas,* 2:245–53.

105. Berthiaume, "Louisiana, or the Shadow Cast by French Colonial Myth," 16.

106. Edgar Morin, in *La rumeur d'Orléans,* argues that certain rumors spread more widely if they express a preconceived prejudice on the part of the public.

107. See Darnton, *Poetry and the Police.*

108. "Quelques avis venus des îles de Mississipi, assurèrent que plus de quinze cents Français des deux sexes avaient été hachés par les sauvages de cette contrée, qui étaient venus en très-grand nombre les surprendre dans leurs nouvelles habitations." Buvat, *Journal de la Régence,* 2:363.

109. "Les actions, qui étaient à plus de cinq cents livres pour cent de profit, baissèrent de cinquante livres, ce qu'on attribuait au bruit qui courut alors que les Espagnols avaient fait du ravage au Mississipi." Buvat, *Journal de la Régence,* 2:424. I thank Arnaud Orain for the translation of this sentence.

110. "La charmante rôtisseuse, / Pour son ami, / Envoie, pour se rendre heureuse, / Son homme à Mississipi." The *Poèmes satiriques du XVIIIe siècle* database contains thirteen songs that mention Quoniam, including ten published in the year 1718.

111. A version of this Quoniam section was published as Jennifer Tsien, "Quoniam le rôtisseur et les prisonniers du Mississippi," in Magnot-Ogilvy, *Gagnons sans savoir comment,* 207–20.

112. "Il n'y a point de nouvelles que celle d'un rôtisseur appelé M. Quoniam. Le pauvre homme avoit pour son malheur épousé une très jolie femme: quelqu'un en grand crédit en est devenu amoureux; on ne sait qui c'est [. . .] il s'est trouvé des gens qui ont enlevé le mari et ont laissé la femme revenir à Paris." Balleroy, *Les correspondants de la marquise de Balleroy,* bk. 1, p. 217.

113. Marcel Giraud finds evidence of the first forced exiles to Louisiana in 1717. The Conseil de marine approved the embarkation of specific types of people: vagabonds, *faux-saulniers* (smugglers who dealt in salt, a commodity that was otherwise subject to taxation), deserters, orphans, and "jeunes libertins" denounced by their families. However, these arrests were made on a case-by-case basis and on a much smaller scale than starting in late 1718, when Law took over control of the Compagnie. Giraud, *Histoire de la Louisiane française,* 2:31–34.

114. In the *Poèmes satiriques du XVIIIe siècle* database, only one song is dated from 1717 (http://satires18.univ-st-etienne.fr/texte/r%C3%B4tisseuse-quoniam -sous-entendu-grivois/sans-titre), but it is unclear whether the collection of songs from which it was taken contains a dating error. The editor of the database, Henri Duranton, confirmed that this was a possibility.
115. "Cette femme a bien du crédit / Un ministre l'a bien servi, / Monsieur son secrétaire aussi." See http://satires18.univ-st-etienne.fr/texte/affaire-du-r%C3 %B4tisseur-quoniam/sans-titre-0.
116. "Un gros monsieur," "fait de magnifiques dépenses." *Recueil Clairambault-Maurepas*, 3:17–24.
117. "Coche [...] obtint, en 1720, une lettre de cachet qui envoyait le pauvre Quoniam dans les provinces de Mississipi" (Coche [...] obtained, in 1720, a *lettre de cachet* that sent poor Quoniam to the provinces of Mississippi). Narbonne, *Journal des règnes de Louis XIV et Louis XV,* 410, quoted in Faure, *La banqueroute de Law,* 418.
118. "Mme Quoniam aurait présenté sa fille au Régent, qui s'y était intéressé, et aurait éloigné Quoniam, non pas en tant que mari mais en tant que père." Rapport de police, Arsenal MS 10243, quoted in Faure, *La banqueroute de Law,* 418.
119. "J'ai raconté ce fait assez peu important, parce que mes ennemis m'en ont attribué le blâme [...] mais je n'ai pas le malheur de ce pauvre mari sur la conscience. Ravannes, qui n'était pas encore conseiller d'Etat, est capable d'avoir fait le coup [...]. Au reste, Massillon, confesseur de la Quoniam, a refusé de m'éclaircir dans mon doute. Si c'était Son Altesse Royale elle-même!" [Lacroix], *Mémoires du cardinal Dubois,* 149. Ravannes was probably the abbé Gabriel Petit de Ravannes. Guy Chaussinand-Nogaret mentions this "auteur satirique des faux mémoires" in his biography *Le cardinal Dubois, 1656–1723,* 14.
120. "Or sus pleurons tous le malheur / De cet aimable rôtisseur / Lan la derirette / Parti pour le Mississipi / Lan la deriri." http://satires18.univ-st-etienne.fr /texte/affaire-du-r%C3%B4tisseur-quoniam/sans-titre-0. We could even apply Mikhail Bakhtin's idea that the combination of laughter and tears is part of carnivalesque activity, which temporarily subverts authority.
121. "Adieu, femme, enfants et ménage, / C'est tout de bon. / L'on m'embarque pour un voyage / Qui sera long. / Pour se défaire d'un mari, / L'on m'envoie à Mississipi." http://satires18.univ-st-etienne.fr/texte/r%C3%B4tisseur -quoniam-fait-divers/quoniam.
122. "Maris, qui savez cette histoire, / Pensez à vous, / Et ne vous faites pas de gloire / D'être jaloux. / Autrement vous irez aussi, / Malgré vous, à Mississipi."
123. "Tous les voisins l'ont poursuivie par toutes les pierres, boue et toute sorte d'ordures dont ils ont rempli la boutique, tout le monde étant persuadé qu'elle a part à l'enlèvement de son mari." Quoted in Faure, *La banqueroute de Law,* 417.

124. "Pour la belle rôtissseuse, / Dont chacun murmure fort, / On la traite en malheureuse, / Tout Paris dit qu'elle a tort." http://satires18.univ-st-etienne.fr/texte/r%C3%B4tisseur-quoniam-fait-divers/quoniam-2.
125. "Il paraît que l'on dut faire garder la boutique par des soldats, pour protéger la *belle rôtisseuse* contre l'irritation publique." *Recueil Clairambault-Maurepas,* 3:24.
126. Giraud, *Histoire de la Louisiane française,* 2:121.
127. Faure, *La banqueroute de Law,* 417–27; Giraud, *Histoire de la Louisiane française,* 3:252–83.
128. For a more extensive review of the plays and stories that used the Mississippi Bubble as a theme, see Orain, *La politique du merveilleux.*
129. "Je m'appelle Arlequin, chevalier d'industrie. Je viens de Paris. J'en étais parti avec deux cents jeunes gens d'élite, tant mâles que femelles que la police avait choisis avec prédilection pour aller fonder d'honnêtes familles au Mississipi." Lesage, *Arlequin roi des Ogres,* 140.
130. "Tout le peuple étoit acharné contre ces gens-là, et avec raison, puisque c'étoit lui ôter la liberté publique de ne pouvoir sortir de chez soi sans être arrêté pour aller à Mississipi." Saint-Simon, *Mémoires,* 37:474–75.
131. See the biography Petitfils, *Le régent;* and Reynaud and Thomas, *Le régent entre fable et histoire.*
132. Lynn Hunt, in *The Family Romance of the French Revolution,* explores the paternal symbolism surrounding the king and specifically mentions that "images of state and familial power were perhaps most closely intertwined in the controversy over the lettres de cachet" (19). Also, she mentions the myth Freud creates in "Totem and Taboo" of the brothers who banded together to kill their father, who had monopolized all the women.
133. See Quétel, *De par le Roy.*
134. Fanny Cosandey and Robert Descimon remark that "les lettres de cachet offraient une parfaite illustration de la mise en œuvre du principe de supériorité du roi sur la loi" (The *lettres de cachet* are a perfect illustration of the way in which the principle that the king is above the law was put into practice). *L'absolutisme en France,* 35.
135. "Nous fûmes surpris de découvrir, en avançant, que, ce qu'on nous avait vanté jusqu'alors comme une bonne ville, n'était qu'un assemblage de quelques pauvres cabanes." Prévost, *Histoire du chevalier des Grieux et de Manon Lescaut,* 433.
136. "C'est au Nouvel Orléans [*sic*] qu'il faut venir, disais-je souvent à Manon, quand on veut goûter les douceurs de l'amour. C'est ici qu'on aime sans intérêt, sans jalousie, sans inconstance." Prévost, *Histoire du chevalier des Grieux et de Manon Lescaut,* 437.
137. "Nos compatriotes y viennent chercher de l'or; ils ne s'imaginent pas que nous y avons trouvé des trésors bien plus estimables." Prévost, *Histoire du chevalier des Grieux et de Manon Lescaut,* 437.

180   Notes to Pages 53–59

138. "Ces allusions à peine voilées [...] au Régent, au lieutenant de police d'Argenson [...] choquer le monde bien-pensant." Sgard, *Vie de Prévost (1697–1763)*.
139. "Une vaste plaine, sans avoir pu trouver un arbre pour nous mettre à couvert," "une campagne couverte de sable." Prévost, *Histoire du chevalier des Grieux et de Manon Lescaut*, 439.
140. Roland Barthes, in *Sur Racine*, describes this feature of French tragedies: there is a center of power where the action happens, usually a royal palace, and there is the place outside of it—it does not matter where it is—where the characters are sent to die or to be punished.
141. "Il est difficile de contrôler l'effet des images lancées en public, et, de fait, la population s'approprie les mythes de façon personnelle [...] la foule détourne à son profit le sens de ce qui lui a été brutalement imposé d'en haut." Farge, *Subversive Words*, 94–95; *Dire et mal dire*, 146–47.
142. "*La rumeur est un rapport à l'autorité* [...]. Elle est souvent une parole d'opposition: les démentis officiels ne la convainquent pas, comme si officiel et crédible n'allaient plus de pair. [...] Information parallèle et parfois opposée à l'information officielle, la rumeur est un *contre-pouvoir*." Kapferer, *Rumors*, 14; *Rumeurs*, 25.
143. Kaiser, "Money, Despotism, and Public Opinion," 2.
144. Kaiser, "Money, Despotism, and Public Opinion," 17.

2. Enlightenment Travelers

1. See, e.g., Berthiaume, "Louisiana, or the Shadow Cast by French Colonial Myth," 21.
2. Sayre, "How to Succeed in Exploration," 53.
3. "Faire plaisir au public," "rendre même quelque service à ma patrie." Charlevoix, *Histoire*, 1:1. For the English, see *History and General Description of New France*, trans. Shea, 1:103.
4. "Si je me dois à la république comme citoyen, ma profession m'oblige aussi à servir l'Église [...] je me suis encore déterminé à entreprendre cet ouvrage par le désir de faire connaître les miséricordes du Seigneur et le triomphe de la religion sur ce petit nombre d'élus, prédestinés avant tous les siècles, parmi tant de nations sauvages, qui jusqu'à l'entrée des Français dans leur pays étaient demeurées ensevelies dans les plus épaisses ténèbres de l'infidélité." Charlevoix, *Histoire*, 1:2; Shea, 1:103–4.
5. "Madame, Vous avez souhaité que je vous écrivisse régulierement par toutes les occasions, que j'en pourrois trouver, & je vous l'ai promis, parce qu'il ne m'est pas permis de vous rien refuser." Charlevoix, *Journal d'un voyage*, 1:163. For the English, see *Charlevoix's (1682–1761) Journal of a Voyage*, trans. True, 85.
6. A note from the original edition identifies her as Gabrielle-Victoire de Rochechouart Mortemart. Charlevoix, *Journal d'un voyage*, 1:103.

The family considered itself nobler than the Bourbons, and her aunt was Louis XIV's important mistress, the marquise de Montespan.

7. "Ce sont là, Madame, de vraies Mines, qui valent mieux, & demandent beaucoup moins de frais, que celles du Perou & de Mexique." Charlevoix, *Journal d'un voyage*, 1:172; True, 91.

8. "Il courut un bruit, il y a quelques années, qu'on y avoit découvert une Mine d'Argent, & faute de Mineurs, on fit partir de Québec, où j'étois alors, un Orfévre, pour en faire l'épreuve: mais il n'alla pas bien loin. Il s'apperçut bientôt aux discours de celui, qui avoit donné l'avis, que la Mine n'existoit que dans le cerveau blessé de cet Homme lequel lui recommandoit sans cesse d'avoir confiance en Dieu. Il jugea que si la confiance en Dieu pouvoit par miracle faire trouver une Mine, il n'étoit pas nécessaire d'aller jusqu'à Anticosty, & il revint sur ses pas." Charlevoix, *Journal d'un voyage*, 1:194; True, 104.

9. Pierre Berthiaume speculates that the minister of the marine did not allow earlier publication of Charlevoix's text, because he did not want news to spread about the absence of mines. Charlevoix, *Journal d'un voyage*, 1:50–52.

10. "Les Lettres de ce Jésuite étaient adressées à la duchesse de Lesdiguières; on les tint fort secrètes. Si elles eussent été publiées alors, la Colonie aurait eu infailliblement une autre destinée; mais cette correspondance ne vit le jour que vingt-cinq ans après." Barbé-Marbois, *Histoire de la Louisiane*, 122.

11. "Il fut facile de cacher au public les calamités sans nombre dont ces Français furent victimes. Les communications avec la métropole étaient rares, la correspondance nulle ou mystérieuse." Barbé-Marbois, *Histoire de la Louisiane*, 120.

12. "Faire éclater la vérité, et, en avertissant les peuples, avertissent les gouvernements eux-mêmes." Barbé-Marbois, *Histoire de la Louisiane*, 120.

13. "Des hommes éclairés et sages portaient cependant un jugement sain sur l'état des affaires de ce pays. Le père Charlevoix, jésuite, le parcourait en 1720, 1721 et 1722. L'extrême discrétion de la Compagnie dont il était membre, ne lui permettait pas de tout dire; mais ce qu'il dit est sincère, et surtout dans le récit de ce qu'il a vu." Barbé-Marbois, *Histoire de la Louisiane*, 120.

14. During the Revolution, he was exiled to Guyana; under Napoleon's rule, he was recalled and was appointed treasury minister, a position from which he negotiated the Louisiana Purchase.

15. Dumont de Montigny, *Memoir of Lieutenant Dumont*, 127.

16. Gordon Sayre remarked that while Le Blanc may not have been Dumont's godfather, he was probably a patron of his family. Sayre, email message to author, January 24, 2020.

17. Documents sometimes spell his name La Motte, sometimes La Mothe, sometimes as one word, sometimes as two. The car manufacturer Cadillac, which is based in Detroit, is named after him.

18. Various accounts describe him as making people angry wherever he was stationed. For instance, Daniel Usner tells us, "Internal tension violently surfaced

in 1715, when Governor Antoine de La Mothe Cadillac traveled upriver without offering presents or accepting the Natchez calumet." Usner, *American Indians in the Lower Mississippi Valley,* 21.

19. "Salmigondis où l'on n'y connaît rien." Antoine Lamothe Cadillac to comte de Pontchartrain, October 26, 1713, ANOM, C13A 3, p. 8. A *salmigondis,* according to the *Dictionnaire de l'Académie française* of 1694, is a "ragoût de plusieurs sortes de viandes réchauffées" (a stew of different sorts of warmed-over meats). https://www.dictionnaire-academie.fr/. It is translated as "a hotchpotch in which one can understand nothing" in Rowland and Sanders, *Mississippi Provincial Archives: French Dominion, 1701–1729,* 2:165 (hereafter *MPA*).

20. "Selon le proverbe, méchant pays, méchantes gens: l'on peut dire que c'est un amas de la lie de Canada, gens de sac et de corde sans subordination pour la religion et pour le gouvernement, adonnés au vice." ANOM, C13A 3, p.13; *MPA,* 2:167.

21. "Il faut bien une dizaine d'années." ANOM, C13A 3, p. 37; *MPA,* 2:177.

22. "Voilà le Paradis terrestre de M. d'Artaguiette et de plusieurs autres, la Pomone de M. de Raimondville et les îles fortunées de M. de Mandeville, et de M. Philippe. Leurs mémoires et leurs relations sont pures fables. Ils ont parlé de ce qu'ils n'ont point vu, et ils ont trop familièrement cru ce qu'on leur a dit." ANOM, C13A 3, pp. 9–10; *MPA,* 2:166.

23. "La Colonie de Louisiane est un monstre qui n'a aucune forme de gouvernement, l'état déplorable où elle se trouve prouve le peu d'attention qu'on a fait à ses mémoires et de ce qu'on a préféré les fables de ceux qui ont dépeint ce pays comme très excellent. Il l'a tout examiné et proteste de n'avoir jamais vu de plus mauvais." ANOM, C13A 4, p. 389; *MPA,* 2:219.

24. "Suspects de Discours inconsidérés contre le Gouvernement de l'État." This arrest report is found in the Bibliothèque de l'Arsenal, Archives de la Bastille, MS 10,631, "1717 La Mothe Cadillac."

25. "Soupçonnés d'avoir tenu des discours peu convenables contre le gouvernement de l'état des colonies, accusé aussi d'avoir fait travailler à des mémoires contraires au bien de l'état." Arrest report, Archives de la Bastille.

26. "La Motte, qui avoit commandé dans le Mississipi du temps que Crozat en étoit le maître, fut mis à la Bastille ces jours passés pour avoir mal parlé sur l'établissement qu'on y veut faire sous le nom de la compagnie d'Occident." Dangeau, *Journal,* 17:168.

27. Banks, *Chasing Empire across the Sea,* 215.

28. Banks, *Chasing Empire across the Sea,* 188.

29. "Speeches and books were assigned real authors [...] only when the author became subject to punishment" (Les textes, les livres, les discours ont commencé à avoir réellement des auteurs [...] dans la mesure où l'auteur pouvait être puni). Foucault, "What Is an Author?," 124.

30. During the ancien régime, *histoire* had the meaning it does now, but it had another one as well: the description of natural objects. The 1694 *Dictionnaire de l'Académie française* includes this definition of *histoire:* "toutes sortes de descriptions des choses naturelles, comme plantes, mineraux &c. *L'Histoire naturelle de Pline. l'histoire des animaux. l'histoire des plantes. histoire des mineraux.*" https://www.dictionnaire-academie.fr/.
31. Dawdy, "Enlightenment from the Ground."
32. Dawdy, "Enlightenment from the Ground," 23.
33. He calls himself "ingénieur Machiniste du Roy; architecte pour le civil et pour l'hydraulique" on the map Gordon Sayre explains in "A Newly Discovered Manuscript Map," 26.
34. Like Valette de Laudun's publishers, Raynal's played a complicated game of hide and seek, putting a foreign city on the title page. Historians of the book note that these place names were false and that some controversial books were published in France with tacit permission. Later editions of Raynal's book really were published in the Netherlands or Switzerland.
35. "J'ai lu par l'ordre de Monseigneur le Chancelier un manuscrit intitulé *Histoire de la Louisiane,* par M. le Page du Pratz. L'histoire d'un pays aussi intéressant pour la France que la Louisiane ne peut être que favorablement reçue du public, et il me paraît qu'elle le doit être d'autant plus que l'auteur a demeuré longtemps dans ce pays, qu'il a vécu avec les sauvages, qu'il a vu par lui-même la plupart des événements qu'il rapporte; ce qui l'a mis en état de constater, de vérifier ou de détruire les notions que nous avions déjà sur cette vaste contrée." Le Page du Pratz, *Histoire de la Louisiane,* 3:452. The translations are mine because the published English translation of Le Page du Pratz's text is very much abridged.
36. "L'intérêt que je prends au bien de ma patrie exige que je lui découvre le nouveau fonds de commerce que la nature lui présente dans les régions éloignées et que l'industrie de l'homme peut préparer pour nous fournir par son moyen un surcroît de commodités et d'abondance." Le Page du Pratz, *Histoire de la Louisiane,* 1:v.
37. An excerpt of his text was first published in the *Journal œconomique,* a physiocratic publication. See Orain, "Le *Journal œconomique.*"
38. "Les faux jugements qu'on a portés sur cette contrée de l'Amérique, semblent même inviter un bon patriote à redresser les idées et à en donner de justes." Le Page du Pratz, *Histoire de la Louisiane,* 1:v.
39. "On sait tout ce que l'on a dit et pensé de désavantageux sur le Missicipi [*sic*], nom que le vulgaire affecte de donner à ce pays, quoique le premier et le véritable soit celui de la Louisiane que je lui confère." Le Page du Pratz, *Histoire de la Louisiane,* 1:vi.
40. "Il est donc absolument nécessaire de détruire ces faux jugements occasionnés par des relations infidèles, souvent pleines de malignité et presque toujours

d'ignorance [...]. On y verra non seulement avec quelle impartialité j'ai considéré la Louisiane, mais encore avec quelle attention j'en ai examiné les productions." Le Page du Pratz, *Histoire de la Louisiane*, 1:xvi.

41. "Je m'estimerai heureux et très dédommagé des peines et des soins que m'ont coûté mes recherches, si cette histoire peut être utile au service du Roi et à l'avantage du commerce de ma patrie, puisque toute ma vie, je n'ai eu d'autre ambition ni d'autres désirs que de pouvoir me rendre utile au service du Roi et de l'Etat." Le Page du Pratz, *Histoire de la Louisiane*, 1:xvi.

42. "Je me crois obligé d'en faire la description pour détromper les incrédules, tels que ceux que j'ai trouvé à Paris & en Province." Le Page du Pratz, *Histoire de la Louisiane*, 1:29.

43. "J'en suis témoin oculaire." Le Page du Pratz, *Histoire de la Louisiane*, 1:30.

44. "Pour le montrer en France, à ceux qui ne croient pas les voyageurs sur cet article." Le Page du Pratz, *Histoire de la Louisiane*, 1:30.

45. "La Bonite trompée par ces appas, voulant avaler la poupée qu'elle prend pour un poisson, se trouve prise elle-même." Le Page du Pratz, *Histoire de la Louisiane*, 1:30.

46. Cañizares-Esguerra, *How to Write the History of the New World*, 14.

47. Le Page du Pratz, *Histoire de la Louisiane*, 1:2.

48. Cañizares-Esguerra, *How to Write the History of the New World*, 1.

49. Cañizares-Esguerra, *How to Write the History of the New World*, 1–2.

50. "Après avoir parlé des huîtres de la Louisiane, nous dirons un mot de celles de S. Domingue que l'on trouve suspendues aux arbres; il me paroît qu'on peut les nommer huîtres branchues." Le Page du Pratz, *Histoire de la Louisiane*, 2:159.

51. "Les critiques s'imagineront avoir beau jeu sur ce petit article." Le Page du Pratz, *Histoire de la Louisiane*, 2:159.

52. "Une chose que je ne concevois pas trop." Le Page du Pratz, *Histoire de la Louisiane*, 2:160.

53. "Tel est le prétendu Phénomène; que l'on ne crie donc point à l'imposture au sujet de mes Huitres branchues; je suis même persuadé que personne ne contestera ce fait qui est connu des Marins[;] il est d'ailleurs naturel & très possible." Le Page du Pratz, *Histoire de la Louisiane*, 2:160–61.

54. "Au lieu que si je disois que les Chats de la Louisiane vont à la pêche de l'Huitre, & qu'ayant mis une de leurs pattes dans l'écaille qui se resserre aussi-tôt, ils restent dans cette position [...] si dis-je, je parlois de la sorte, on seroit autorisé à ne pas me croire." Le Page du Pratz, *Histoire de la Louisiane*, 2:161.

55. "Je ne puis en vérité m'imaginer comment un Auteur peut avoir le front de faire présent au Public d'inventions aussi impertinentes qu'elles sont impossibles. Pour moi je souscris volontiers à ma condamnation, lorsque dans les faits ou descriptions que je rapporte on trouvera la moindre contradiction; je n'avance rien à tort & à travers, dont je ne sois assuré; je fais profession de dire ce que je sçais, & rien de plus." Le Page du Pratz, *Histoire de la Louisiane*, 2:161–62.

56. "Je vis un phénomène qui épouvanta fort les superstitieux." Le Page du Pratz, *Histoire de la Louisiane*, 1:194.
57. "Le phénomène fut aperçu vers sa fin de beaucoup de personnes qui le virent avec frayeur." Le Page du Pratz, *Histoire de la Louisiane*, 1:196.
58. "Les savants pourront exercer leurs talens à en découvrir les causes." Le Page du Pratz, *Histoire de la Louisiane*, 1:194.
59. "Les comètes sont des présages, disaient les gens crédules, des présages envoyés d'en-haut pour annoncer quelque grand châtiment mérité par les hommes." Hazard, *La crise de la conscience européenne*, 108.
60. Jean Le Rond d'Alembert, "Discours préliminaire," in Diderot and d'Alembert, *Encyclopédie*, 1:vi. See https://www.dictionnaire-academie.fr/.
61. "Pour moi, je suis fort porté à croire qu'elle n'existe qu'en imagination." Le Page du Pratz, *Histoire de la Louisiane*, 3:138.
62. "Mettons à profit ce que nous avons sous la main; une utilité réelle ne sera-t-elle point préférable à des avantages chimériques qu'il faudroit aller chercher bien loin, & qui même n'existeront jamais?" Le Page du Pratz, *Histoire de la Louisiane*, 3:139–40.
63. Mapp, *Elusive West*, 197.
64. Cañizares-Esguerra, *How to Write the History of the New World*, 3.
65. "Des hommes qui savent faire un très bon usage de leur raison," "certaines Nations policées." Le Page du Pratz, *Histoire de la Louisiane*, 1:88.
66. "Ils me répondoient qu'ils étoient sortis de dessous terre." Le Page du Pratz, *Histoire de la Louisiane*, 2:216–17.
67. "Pour exprimer avec quelle surprise on les avoit vu paroître tout d'un coup." Le Page du Pratz, *Histoire de la Louisiane*, 2:216–17.
68. "Du nombre de ces charitables voisins était le R.P. de Ville; ce digne religieux était plein d'érudition, et il était membre d'une société qui a produit un si grand nombre de savants, que sa science ne fut pas pour moi un sujet d'étonnement." Le Page du Pratz, *Histoire de la Louisiane*, 1:130.
69. "Je me faisais un devoir d'écouter beaucoup et de faire plus de questions que de donner des décisions." Le Page du Pratz, *Histoire de la Louisiane*, 1:131.
70. For a published response to Le Page du Pratz's heliocentric ideas, see *Lettre du R.P. **** de la congregation de l'oratoire*, which can be found in the Bibliothèque Nationale de France. I thank Gordon Sayre for this discovery.
71. "Dieu étant l'auteur de cette machine, il en connaissait parfaitement toutes les parties et le méchanisme, et qu'il inspira à Josué d'arrêter la machine du monde, par son premier mobile; c'est à dire que le soleil étant au centre du monde et tournant sur lui-même, donnait le mouvement à toutes les parties de l'univers; or il est de la prudence d'un sage et savant mécanicien d'arrêter sa machine par le premier mobile plutôt que par une pièce éloignée, qui doit avoir un mouvement beaucoup plus rapide." Le Page du Pratz, *Histoire de la Louisiane*, 1:132.

72. "On ne peut douter, lui dis-je, que l'Univers ne soit une machine, dont toutes les parties sont intimement liées les unes aux autres." Le Page du Pratz, *Histoire de la Louisiane,* 1:132.

73. "Dès qu'ils furent près de l'établissement des Français, ils se parèrent chacun d'une des pièces de la chapelle: celui qui avait sur sa peau la plus belle chasuble marchait à la tête; ceux qui portaient les chasubles le suivaient, venaient ensuite les porte-étoles suivis de ceux qui avaient leur manipules à leur col; on voyait après ceux-ci trois ou quatre naturels revêtu d'aubes, d'autres de surplis; les acolytes, contre l'ordinaire, marchaient à la queue de *cette procession d'un goût si nouveau,* ne se trouvant point assez paré de porter à la main, en dansant en cadence, une croix ou un chandelier." Le Page du Pratz, *Histoire de la Louisiane,* 2:249.

74. "Un d'eux avait trouvé le secret de percer la patène qu'il portait pendue à son col." Le Page du Pratz, *Histoire de la Louisiane,* 2:249.

75. "Cette procession d'un goût nouveau," "cette troupe de mascarades d'une mode nouvelle." Le Page du Pratz, *Histoire de la Louisiane,* 2:250.

76. "Que l'on s'imagine le spectacle ridicule que pouvait offrir aux yeux l'ordre bizarre de cette procession telle que je viens de la décrire." Le Page du Pratz, *Histoire de la Louisiane,* 2:250.

77. "Son chagrin s'évanouit, il eut même bien de la peine à s'empêcher d'en rire comme les autres." Le Page du Pratz, *Histoire de la Louisiane,* 2:250.

78. The same message was conveyed several years later in the illustrations of Diderot and d'Alembert's *Encyclopédie,* where supposedly sacred objects used during Mass are classified under ordinary *orfèvre grossier,* or metalwork. In these illustrations from the *Encyclopédie,* there is nothing to indicate that anything distinguishes a crucifix or a chalice from a simple gravy boat, since they are made of the same material and by the same artisan. See https://encyclopedie.uchicago.edu/.

79. "Avant que les Chactas se déterminassent à donner sur les Natchez, ils étaient allés chez eux porter le calumet. Ils y furent reçus d'une manière assez nouvelle: ils les trouvèrent eux et leurs chevaux parés de chasubles et de devants d'autel: plusieurs portaient à leur col des patènes, buvaient et donnaient à boire de l'eau-de-vie dans des calices et des ciboires. Les Chactas eux-mêmes, quand ils eurent pillé nos ennemis, renouvelèrent cette profanation sacrilège, en faisant dans leurs danses et dans leurs jeux le même usage de nos ornements et de nos vases sacrés." Letter of the père Le Petit, New Orleans, July 12, 1730, in *Lettres édifiantes et curieuses,* 20:183–84.

80. "Je m'attachai à le cultiver, sans déroger à la supériorité que nous avons naturellement sur eux par nos lumières, nos sciences, et nos arts." Le Page du Pratz, *Histoire de la Louisiane,* 2:322.

81. "Je ne manquai point à ce sujet, non plus que sur celui des esprits aeriens, et les prières qu'ils leur adressaient, de rectifier ses idées et de les ramener à la vérité que

la religion nous enseigne et que les livres saints nous ont transmise. Il m'écouta avec une grande attention et me promit d'apprendre tout ce que je lui disais aux vieillards de la nation." Le Page du Pratz, *Histoire de la Louisiane*, 2:330.
82. "Cet événement extraordinaire avait paru lui annoncer quelque chose de sinistre; et de la ferme persuasion où le peuple est que l'extinction du feu sacré entraîne infailliblement la mort d'un grand nombre d'hommes lui avait fait appréhender que ce second accident se joignant au premier, toute la nation ne pérît." Le Page du Pratz, *Histoire de la Louisiane*, 2:337–38.
83. "Je ne puis passer sous silence l'étonnement où je le jettai, en lui disant que rien n'étoit moins extraordinaire que de faire descendre du feu du Soleil, et que j'étais en état de le faire toutes les fois qu'il me plaisait. Sa surprise fut extrême. 'Cela me passe' dit-il; 'est-il possible qu'un mortel puisse faire venir du feu du soleil?'" Le Page du Pratz, *Histoire de la Louisiane*, 2:341–42.
84. "Je prononçai d'un ton ferme le mot *Caheuch* qui signifie *viens*, comme si j'eusse commandé au feu de descendre. Un instant après l'amadou fuma, je soufflai et le feu parut au grand étonnement du Grand Soleil et de toute sa suite, dont une partie tremblait, et leur prince ne paraissait guères plus assuré." Le Page du Pratz, *Histoire de la Louisiane*, 2:342.
85. "Tout homme le pouvait [. . .]. Je le rassurai de façon qu'il se détermina à en faire l'épreuve lui-même." Le Page du Pratz, *Histoire de la Louisiane*, 2:343.
86. "J'eus bien de la peine à m'empêcher de rire; mais mon intérêt demandait que j'eusse un air mystérieux." Le Page du Pratz, *Histoire de la Louisiane*, 2:344.
87. "Ils tinrent conseil," "Je profitai de ces moments pour aller dans mon champ, comme si j'y eusse eu une affaire; mais dans le fond pour y rire à mon aise de la scène que je venais d'occasioner." Le Page du Pratz, *Histoire de la Louisiane*, 2:349.
88. "Il me promit aussi de n'en rien dire aux Français, de peur que l'on ne me sût mauvais gré de m'être défait d'une chose si précieuse." Le Page du Pratz, *Histoire de la Louisiane*, 2:348.
89. "Que l'homme se mette à leur place pour un moment: si nous eussions eu aussi peu d'éducation que ces peuples, et que nous n'eussions jamais rien vu d'extraordinaire dans aucun genre [. . .] nous serions certainement aussi surpris qu'ils le sont la première fois qu'ils voient des choses réellement très surprenantes." Le Page du Pratz, *Histoire de la Louisiane*, 2:345.
90. "Une gravure le représente, l'arc et la flèche à la main, piétinant le sceptre et le code des lois, symboles de l'autorité royale et scriptuaire. Au-dessus de sa tête, une formule choc résume bien les développements subséquents de la critique: *Et leges et sceptra terit* ('Il foule aux pieds et la loi et le sceptre')." Lahontan, *Nouveaux voyages*, in *Œuvres complètes*, 1:54.
91. "Les Souverains étoient despotiques, & avoient depuis long-tems établi la funeste coutûme de faire mourir avec eux un nombre de leur Peuple." Le Page du Pratz, *Histoire de la Louisiane*, 2:224.

92. "Ces Peuples sont élevés dans une si parfaite soumission à leur Souverain, que l'autorité qu'ils exercent sur eux est un véritable despotisme qui ne peut être comparé qu'à celui des premiers Empereurs Ottomanes." Le Page du Pratz, *Histoire de la Louisiane*, 2:352.

93. Usner, *American Indians in the Lower Mississippi Valley*, 15–16.

94. "Quand les sauvages de la Louisiane veulent avoir du fruit, ils coupent l'arbre au pied et cueillent le fruit." Diderot and d'Alembert, *Encyclopédie*, 4:887.

95. "Dans des pays où le prince se déclare propriétaire des fonds et l'héritier de ses sujets, il en résulte nécessairement l'abandon de la culture des terres, tout y est en friche, tout y devient désert." Diderot and d'Alembert, *Encyclopédie*, 4:887.

96. "Voilà le gouvernement *despotique,* dit l'auteur de l'esprit des lois." Diderot and d'Alembert, *Encyclopédie*, 4:887.

97. "*Idée du despotisme.* Quand les sauvages de la Louisiane veulent avoir du fruit, ils coupent l'arbre au pied, et cueillent le fruit. Voilà le gouvernement despotique." Montesquieu, *De l'esprit des lois,* pt. 1, bk. 5, ch. 13, in *Œuvres complètes* (ed. Caillois), 2:292.

98. "Il faut d'abord en faire des hommes," "maîtres absolus d'eux-mêmes, sans être assujettis à aucune loi," "l'indépendance dans laquelle ils vivent, les asservit aux passions les plus brutales." Le père Gabriel Marest, Kaskaskia, Illinois, November 9, 1712, in *Lettres édifiantes et curieuses*, 11:305.

99. "Nos sauvages ne sont pas accoutumés à cueillir le fruit aux arbres; ils croient faire mieux d'abattre les arbres mêmes: ce qui est cause qu'il n'y a presque aucun arbre fruitier aux environs des villages." *Lettres édifiantes et curieuses,* 2:315.

100. "Si l'on croit les relations, le gouvernement de ces peuples sauvages est despotique. Leur chef dispose des biens de tous ses sujets, & les fait travailler à sa fantaisie; ils ne peuvent lui refuser leur tête." Chevalier de Jaucourt, "Matchez," in Diderot and d'Alembert, *Encyclopédie,* 11:35.

101. "Vous diriez que c'est le grand Sésostris," "Ce chef est traité dans sa cabane avec les cérémonies qu'on feroit à un empereur du Japon ou de la Chine." Chevalier de Jaucourt, "Matchez," in Diderot and d'Alembert, *Encyclopédie,* 11:35.

102. Montesquieu, *De l'esprit des lois,* pt. 3, bk. 18, chap. 18.

103. "Un peuple de la Louisiane […]. Leur chef dispose des biens de tous ses sujets, & les fait travailler à sa fantaisie […]. Les préjugés de la superstition sont supérieurs à tous les autres préjugés, & ses raisons à toutes les autres raisons. Ainsi, quoique les peuples sauvages ne connaissent point naturellement le despotisme, ce peuple-ci le connaît. Ils adorent le soleil: &, si leur chef n'avait pas imaginé qu'il était le frère du soleil, ils n'auraient trouvé en lui qu'un misérable comme eux." Montesquieu, *De l'esprit des lois,* pt. 1, bk. 5, chap. 18.

104. Shannon Lee Dawdy mentions that the Natchez's subjection to a sun king can be interpreted as a metaphor for the French in "Enlightenment from the Ground," 24–25.

105. "La crédulité des peuples le maintient dans l'autorité despotique qu'il se donne." Letter of the père Le Petit, New Orleans, July 12, 1730, in *Lettres édifiantes et curieuses*, 20:107.
106. "Un des principaux articles de leur religion, surtout pour les domestiques du grand chef, est d'honorer les funerailles, en mourant avec lui pour aller les servir dans l'autre monde [. . .] dès qu'il naît au grand Chef un héritier présomptif, chaque famille qui a un enfant à la mamelle doit lui en faire hommage. On choisit parmi tous ces enfants un certain nombre qu'on destine au service du jeune prince [. . .] s'il vient à mourir, tous ces domestiques s'immolent avec joie pour suivre leur cher maître." *Lettres édifiantes et curieuses*, 20:112–13.
107. "Les femmes se font toujours étrangler pour les suivre [. . .]. [On voit des femmes] qui étranglent elles-mêmes leurs enfants, pour ne pas perdre le droit de s'immoler dans la place selon les cérémonies ordinaires et ainsi que la loi l'ordonne." *Lettres édifiantes et curieuses*, 20:115.
108. "Le principe des états despotiques est qu'un seul prince y gouverne tout selon ses volontés, n'ayant absolument d'autre loi qui le domine, que celle de ses caprices." Chevalier de Jaucourt, "Despotisme," in Diderot and d'Alembert, *Encyclopédie*, 4:886–87.
109. "Entre ces nations, la plus remarquable étoit celle des Natchez. Elle obéissoit à un homme qui s'appelloit GRAND SOLEIL [. . .]. La police, la guerre, la religion: tout dépendoit de lui. Peut-être le globe entier n'eût-il pas offert un souverain plus absolu." Raynal, *Histoire des deux Indes*, vol. 4, bk. 16, p. 97.
110. "Lorsqu'il mouroit, lui ou sa femme, il falloit que plusieurs de leurs sujets terminâssent aussi leur carrière, pour les aller servir dans un autre monde." Raynal, *Histoire des deux Indes*, vol. 4, bk. 16, p. 97.
111. "La religion des Natchez se bornoit à l'adoration du soleil: mais cette croyance étoit accompagnée de beaucoup de culte & par conséquent suivie de mauvais effets. Cependant il n'y avoit qu'un temple pour toute la nation. Il fut embrâsé un jour par le feu qu'on y entretenoit perpétuellement, du moins habituellement; & la consternation fut générale. On faisoit de vains efforts pour arrêter l'incendie. Quelques mères y jettèrent leurs enfans, & le feu s'éteignit enfin. L'éloge de ces barbares héroïnes fut prononcé le lendemain par le pontife despote. C'est ainsi qu'il régnoit. On s'étonne qu'un peuple aussi pauvre, aussi sauvage fût si cruellement asservi: mais la superstition explique tout ce que la raison trouve inconcevable. Elle seule pouvoit ôter la liberté à des hommes qui n'avoient guère à perdre que la liberté." Raynal, *Histoire des deux Indes*, vol. 4, bk. 16, p. 97.
112. Mehta, "Spanish Conquistadores, French Explorers, and Natchez Great Suns."
113. "Et toi, tyran aveugle! parce que tes prêtres n'ont pas l'art persuasif qui feroit triompher leurs raisons; parce qu'ils ne peuvent effacer de l'esprit de ces innocens les traces profondes que l'éducation y a gravées; parce que ceux-ci ne veulent être ni des lâches, ni des hypocrites, ni des infames; parce qu'ils aiment mieux obéir à leur Dieu qu'à toi, il faut que tu les spolies, que tu les enchaînes, que tu

les brûles, que tu les pendes; que tu traînes leurs cadavres sur une claie. [...] Le malheur de l'état voulut que la superstition de Louis XIV, que la foiblesse du régent fissent rejetter ces propositions." Raynal, *Histoire des deux Indes,* vol. 4, bk. 16, pp. 110–12.

3. Louisiana Finds Its Voice

1. Vidal, *Caribbean New Orleans,* 493.
2. On the dire conditions of the colony leading up to the Spanish takeover, see J. Moore, *Revolt in Louisiana.*
3. Several incidents in Ulloa's life indicate that he was far more successful as a scientist than as an administrator. For example, his scathing report of the corrupt management of the Huancavelica mine in Peru resulted in his ouster by the local officials. Whitaker, "Antonio de Ulloa."
4. Marc Villiers du Terrage quotes the letter from French governor Aubry recounting the events and explaining the document that both men signed. *Les dernières années de la Louisiane française,* 240–41.
5. Acadians were French residents of present-day Nova Scotia, who refused to pledge allegiance to Britain when France ceded control of this territory in the 1750s. Many Acadians migrated to southern Louisiana and are now known as Cajuns. See Brasseaux, *Founding of New Acadia.*
6. "Une conspiration générale," "Une révolte générale de tous les habitants de la colonie, contre le gouvernement et sa nation, laquelle a éclaté tout d'un coup le 28 et le 29 octobre." Handwritten letter from Charles-Philippe Aubry, New Orleans, November 25, 1768, ANOM, C12 A 48, p. 24.
7. "Il s'est trouvé tant de la ville que de la campagne près de neuf cents hommes armés, tous les officiers de milice à leur tête, avec un pavillon blanc qu'ils ont arboré sur une place, criant tous généralement Vive la France et qu'ils ne voulaient point d'autre roi, paraissant même disposés à faire craindre pour la vie des Espagnols, si on n'avait pas d'égard à leur demande." MS letter from Aubry, November 25, 1768, ANOM.
8. "Députés des Habitans de la *Louisiane,* chargés de porter au pied du Trône les larmes & les respectueuses Suppliques de la Colonie [...] ont ordre d'exprimer le vœu unanime de leurs Concitoyens de vivre & de mourir avec le titre de *François.*" *Gazette d'Amsterdam* 38 (May 5, 1769).
9. "Afin que S.M. daignât les prendre sous sa protection & les regarder toujours comme ses fidèles Sujets." *Gazette d'Amsterdam* 39 (May 8, 1769).
10. Brasseux explains the divide between what he calls the Francophiles and the Hispanophiles, who take the two sides on this affair. *Denis-Nicolas Foucault and the New Orleans Rebellion of 1768,* 3–8.
11. The French edition was first published in 1846; the expanded English edition appeared in 1866.

12. Fortier, *History of Louisiana*, 1:175–76.
13. Vidal, "Francité et situation coloniale."
14. The copy of the *Mémoire des habitants* that a French author, Jean Bochart de Champigny, included in his text bears the dedication "A l'Univers," but it is probable that Champigny added these words, since they do not appear in other copies of the manifestos. I examine Champigny's works at length in the next chapter.
15. "En Louisiane, où l'instruction est peu répandue, où la population n'a surtout aucun moyen de s'instruire." Giraud, *Histoire de la Louisiane française*, 2:94. We do know that some schools existed, though. On the Ursuline school for girls, for example, see Clark, *Masterless Mistresses*.
16. Vidal, *Caribbean New Orleans*, 491.
17. "Lorsque la Louisiane fut cédée à l'Espagne et à la Grande-Bretagne en 1762–1763, la première génération d'élites créoles, c'est-à-dire nées sur place, venait donc juste de commencer à hériter des biens de ses parents et à occuper les postes de responsabilité dans la colonie à la place des officiers natifs de métropole." Vidal, "Francité et situation coloniale," 1029.
18. Vidal, *Caribbean New Orleans*, 444.
19. Vidal, *Caribbean New Orleans*, 447.
20. Mills, "Chauvin Brothers."
21. Mills, "Chauvin Brothers," 124.
22. "Déplorent [. . .] la nécessité de maintenir dans les fonctions de conseillers [. . .] l'ancien 'garçon meunier' La Fresnière, qui, pratiquement illéttré, ne conviennent pas à la 'dignité d'un Conseil Supérieur.'" Giraud, *Histoire de la Louisiane française*, 2:94.
23. Leumas, "Ties That Bind."
24. Klooster, *Revolutions in the Atlantic World*.
25. On Denis Braud, see Beer, "History of Libraries in Louisiana"; McMurtrie, *Pioneer Printer of New Orleans;* and Dart, "Adventures of Denis Braud."
26. As I have discussed elsewhere, the printing press had an ambiguous legacy. For example, in the eighteenth century, publication certainly made Enlightenment ideas far more accessible to a growing reading public than before, but *philosophes* often expressed hostility toward an instrument that allowed books of low quality to flood the marketplace. See Tsien, *Bad Taste of Others*, 14–38.
27. The first text can be found in ANOM, C13A 48, and it is quoted in its entirety in Gayarré, *Histoire de la Louisiane*, 2:215–28; the second can be found as an annex to the third text, beginning on page 49; and the third, published in New Orleans by Braud in 1768, is available in many libraries, in printed and scanned versions.
28. Vidal states in a note that according to evidence presented at the trial of the revolt's leaders, the authors were the merchant Pierre Caresse and the lawyer

Julien-Jérôme Doucet, very likely with the support of La Frénière. *Caribbean New Orleans*, 482n51.

29. "Témoins oculaires des calamités qui nous affligent, les magistrats du Conseil Supérieur de la Louisiane n'ont pu se refuser plus longtemps aux cris plaintifs d'un peuple opprimé." *Mémoire*, 1. The English translation is from Fortier, *A History of Louisiana*, 1:177. From this point on, I modernize the spelling in the French text.

30. "Leurs soins diligents ne se sont pas bornés à calmer les inquiétudes d'un peuple gémissant, ils l'ont encore autorisé à porter sa supplique et ses vœux au pied du Trône, bien persuadés que le regard compatissant de leur Souverain naturel, se détournerait sur des sujets aussi dévoués et que leurs amour respectueux pour leur Monarque, ne serait pas rejeté par Sa Majesté bienfaisante, l'image en terre pour ses Peuples de l'Etre conservateur." *Mémoire*, 2; Fortier, *History of Louisiana*, 1:178.

31. Lynn Hunt has famously examined the importance of the "ideal of the good father" in both novels and political discourse of the era leading up to the Revolution. Hunt sees a transformation of the father figure in the 1750s and 1760s, with a new emphasis on "affection and concern rather than unquestioned authority." Hunt, *Family Romance of the French Revolution*, 21, 25.

32. "Extrapolation ou analogie [...] une référence essentielle à l'amour naturel et réciproque des pères-princes et des sujets-enfants." Cosandey and Descimon, *L'absolutisme en France*, 261.

33. An excellent overview of the paternal model evoked in political treatises about absolutist monarchy can be found in Crest, *Modèle familial et pouvoir monarchique*.

34. "Réclam[ent] nos lois, notre patrie, notre souverain et de lui vouer la persévérance de notre amour." *Mémoire*, 41; Fortier, *History of Louisiana*, 1:199.

35. "Le Roi Très Chrétien étant dans la ferme résolution de resserrer de plus en plus, et de perpétuer les liens de la tendre amitié qui l'unissent au Roi Catholique son Cousin [...]." Fortier, *History of Louisiana*, 1:263.

36. Fortier, *History of Louisiana*, 1:264.

37. "Mi mui caro y mui amado Primo." Fortier, *History of Louisiana*, 1:264.

38. "Puro efecto de la nobleza de su Corazon y del amor y amistad en que vivimos." Fortier, *History of Louisiana*, 1:264.

39. "Mon tres Cher et tres Amé [sic] Cousin." Fortier, *History of Louisiana*, 1:265.

40. "Amité [sic] et affection de Sa Majesté Catholique." Fortier, *History of Louisiana*, 1:266.

41. "Que les habitants soient gardés et maintenus dans leurs possessions." Fortier, *History of Louisiana*, 1:267.

42. "Esperant au Surplus que Sa Majesté voudra bien donner a Ses Nouveaux Sujets de la Louisiane les mêmes Marques de protection et de bienveillance qu'ils ont éprouvé sous ma domination." Fortier, *History of Louisiana*, 1:267.

43. "Notre grand Roi, dans sa lettre qui nous l'annonce [la cession], semblait pressentir nos alarmes. Il [...] nous faisait espérer de sa part les mêmes marques

de bienveillance et de protection que celles goûtées sous sa chère domination. Ces sentiments augustes doivent enhardir notre amour." *Mémoire*, 3; Fortier, *History of Louisiana*, 1:178.
44. "Bien persuadés que le regard compatissant de leur Souverain naturel, se détournerait sur des sujets aussi dévoués." *Mémoire*, 2; Fortier, *History of Louisiana*, 1:178.
45. *Mémoire*, 3; Fortier, *History of Louisiana*, 1:178.
46. "Cette domination chérie, sous laquelle nous voulons vivre & mourir." *Mémoire*, 3; Fortier, *History of Louisiana*, 1:179.
47. "Les vœux du public se sont toujours accordés avec le choix du prince, à lui donner le commandement en chef de la Louisiane." "Louis, par la grâce de Dieu," 66.
48. "Le Français naît libre et soumis." ANOM, "Très-humbles représentations," 151. On the connection between political submission and sexual masochism in Rousseau's writings, see Falaky, *Social Contract, Masochist Contract*.
49. "Cette noble résistance aux volontés des souverains naturels, loin d'allumer leur colère, a réveillé leur tendresse." *Mémoire*, 41; Fortier, *History of Louisiana*, 1:199–200.
50. Locke's *Two Treatises of Government* appeared in several French-language editions, notably the translation by David Mazel in 1691. The ideas contained in these texts were also popularized by writers such as Barbeyrac and Montesquieu, according to Hutchinson, *Locke in France*. More than any of the prominent French *philosophes*, Locke addresses and dismantles the metaphor of the king as father.
51. In the first treatise, Locke argues against Robert Filmer's idea that since Adam was the original patriarch, all future generations have inherited the state of subjection from him: "A father cannot alien the power he has over his child." In the second treatise, Locke states that conquest by a foreign power is illegitimate and that the conquered people are not subjected to the laws of their conquerors. Locke, *Two Treatises*, 69, sec. 100; 205–15, secs. 175–96.
52. As Lynn Hunt does for the French Revolution, Christopher L. Miller reads documents from the eighteenth-century Atlantic triangle in a Freudian way, specifically applying the concept of the Oedipus complex. "The history of colonialism is rife with metaphors casting Europe in the role of father, Africa as mother [. . .], and the new *creole* (from Spanish *criar*, 'to breed,' 'to raise') colonies as children." Miller, *French Atlantic Triangle*, 5.
53. "Tous les mémoires, placets et lettres envoyés en métropole par les insurgés témoignaient donc apparemment d'un grand attachement envers Louis XV dont ils semblaient attendre beaucoup, alors même que certaines de leurs revendications remettaient en cause ses prétentions absolutistes." Vidal, "Francité et situation coloniale," 1046.
54. "Nos gouverneurs, commandants et magistrats ont toujours été regardés par nous comme nos pères." *Mémoire*, 33; Fortier, *History of Louisiana*, 1:195.

55. "Un peuple dont le Conseil est le père." "Louis, par la grâce de Dieu," 49.
56. In "The Politics of Patriotism in France (1770–1788)," Peter R. Campbell explains the historical connections between the words *patriote, pères de la patrie,* and *despotisme* in the struggles of the French parlements.
57. "They acted this way in order to subscribe to the views of the Parlement de Paris, which claimed to embody the whole nation, in opposition to the king." Vidal, "Francité et situation coloniale," 1047.
58. "Les Habitans sont résolus d'aller se ranger parmi les Sauvages qui vivent en liberté." *Gazette d'Amsterdam* 38 (May 12, 1769).
59. "Bien conscients du faible intérêt de ce qu'ils [the rebels] avaient à offrir et de la forte possibilité que leur requête ne fût pas entendue, ils prévinrent le duc d'Orléans en termes voilés que leur seul recours en cas de refus serait de '[vivre] dans l'indépendance.'" Vidal, "Francité et situation coloniale," 1048–49.
60. The *Mémoire* calls October 28 "le jour de la révolution" (3); however, we must keep in mind that in dictionaries of the time the word *révolution* meant something similar to "event." For example, the definition in the 4th edition of the *Dictionnaire de l'Académie française* (1762) reads, "changement qui arrive dans les affaires publiques, dans les choses du monde. *Grande, prompte, subite, soudaine, étrange, merveilleuse, étonnante, heureuse révolution.*"
61. "La conservation de cette colonie par la France garantit mieux les possessions d'Espagne de ce côté." *Mémoire,* 41–42; Fortier, *History of Louisiana,* 1:200.
62. J. Moore, *Revolt in Louisiana,* 173, quoting from Rodríguez Casado, *Primeros años de dominación española en la Luisiana,* 224.
63. Part of a speech by La Frénière that is quoted in the document "Louis, par la grâce de Dieu" confusingly adds more members to the metaphorical family: "La liberté et la concurrence sont les mères nourricières des deux états; l'exclusion, le tyran et la marâtre." "Louis, par la grâce de Dieu," 77.
64. Cosandey and Descimon, *L'absolutisme en France,* 265.
65. "Les rapports des doctrines absolutiste et mercantiliste semblent au cœur de la vision politique du 'grand roi.'" Cosandey and Descimon, *L'absolutisme en France,* 265.
66. "Des punitions sévères, des châtiments inconnus sous la domination française encore subsistante, sont infligés déjà par son ordre, aux fautes les plus légères." *Mémoire,* 20–21; Fortier, *History of Louisiana,* 1:188.
67. "Aucun lien ne nous attache encore à son autorité; rien autre chose qu'une déférence respectueuse pour le caractère dont on le croit revêtu." *Mémoire,* 20; Fortier, *History of Louisiana,* 1:188.
68. "La Loi d'Espagne peut avoir ses agréments et ses avantages que nous ne connaissons pas; mais l'antipathie pour l'humanité, et la disposition naturelle à faire du mal, reconnue et avérée dans la personne chargée de nous présenter cette Loi, nous en a fait sentir les conséquences les plus dures, en ne paraissant

agir que par ces mêmes conséquences." *Mémoire*, 21; Fortier, *History of Louisiana*, 1:188.
69. "Glaive vengeur." *Mémoire*, 37; Fortier, *History of Louisiana*, 1:197.
70. "Le terme de tyrannie paraîtra fort, joignons-y celui de vexation pour correspondre à la vérité des faits." *Mémoire*, 36; Fortier, *History of Louisiana*, 1:197.
71. "Etait-ce pour nous insulter, ou pour en imposer à nos murmures?" *Mémoire*, 37; Fortier, *History of Louisiana*, 1:197.
72. "Etait diamétralement opposée à notre bien être, et capable de prime abord d'exciter *nos* murmures." *Mémoire*, 38; Fortier, *History of Louisiana*, 1:198.
73. Fortier, *History of Louisiana*, 1:167.
74. Fortier, *History of Louisiana*, 1:217.
75. Fortier, *History of Louisiana*, 1:226.
76. I use the twentieth-century term *disinformation*, defined by the *Oxford English Dictionary* as "the dissemination of deliberately false information, esp. when supplied by a government or its agent to a foreign power or to the media, with the intention of influencing the policies or opinions of those who receive it" (http://www.oed.com/view/Entry/54579?redirectedFrom=disinformation#eid), whose French near equivalent is *intox*, or "campagne systématique de mise en condition de l'opinion publique par la diffusion d'opinions tantôt vraies tantôt fausses et plus ou moins alarmantes" (http://www.lexilogos.com/francais_langue_dictionnaires.htm). The terms did not exist in the eighteenth century, but the concepts did.
77. "Nous n'ignorons pas que l'envoyé d'Espagne ait pris avant son départ, et recueilli encore par émissaires, des certificats de quelques particuliers qui résident parmi nous." *Mémoire*, 47; Fortier, *History of Louisiana*, 1:203.
78. "Certificats peu authentiques." *Mémoire*, 47; Fortier, *History of Louisiana*, 1:203.
79. "Clients mercenaires qu'il s'est attaché par des promesses brillantes et qui cherchent ici des prosélytes, en persuadant les simples et en effrayant les faibles." *Mémoire*, 47; Fortier, *History of Louisiana*, 1:203.
80. "Ils ne démentiront jamais la voix générale & la notoriété publique." *Mémoire*, 47; Fortier, *History of Louisiana*, 1:203.
81. "En este tiempo, se dio al público un libelo infamatorio, su titulo, *Memorias de los habitantes y negociantes de la Luisiana* [. . .] satirizando con imposturas a D[on] Antonio de Ulloa, y toda la Nacion." Joseph Melchior de Acosta, "Relacion diaria, veridica, y circunstanciada de todos los acaecimientos hauidos en la Luisiana," in Serrano y Sanz, *Documentos históricos de la Florida y la Luisiana*, 288.
82. Fortier, *History of Louisiana*, 1:214–15.
83. Fortier, *History of Louisiana*, 1:217.
84. J. Moore, *Revolt in Louisiana*, 151.
85. "Estas sencillas gentes [. . .] habiendo sido engañados por la primera vez, no querían experimentar otro engaño a la segunda." Acosta, "Relacion diaria, veridica, y circunstanciada," 292.

86. Villiers du Terrage, *Les dernières années de la Louisiane française*, 268.
87. "Pour mettre le comble à tant de tribulations [...] avec le temps on réduira les colons de la Louisiane à la simple nourriture de la tortilla, tandis que l'aliment le plus sobre ne fera jamais leur peine." "Louis, par la grâce de Dieu," 65.
88. "La misère devint si grande que la moitié de la colonie se trouva réduite au riz et au mahy [maïs], et sans les sages précautions de M. Foucault qui en fit descendre de la côte des Allemands, les pères et mères n'auraient eu que des larmes à offrir au cri plaintif de l'enfant affamé [...]. Votre conseil supérieur, Sire, doit-il dire à Votre Majesté que votre peuple est persuadé que M. Ulloa [...] était décidé à réduire vos sujets à la nourriture de la tortilla?" "Très-humbles représentations," 154–55.
89. Giraud, *Histoire de la Louisiane française*, 1:176.
90. Villiers du Terrage, *Les dernières années de la Louisiane française*, 269n. Bernardin de Saint-Pierre, in his 1773 *Voyage à l'Île de France*, even while praising the value of corn, remarks about "Le maïs, ou blé turc": "Il sert à nourrir les noirs, les poules et les bestiaux" (218; Corn, or Turkish wheat: It is used to nourish Blacks, chickens, and livestock).
91. Kaplan, *Bakers of Paris*, 23.
92. A translation of a letter by Ulloa that recounts the events appears in Chandler, "Ulloa's Account of the 1768 Revolt"; the passage quoted is from pp. 412–13. The original document can be found as "Noticia de los acaecimientos de la Luisiana en el año de 1769," legajo 2542, 30–124, in the Archivo General de las Indias, Seville (hereafter AGI). "In a kind of foreword," writes Chandler, "it is stated that Ulloa prepared this lengthy report for publication, but it never saw the light of day" (409n8).
93. On the symbolic importance of wine to French colonists in the Americas, see Brazeau, *Writing a New France*.
94. "Il se hâta de caractériser son antipathie en demandant à la Havane une nourrice, pour que son enfant ne pût sucer aucune goutte du lait français, quels pernicieux principes! Quelles barbares dispositions pour gouverner des sujets français!" "Très-humbles représentations," 154. Champigny refers to this incident in his notes to the *Mémoire*. Champigny, *État présent de la Louisiane*, 142–43.
95. See Dubos, *Réflexions critiques*, 2:238–40.
96. "Il ya encore fait conférer le sacrement de mariage par son aumônier, à deux personnes, dont la femme était une négresse esclave et l'homme un blanc, sans la permission du curé, sans aucune publication de ban, sans aucunes formes ni solennités requises par l'église, au grand scandale du public, au mépris du Concile de Trente, et contre la disposition précise de nos ordonnances, tant civiles que canoniques." *Mémoire*, 40; Fortier, *History of Louisiana*, 1:199.
97. "[Ulloa] a accordé la protection la plus ouverte aux nègres non-mutilés sur leurs simples plaintes et sans jamais avoir entendu les maîtres. Quel

bouleversement funeste! Vos sujets étaient menacés de l'esclavage et leurs nègres acquerraient des degrés d'hommes libres." "Très-humbles représentations," 154.
98. Fortier, *History of Louisiana*, 1:173.
99. Later authors that I deal with in the following chapters take up the animal metaphor when referring to the king's mistreatment of colonists, who were metaphorically bought and sold.
100. The depositions can be found in ANOM, C13A 48, pp. 100–148.
101. "Nous prenait-il pour les sauvages du Pérou & du Mexique?" *Mémoire*, 37; Fortier, *History of Louisiana*, 1:197.
102. "L'importion [*sic*] des Negres" is "l'aliment le plus propre à son accroissement." "Louis, par la grâce de Dieu," 54.
103. "The introduction des Negres [...] l'embonpoint." "Louis, par la grâce de Dieu," 61.
104. In *Poems of Nation, Anthems of Empire,* Suvir Kaul describes a parallel situation: he points out how the song "Rule, Britannia," with the refrain "Britons never, never, never shall be slaves," establishes a "negative definition of the national self" (2). In other words, national self-assurance rests on keeping away the fear of enslavement.
105. "Tremblant de ses menaces, [les Acadiens] croyaient déjà les voir effectuer sur la liberté de leurs familles et se voir vendre à l'encan, pour acquitter les rations du roi. Sommes-nous à Fez ou au Maroc?" *Mémoire*, 39; Fortier, *History of Louisiana*, 1:198.
106. See Maziane, "Les captifs européens en terre marocaine."
107. "Ce peuple, si longtemps le jouet des événements, s'est déterminé, par un esprit patriotique, [de] venir vivre sous les heureuses lois de leur ancien maître." "Louis, par la grâce de Dieu," 63.
108. "Les a menacés de les chasser de la colonie et de les faire vendre comme des esclaves." "Louis, par la grâce de Dieu," 63–64.
109. "L'affection des Naturels." *Mémoire*, 7; Fortier, *History of Louisiana*, 1:181.
110. Aravamudan, *Tropicopolitans*, 39.
111. In fact, the *Mémoire* surreptitiously (or unintentionally) signals this link to us by referring to the "mines" of gold once thought to exist in Louisiana. At this point, hope of finding actual mines has been extinguished, but it lives on in the metaphor. The established trade agreements with the Natives, the authors of the *Mémoire* claim, are a valuable asset: "C'est une mine abondante [...] qui même promet des trésors plus estimables que les métalliques du Potose" (It is an abundant mine [...] which promises treasures more valuable than those of Potosi). *Mémoire*, 7; Fortier, *History of Louisiana*, 1:181.
112. "Dans les colonies de peuplement du 'Nouveau Monde,' les colons d'origine européenne se trouvaient dans la position particulière d'être à la fois des colonisateurs par rapport aux Amérindiens et aux Africains et des colonisés vis-à-vis de la métropole." Vidal, "Francité et situation coloniale," 1022.

113. Anderson, *Imagined Communities*.
114. Aravamudan, *Tropicopolitans*, 270–71.
115. "Que vehia en él la historia del Marqués de Poncalet en la sublevacion de Bretaña en Francia." Acosta, "Relacion diaria, veridica, y circunstanciada," 287.
116. See Guillorel, "Complaintes de tradition orale en Bretagne." The song also exists in popular culture, as we can see in YouTube clips and in Bernard Tavernier's film *Que la fête commence,* which imaginatively conflates the Pontcallec conspiracy with the forced emigrations to Louisiana discussed in chapter 2.
117. Vidal, *Caribbean New Orleans*, 493.
118. Vidal discovered a letter from the Spanish minister Grimaldi in which he worried about "the consequences that the bad example of Louisiana could entail in other possessions of America, even those belonging to different powers where the spirit of sedition and independence was beginning to spread." Vidal, *Caribbean New Orleans,* 494, quoting from Jerónimo Grimaldi, "Copie de la lettre de M. le marquis de Grimaldi à M. le comte de Fuentes," ANOM, C13A 50, fol. 47r. We will see in chapter 5 how the Spanish governor of Louisiana would fear the effects of the Saint-Domingue revolt in the 1790s on Louisiana. The Haitian exiles would not settle in large numbers in New Orleans until 1809. Vidal, *Caribbean New Orleans,* 498.

4. The Sentimental Aftermath of the Revolt

1. In France, plays could be staged in theaters only if the government censors approved of them, so any subversive content would have been prohibited.
2. Vincent-Buffault, *Histoire des larmes,* 9.
3. Vincent-Buffault, *Histoire des larmes,* 14.
4. Vincent-Buffault, *Histoire des larmes,* 13.
5. This idea of natural law was a potentially problematic view of human nature as universal, because in this view all persons presumably felt the same law in their heart, and they would all come to the same conclusion, given the right circumstances. Dan Edelstein explores how politicians used this concept to justify the most violent phase of the French Revolution in *The Terror of Natural Right*.
6. "C'est la forme littéraire surtout qui garantit le succès d'un mémoire judiciaire. Là-dessus, les contemporains sont unanimes: un bon mémoire a les qualités d'une œuvre littéraire, il touche, émeut, fait frémir et pleurer." Maza, "Le tribunal de la nation," 82.
7. "A travers la critique sociale se profile donc une critique politique qui oppose la loi, expression de la volonté générale, à la cour, domaine des intérêts particuliers." Maza, "Le tribunal de la nation," 84.
8. "L'innocence persécutée." Maza, "Le tribunal de la nation," 86.
9. "Désacralisation des institutions centrales de l'Ancien Régime, à commencer par la monarchie elle-même." Maza, "Le tribunal de la nation," 87.

10. Wahnich, *Les émotions, la Révolution française et le présent*, 18.
11. Wahnich, *Les émotions, la Révolution française et le présent*, 17.
12. See Duchet, *Anthropologie et histoire*.
13. "La Louysiane est une vaste contrée, bornée au midi par la mer, au levant par la Floride & la Caroline, au couchant par le nouveau Mexique, au nord par le Canada & par des terres inconnues qui doivent s'étendre jusqu'à la baie d'Hudson." Raynal, *Histoire des deux Indes,* vol. 4, bk. 16, p. 92.
14. Unlike most other authors included in this study, Raynal never left Europe but instead depended on explorers' journals for his information. His judgments therefore imply that he chose certain eyewitness views over others.
15. "Le sol en est sablonneux & le climat brûlant. On n'y voit que quelques cèdres, quelques pins épars [. . .]. Cette position, la plus triste, la plus stérile de ces contrées est celle qu'on choisit pour fixer le petit nombre d'hommes qu'Iberville avoit amenés sous l'appât des plus grandes espérances [. . .]. Une colonie, fondée sur de si mauvaises bases, ne pouvoit prospérer." Raynal, *Histoire des deux Indes,* vol. 4, bk. 16, pp. 86–87.
16. "La cour de Versailles annonça, le 21 avril 1764, aux habitants de la Louysiane, que par une convention secrète du 3 novembre 1762, on avoit abandonné à celle de Madrid, la propriété de leur territoire." Raynal, *Histoire des deux Indes,* vol. 4, bk. 16, p. 116.
17. "Mais de quelque manière que la politique veuille envisager cet événement, ce sera toujours au tribunal de la morale un crime d'avoir vendu ou donné des citoyens à une puissance étrangère. De quel droit, en effet, un prince dispose-t-il d'un peuple qui ne consent pas à changer de maître? Les nations doivent-elles tout aux rois, & les rois ne doivent-ils rien aux nations? Que signifie donc le droit des gens? N'est-il que le droit des princes?" Raynal, *Histoire des deux Indes,* vol. 4, bk. 16, p. 116.
18. Raynal, *Histoire des deux Indes,* vol. 4, bk. 16, p. 117.
19. "Ne tiennent, disent-ils, leur pouvoir que de Dieu seul." Raynal, *Histoire des deux Indes,* vol. 4, bk. 16, p. 116.
20. "Cette maxime, imaginée par le clergé, qui ne met les rois au-dessus des peuples, que pour commander aux rois même au nom de la divinité." Raynal, *Histoire des deux Indes,* vol. 4, bk. 16, p. 116.
21. "La religion étant l'unique frein du despotisme." Raynal, *Histoire des deux Indes,* vol. 4, bk. 16, p. 117.
22. "Mais pourquoi l'autorité voudroit-elle se déguiser qu'elle vient des hommes? La nature, l'expérience, l'histoire, le sentiment intérieur, apprennent assez aux rois qu'ils tiennent des peuples tout ce qu'ils possèdent." Raynal, *Histoire des deux Indes,* vol. 4, bk. 16, p. 118.
23. "C'est donc en vain que les princes ont recours au ciel pour rappeler leurs droits, quand ils manquent à leurs devoirs. La loi qu'ils invoquent s'élève contre eux. Elle tonne, & les foudroie par la bouche des pontifes. Elle crie au

fond des cœurs d'un peuple qui gémit." Raynal, *Histoire des deux Indes,* vol. 4, bk. 16, p. 117.

24. "Puisqu'on reçoit du peuple tous les fruits de l'obéissance, pourquoi ne pas accepter de lui seul tous les droits de l'autorité? Qu'a-t-on à craindre des volontés qui se donnent, & que gagne-t-on à l'abus d'une puissance qu'on usurpe? Ne faut-il pas la retenir par la violence, quand on s'en est emparé par surprise? Et quel est le bonheur d'un prince qui ne commande que par la force, & qui n'est obéi que par la crainte?" Raynal, *Histoire des deux Indes,* vol. 4, bk. 16, p. 118. It is ironic that the New Orleans revolt of 1768 involved the actual family of the Bourbon kings, with their official Pacte de Famille: the Spanish and the French cousins even mention their love for each other in the peace treaty that ceded Louisiana, as I stated in the previous chapter.

25. "Qu'une chaîne de fer, qui tient une nation entière sous les pieds d'un seul homme? Ce n'est donc plus un lien réciproque d'amour & de vertu, d'intérêt & de fidélité." Raynal, *Histoire des deux Indes,* vol. 4, bk. 16, p. 116.

26. I expand my analysis of Raynal's section on Louisiana, with a special focus on the eighteenth-century concept of imagination, in "Louisiana as a Figment of the Imagination."

27. "Une voix qui crie du fond de l'Amérique; c'est la voix d'une nombreuse colonie." Raynal, *Histoire des deux Indes,* vol. 4, bk. 16, p. 119; Isaiah 40:3.

28. "Que t'ai-je fait, pour me livrer à un étranger? Ne suis-je pas sortie de ton sein? N'ai-je pas semé, planté, cultivé, moissonné pour toi seule? [. . .] Mais non, tu m'as abandonnée. Tu m'as engagée à mon insu, par un marché, dont le secret même était une trahison. Mère insensible, ingrate, as-tu pu rompre, contre le vœu de la nature, les nœuds qui m'attachaient à toi par ma naissance même? [. . .] Tu m'as arrachée à ma famille. [. . .] Rends-moi mon père, cruelle. [. . .] Je languirai, je périrai de douleur & faiblesse." Raynal, *Histoire des deux Indes,* vol. 4, bk. 16, p. 119.

29. Michel Delon comments on this passage in "L'appel au lecteur dans l'*Histoire des deux Indes.*"

30. Various editions, with changes in the content, appeared from 1770 on. I quote from the 1780 edition; the section I quote is the same as in the 1770 editions.

31. "Effusion collective naît de l'image familiale (amour conjugal, ou filial) que présentent quelques hommes publics, et qui fait fondre en larmes toute l'assistance: elle s'apparente à une sorte de comédie larmoyante." Vincent-Buffault, *Histoire des larmes,* 89.

32. Quintilian, *Institutio Oratoria,* 9.30. See http://www.perseus.tufts.edu/hopper/text?doc=urn:cts:latinLit:phi1002.phi0019.perseus-eng1:2.

33. Quintilian, *Institutio Oratoria,* 9.33.

34. Quintilian, *Institutio Oratoria,* 9.31.

35. Quintilian, *Institutio Oratoria,* 9.32.

36. Riffaterre, "Prosopopeia," 117.

37. Riffaterre, "Prosopopeia," 108.
38. "Voit-on qu'ils aient le droit d'acheter, de vendre & d'échanger les peuples sans les consulter? Quoi, les princes s'arrogeront le droit barbare d'aliéner ou d'hypothéquer leurs provinces & leurs sujets, comme des biens meubles & immeubles [...] contre le droit de la nature, contre le droit des gens, vous disposez de vos colons comme d'un troupeau de bêtes, vous les cédez sans leur consentement." Raynal, *Histoire des deux Indes,* vol. 4, bk. 16, pp. 118–23.
39. "Des hommes généreux, dont tout le crime étoit d'avoir eu un attachement sans bornes pour leur métropole." Raynal, *Histoire des deux Indes,* vol. 4, bk. 16, p. 121.
40. "Barbares, sanguinaires, perfides Espagnols." Raynal, *Histoire des deux Indes,* vol. 4, bk. 16, p. 123.
41. "On vouloit des victimes." Raynal, *Histoire des deux Indes,* vol. 4, bk. 16, p. 122.
42. "Vos yeux désignoient dans la foule les premières victimes de votre autorité." Raynal, *Histoire des deux Indes,* vol. 4, bk. 16, p. 123.
43. "Maîtres inhumains," "ordonné cette horrible tragédie!," "le ministère François n'en conçut aucune indignation!" Raynal, *Histoire des deux Indes,* vol. 4, bk. 16, p. 122.
44. "On entraîne à l'échafaud, on va précipiter dans des fosses obscures, vos amis, vos parens, vos chefs, vos défenseurs, les objets de votre tendresse, de votre vénération; & vous êtes immobiles! quand & pourquoi, vous exposerez-vous donc à mourir?" Raynal, *Histoire des deux Indes,* vol. 4, bk. 16, p. 123.
45. "Mais peut-on plaindre bien vivement la triste situation de ces colons qui ont laissé égorger leur compatriotes [...]? La conscience, ce juge sévère de tous les devoirs, ne leur crie-t-elle pas, sans interruption: '[...] C'étoient ton père, ton frère, ton enfant; & tu les as vus tranquillement conduire à l'échafaud ou charger de chaînes! & tu t'inclines froidement sur la pierre qu'ils ont teinte de leur sang!'" Raynal, *Histoire des deux Indes,* vol. 4, bk. 16, p. 126.
46. This book was not published in English translation until 1853 as *Memoir on the Present State of Louisiana.*
47. Chaix d'Est-Ange, *Dictionnaire des familles françaises anciennes ou notables,* s.v. "Bochart de Champigny" (5:9–11).
48. F. Moore, *Life of Oliver Goldsmith,* 308.
49. Prior, *Life of Oliver Goldsmith, M.B.,* 2:142.
50. To ensure an income for themselves, eighteenth-century authors wrote a prospectus for a book in progress, then solicited subscribers to pay ahead of time, which would allow the author to finish his book and then deliver it to his customers.
51. See https://founders.archives.gov/index.xqy?q=champigny&s=1111211111&sa=&r=1&sr=].
52. See https://founders.archives.gov/documents/Franklin/01-27-02-0135.
53. "Quelques mauvais romans." Champigny, *État présent de la Louisiane,* iii.

54. "Des faits purement historiques, & arrivés pour ainsi dire sous mes yeux; ils sont même si récens, que les pleurs qu'ils ont fait répandre, tant en Amérique qu'en Europe, ne sont pas encore séchés. Je n'avance ici rien que de vrai, il ne me reste donc qu'à communiquer au Lecteur par quelle voie ce manuscrit m'est parvenu." Champigny, *État présent de la Louisiane*, 3.

55. The reference to an honorable English friend reflects a possible reality, which Champigny mentions in the London edition of his text. In that edition, the author dedicates his work to a friend, "Mylord Romney, Président de la Société des Arts, et colonel de la milice du Comté."

56. "J'écris pour les ames sensibles." Champigny, *État présent de la Louisiane*, x.

57. "En transmettant à la postérité ces traits héroiques & sublimes qui feront l'objet de cet Ouvrage." Champigny, *État présent de la Louisiane*, ix.

58. "Sans dignité, sans générosité [. . .] voilà l'homme quant à l'âme. Quant au corps . . . . il est difficile d'être plus petit et plus mince que l'était Dom Antonio d'Wlloa, une voix faible et aigre annonçait son caractère. Sa physionomie, quoiqu'assez régulière, avait cependant quelque chose de faux; de gros yeux, qui toujours baissés vers la terre, ne lançaient que des regards échappés [. . .]. Une bouche dont le ris forcé annonçait quelque fourberie, la duplicité et l'hypocrisie, terminait le portrait de Dom Antonio d' Wlloa." Champigny, *État présent de la Louisiane*, 37–38.

59. "M. Aubry était un petit homme sec, maigre, laid, sans noblesse, sans dignité, sans maintien." Champigny, *État présent de la Louisiane*, 38.

60. "Voilà le portrait des deux hommes qui ont fait la perte de la colonie de la Louisiane, le premier par méchanceté, le second par faiblesse." Champigny, *État présent de la Louisiane*, 38.

61. "Figure noble," "port majestueux." Champigny, *État présent de la Louisiane*, 64.

62. "Un guerrier," "galant homme." Champigny, *État présent de la Louisiane*, 65.

63. "Déjà les Cocardes blanches s'arboraient, déjà on se préparait à marcher aux ennemis, quand M. de La Frénière [. . .] arrêta cette fougue par un discours dont voici la substance:" Champigny, *État présent de la Louisiane*, 58.

64. "Obéir aux ordres de notre roi [. . .]. Attendons tout d'un roi bienfaisant, d'un roi du même sang que le nôtre, écoutons les promesses de celui qui le représente, et tâchons d'en mériter l'exécution par une conduite soumise et respectueuse." Champigny, *État présent de la Louisiane*, 61.

65. "Nous approchons du moment terrible qui va décider pour jamais du sort de la colonie. Avant de porter nos regards sur les scènes d'horreur qui me restent à tracer, transportons-nous à la Louisiane, et voyons à quoi s'occupent les habitants depuis le départ de M. d'Ulloa.

J'admire tout le long du fleuve les fruits heureux de la liberté et du contentement; chacun a redoublé d'effort: les cultures sont dans le plus bel état; les revenus seront plus considérables qu'ils ne l'avaient été dans les temps

d'engourdissement marqués par le séjour d'Ulloa. Je vois respirer partout la joie et la tranquillité." Champigny, *État présent de la Louisiane,* 54–55.
66. "Quel est cet édifice que je vois s'élever au milieu de la ville? C'est le temple du Seigneur." Champigny, *État présent de la Louisiane,* 55.
67. "Plus loin je découvre un autre bâtiment, la curiosité m'y porte; on lit sur l'entrée cette belle inscription: AZYLE DU PAUVRE ET DE L'ORPHELIN." Champigny, *État présent de la Louisiane,* 55.
68. "Sans tumulte et sans confusion." Champigny, *État présent de la Louisiane,* 55–56.
69. "Tout cela se passa sans la moindre insulte au pavillon espagnol, ni aux Espagnols qui demeurèrent dans la colonie. [...] Le rapport unanime de tous les étrangers fait de cet événement la chose la plus extraordinaire et la plus surprenante pour le bon ordre, à la décence et à la modération [...]. Ces témoignages d'attachement au Roi de France furent les seules clameurs qui troublèrent la tranquillité et le silence pendant trois jours que les habitants furent assemblés à la Nouvelle-Orléans. Aussitôt le départ de M. Ulloa, le calme et la tranquillité régnèrent." Champigny, *État présent de la Louisiane,* 51–52.
70. "Un accord unanime a fait ces fondations: le cri général les a proposées." Champigny, *État présent de la Louisiane,* 56.
71. "L'amour que nous avons les uns pour les autres." Champigny *État présent de la Louisiane,* 56.
72. "Chacun a fourni selon ses facultés, sans taxes, sans impôts. L'un a donné le bois nécessaire pour la charpente, l'autre les matériaux pour la maçonnerie; celui-ci des lits, celui-là les autres meubles. Chacun a concouru à l'envie, et on a pourvu aux fonds nécessaires pour la dépense qui se fait dans cet hôpital." Champigny, *État présent de la Louisiane,* 56.
73. "La nature ne fournissait pas moins à leurs désirs qu'à leurs besoins. Dans ce pays heureux, la cupidité était étrangère: ils se faisaient des présents, où celui qui donnait croyait toujours avoir l'avantage. Le peuple troglodyte se regardait comme une seule famille; les troupeaux étaient presque toujours confondus; la seule peine qu'on s'épargnait ordinairement, c'était de les partager." Montesquieu, *Lettres persanes,* letter 12, p. 168; *Persian Letters,* 58. In letters 11–14 of *Lettres persanes,* the Troglodytes live at first in a Hobbesian dystopia of violence and extreme self-interest. Then they die off until only a few virtuous ones remain to create a utopian society. The parable ends when their population grows enough to seek a leader. The old man who is chosen begins to weep because he says that from now on, people will be virtuous because of the law, not by free choice.
74. "O vertu! M'écriai-je plein d'enthousiasme, ô divin patriotisme! De quoi ton feu sacré ne nous rend-il pas capables lorsqu'il nous embrase? Parmi quels hommes suis-je transporté?" Champigny, *État présent de la Louisiane,* 56.
75. "Ô monarque heureux qui règne sur les Français, que de tels sujets sont dignes de ton appui! [...] Leur sort doit être à jamais, de voir croître sous ta domination

les sentiments de religion, d'humanité, de charité et de générosité que je vois briller en eux dans un moment où leur volonté n'a d'autre guide que le mouvement de leurs cœurs et d'autre frein que le désir de prouver à l'univers entier combien ils te chérissent." Champigny, *État présent de la Louisiane,* 56–57.

76. "Mais d'où vient ce murmure général dans toute la ville? Chacun se parle à l'oreille, on craint d'élever la voix [...] la pâleur est sur tous les visages, bientôt je vois couler des larmes. Les sanglots étouffent les cris de douleur; je prends part à l'effroi public." Champigny, *État présent de la Louisiane,* 57.

77. "'La mort n'a rien d'effrayant pour nous,' disoit M. le Marquis, en demandant une prise de tabac, avec ce sang froid qui n'a point d'exemple. 'Sachez que, quoiqu'étranger, mon cœur est François; il a toujours été pour LOUIS LE BIEN-AIMÉ, au service duquel j'ai sacrifié trente et quelques années de ma vie, que je me fais gloire que mon amour pour lui soit cause de ma mort.'" Champigny, *État présent de la Louisiane,* 78–79.

78. "Puisse notre Roi Bien-aimé apprendre combien il nous fut cher, combien nous nous glorifions de mourir ses fideles Sujets. [...] Mourir pour le Roi..... mourir François..... quoi de plus glorieux! Cette idée élève tellement mon âme que si dans ce moment terrible où je suis prêt à paraître devant l'Éternel, les Espagnols m'offraient la vie pour cesser d'être François, je leur dirois avec la même fermeté que je leur dis dans ce moment-ci... *Tirez.*" Champigny, *État présent de la Louisiane,* 79.

79. "Palpitant encore, [il] porta la main sur son coeur; on crut lui entendre dire, 'Il est François.'" Champigny, *État présent de la Louisiane,* 79.

80. "Donnons ici un libre cours à nos larmes." Champigny, *État présent de la Louisiane,* 80.

81. "M'a juré avoir été présent à cette cruelle exécution, et m'a permis de faire usage de son nom, pour rendre ce fait encore plus authentique." Champigny, *État présent de la Louisiane,* 79.

82. "Tigre altéré de sang," "âme sauvage et barbare." Champigny, *État présent de la Louisiane,* 83.

83. "Assouvis ta rage & ta cupidité ... fais plus de mal en un jour, que n'en eussent faits [*sic*] les Calligula et les Nérons ... ose plus; ose dire que l'arrêt sorti de ta bouche infâme avoit été dicté par ton Roi... il ne te manquoit plus que ce blasphême horrible." Champigny, *État présent de la Louisiane,* 83.

84. "Il est de toute impossibilité qu'un Conseil aussi éclairé & aussi équitable que celui de Madrid, auquel préside un Roi juste & clément, ait prononcé un jugement sanguinaire contre des gens accusés." Champigny, *État présent de la Louisiane,* 85.

85. "Écartons d'un ouvrage dicté par la vérité cette maxime politique que nous avons vu débiter dans un siécle philosophe & éclairé, maxime barbare, que les nations les moins civilisées ont rejettée avec le plus grand soin, mais que les Espagnols adoptent avec un aveuglement impardonnable. 'Quelque chose

qui arrive,' dit quelqu'un, 'un chef ne doit jamais avoir tort, & il est dangereux de le laisser croire.'" Champigny, *État présent de la Louisiane*, 88–89.

86. "L'univers a vu avec surprise le ministere François demeurer dans le silence sur la conduite de M. Oreilly, n'exiger aucune réparation de son inhumanité, se taire sur son infraction au droit des gens." Champigny, *État présent de la Louisiane*, 90.

87. "Disons qu'on a ignoré jusqu'ici la vérité, disons que le ministere François a lui-même été trompé." Champigny, *État présent de la Louisiane*, 90.

88. "Ce n'est qu'en tremblant, cher ami, que je vous fais le détail de cette sanglante tragédie, car la douleur qui me pénètre me fait verser des larmes de regret lorsque je me représente les fatals poteaux teints de sang des victimes et percés de balles meurtrières qui ont donné la mort à nos illustres camarades, plus malheureux que criminels, qui firent paraître dans cet instant terrible la vertu la plus courageuse et la fermeté la plus héroïque." Bossu, *Nouveaux voyages dans l'Amérique septentrionale*, 20.

89. "Il ne voulut jamais qu'on lui bandât les yeux, disant: qu'ayant tant de fois bravé la mort pour le service du Roi de France son maître, il ne les avait jamais fermés ni détournés devant ses ennemis. [...] mourons en homme [...].
Messieurs les Espagnols, continua-t-il, soyez témoins que nous mourons pour avoir voulu être toujours français; oui, sachez-le, quoiqu'étranger, mon cœur est français; il a été toujours pour Louis le bien aimé, au service duquel j'ai sacrifié trente et quelques années, et je me fais une gloire que mon amour pour lui soit la cause de ma mort." Bossu, *Nouveaux voyages dans l'Amérique septentrionale*, 20–21.

90. "Après ces paroles, ce brave officier déchira sa chemise et montra son estomac cicatrisé de blessures reçues à la guerre, en disant, *tirez bourreaux*." Bossu, *Nouveaux voyages dans l'Amérique septentrionale*, 21.

91. "Je n'exagère en rien l'impression de douleur et d'effroi répandue, en ces tems malheureux, dans toute la Colonie, impression si forte en elle-même, que j'ai vue et vois journellement d'anciens Colons, témoins de ces scènes tragiques, en être tellement frappés, qu'après un espace de trente années et plus, ils n'en font le récit qu'avec des témoignages sensibles de la tristesse, de l'épouvante, et de l'horreur, dont ils furent tous pénétrés, à cette ère vraiment affreuse pour eux, et gravée dans leur mémoire en caractères ineffaçables." Berquin-Duvallon, *Vue de la colonie espagnole*, 4.

92. Vidal, *Caribbean New Orleans*, 496.

93. The textual source that Baudry de Lozières cites, the *Mémoires de M. de Vergennes*, while openly sympathetic to the rebellion, does not contain the above description of La Frénière.

94. "M. Chauvin de La Frénière, procureur-général au Conseil Supérieur, créole et d'une bravoure à remarquer même parmi les Louisianais [...]. M. de la Frénière était un des plus beaux hommes que la nature se soit plu à former. Grand, bien

fait, l'air noble, imposant et brave [...]. Son physique était si remarquable que, ne sachant à qui le comparer, on l'appelait vulgairement *Louis XIV,* parce qu'il avait réellement cette majesté qu'on prête aux souverains." Baudry de Lozières, *Voyage à la Louisiane,* 122–23.

95. "Il savait prononcer agréablement des discours séduisants. [...] Il avait fait ses études en France, et il en avait rapporté les charmes et le goût qu'il répandait dans tout ce qu'il disait et tout ce qu'il écrivait. [...] rien, pour ainsi dire, ne pouvait résister au torrent de son éloquence." Baudry de Lozières, *Voyage à la Louisiane,* 123.

96. As I explained in the last chapter, La Frénière's father and uncles were humble *voyageurs* (roaming fur traders) named Chauvin. They took on additional last names in order to distinguish among themselves.

97. "Il faut convenir que le nom d'un souverain n'est souvent qu'un prétexte apparent qui couvre bien des sottises. [...] M. de Choiseul abusa du nom du roi comme on abuse ailleurs d'un autre talisman, et la Louisiane fut réellement vendue. [...] M. de Choiseul [...] parvint, à force d'intrigue, à tromper le prince sur cet objet. Le roi ne se doutait pas du tort qu'il causait aux Louisianais, de l'attachement de ces braves Français." Baudry de Lozières, *Voyage à la Louisiane,* 116.

98. "La tyrannie la plus révoltante." Baudry de Lozières, *Voyage à la Louisiane,* 121–22.

99. "Tyrannique," "recherches inquisitoriales," "terreur générale." Berquin-Duvallon, *Vue de la colonie espagnole,* 4.

100. It was common practice for eighteenth-century writers to steal whole sections from other writers' books, but they tended to do it word for word.

101. "Les larmes des femmes, des mères et des enfants ne firent qu'irriter son âme féroce," "rien n'attendrit le tigre." Baudry de Lozières, *Voyage à la Louisiane,* 136.

102. "Quel que soit celui qui se cache sous le nom imposant de M. de Vergennes, il ne rend pas moins des services." Baudry de Lozières, *Voyage à la Louisiane,* 5.

103. "Ne voulant point se soumettre au joug espagnol." Vergennes, *Mémoire historique et politique,* viii.

104. "Comme il n'y avait point de bourreau dans la colonie, on s'adressa à un nègre, qui refusa: on le menaça de le pendre lui-même s'il n'obéissait; après un quart-d'heure d'absence, ce nègre, atrocement sublime, revient et jette au milieu du conseil son poing et la hache dont il venait de se l'abattre. 'Maintenant, leur dit-il, vous ne ferez plus de moi un bourreau.' On fusilla les Français." Vergennes, *Mémoire historique et politique,* viii–ix.

105. In terms of Greek tragedy, we could compare this heroic self-mutilation to Œdipus's destruction of his own eyes. The trope also plays a major role in one story popular in the eighteenth century, "Oroonoko," by Aphra Behn (1688), in which an African prince is enslaved in Surinam and revolts against his enslavers. Rather than surrender, he stoically cuts off parts of his own body. This story

was adapted into a highly successful tragedy by Thomas Southerne in 1695. See Harrol, "Passion of 'Oroonoko.'"
106. "Je tiens ces faits d'un ami de M. de Saintelette." Vergennes, *Mémoire historique et politique*, ix, n. 1.
107. "Ah! Sire, peut-être que les noms des cinq malheureux Français qui furent exécutés ne sont jamais parvenus jusqu'à votre majesté; daignez jeter quelques fleurs sur leurs tombeaux, en daignant dire: 'Lafrenière, Noyant, Caresse, Villeret, Marquis et Millet, ont été massacrés par les ordres du barbare Orelli [sic], pour avoit regretté mon service et pour avoir voulu soutenir les lois qu'un monstre voulait anéantir.'" Vergennes, *Mémoire historique et politique*, 168.
108. Reddy, *Navigation of Feeling*, 143.
109. Reddy, *Navigation of Feeling*, 171.
110. Reddy, *Navigation of Feeling*, 108.
111. "Très vite, les meneurs devinrent, dans l'imaginaire louisianais, des patriotes assoiffés de liberté et d'indépendance, des précurseurs de l'indépendance américaine, de véritables George Washington. Et très vite les Louisianais trouvèrent l'interprétation qu'il leur fallait dans un pamphlet publié à Londres en 1773, *La Louisiane ensanglantée* [...]. Dans ce pamphlet destiné à servir de suite aux chapitres de l'*Histoire des deux Indes,* comme l'explique Champigny, l'auteur vante les 'vertus patriotiques de ces généreux Français que les Espagnols ont sacrifiés à leur ressentiment.'" Allain, "Le passé louisianais, création et recréation," 148.

5. In the Age of Revolutions

1. Ritter, "American Revolution on the Periphery of Empires."
2. See Caughey, *Bernardo de Gálvez in Louisiana;* DuVal, *Independence Lost;* and Quintero Saravia, *Bernardo de Gálvez.*
3. Quintero Saravia, *Bernardo de Gálvez*, 5.
4. Weber, *Bárbaros*, 2.
5. The poems can be found in Tinker, *Louisiana's Earliest Poet.*
6. Kathleen DuVal explains the geopolitical strategy of Spanish intervention in the American Revolution in *Independence Lost.*
7. Quintero Saravia, *Bernardo de Gálvez*, 4.
8. Genêt had previously worked as a translator and as a diplomat stationed in Russia. His sister was the famous educator Madame Campan.
9. Most scholarship on this mission refers to Frederick J. Turner's foundational article, "The Origin of Genêt's Projected Attack on Louisiana and the Floridas." A more recent article is W. Campbell, "Origin of Citizen Genet's Projected Attack on Spanish Louisiana."
10. "Le moment est arrivé où le despotisme doit disparaître de la terre," "La France devenue libre [...] annonce à tous les peuples qu'elle est prête à faciliter par son

208   Notes to Pages 139–141

11. puissant appui les efforts de ceux qui voudront suivre son vertueux exemple." [Genêt], *Les Français libres*, 3.
11. "Votre heure est enfin arrivée," "Montrez-vous donc, habitants de la Louisiane." [Genêt], *Les Français libres*, 4, 7.
12. "La nation française connaît vos sentiments." [Genêt], *Les Français libres*, 3–4.
13. "Il est temps que vous ne soyez plus conduits comme des troupeaux." [Genêt], *Les Français libres*, 4.
14. Baudry de Lozières would also compare the colonists to sheep in his 1802 account of the transfer: "comme un fermier se défait d'une partie de ses moutons!" (like a farmer who gets rid of some of his sheep!) Baudry de Lozières, *Voyage à la Louisiane*, 115.
15. "Chaînes [...] pesantes," "Il est temps que vous cessiez d'être esclaves d'un gouvernement auquel vous avez été indignement vendus." [Genêt], *Les Français libres*, 4.
16. "Soutenus par la France tant que votre faiblesse ne vous permettra pas de pouvoir vous défendre vous-mêmes." [Genêt], *Les Français libres*, 8.
17. "Children, I confess, are not born in this full state of equality, though they are born to it. Their parents have a sort of rule and jurisdiction over them when they come into the world, and for some time after; but it is but a temporary one. The bonds of this subjection are like the swaddling-clothes they are wrapt up in, and supported by, in the weakness of their infancy: age and reason, as they grow up, loosen them, till at length they drop quite off, and leave a man at his own free disposal." Locke, *Two Treatises*, pt. 55, p. 123.
18. [Genêt], *Les Français libres*, 7.
19. "Prouve[r] [...] que vous avez conservé dans votre cœur la valeur, le courage et l'intrépidité française." [Genêt], *Les Français libres*, 7.
20. "Français de la Louisiane vous aimez encore votre ancienne patrie, cet attachement est inné dans vos cœurs." [Genêt], *Les Français libres*, 3.
21. "Gravé dans vos âmes le sentiment profond d'une honorable vengeance." [Genêt], *Les Français libres*, 5.
22. "Vous frémissez d'indignation," "la crainte d'échouer, la crainte de ne pas être soutenus amortit votre zèle." [Genêt], *Les Français libres*, 7.
23. "Les hommes étaient nés pour s'aimer, s'unir, être heureux et ils le seraient si ceux qui se disent les images de Dieu sur la terre, si les rois ne cherchaient à les diviser et à s'opposer à leur félicité." [Genêt], *Les Français libres*, 6.
24. "Un roi parjure, des ministres prévaricateurs, des courtisans vils et orgueilleux qui s'engraissaient des sueurs et du sang du peuple." [Genêt], *Les Français libres*, 4.
25. [Genêt], *Les Français libres*, 4.
26. "Le despotisme espagnol a surpassé en atrocité, en stupidité tous les despotismes connus. Ce gouvernement qui a rendu le nom espagnol exécrable sur tout le continent de l'Amérique n'y a-t-il pas marqué tous ses pas par des barbaries? N'est-ce pas sous le masque hypocrite de la religion qu'il a ordonné

ou permis le massacre de plus de 20 millions d'hommes? N'est-ce pas pour assouvir son insatiable avidité qu'il a dépeuplé, appauvri, dégradé des nations entières?" [Genêt], *Les Français libres,* 4–5.

27. "La haine de tous les rois et de leurs complices." [Genêt], *Les Français libres,* 7.
28. "Lorsque les sauvages veuillent cueillir des fruits ils coupent l'arbre au pied[:] voilà le tableau du despotisme." [Genêt], *Les Français libres,* 5.
29. "En effet peu importe à la tyrannie le sort des nations, tout doit être sacrifié à des jouissances passagères, tout doit fléchir sous sa volonté." [Genêt], *Les Français libres,* 5.
30. Melvin Richter informs us that while the ancient Greeks made a distinction between tyranny (personal rule by one usurper) and despotism (a whole political system, regardless of ruler, often applied to "the Orient"), people in late-eighteenth-century France used both terms somewhat indiscriminately. Genêt appears to use them as synonyms. Richter, "Concept of Despotism and l'abus des mots."
31. "Le *despotisme* doit disparaître de la terre." [Genêt], *Les Français libres,* 3.
32. "Prouvez que le despotisme ne vous a point abrutis." [Genêt], *Les Français libres,* 7.
33. "Il se persuada [qu'il] trouverait, non seulement parmi les habitants des contrées de l'Ouest, mais à la Nouvelle-Orléans même, un parti nombreux prêt à le seconder. On l'assurait que toute la Louisiane désirait de rentrer sous la domination de la France, et il se disposa sérieusement à en faire la conquête." Barbé-Marbois, *Histoire de la Louisiane,* 168.
34. Hanger, "Conflicting Loyalties," 7.
35. "Pour célébrer l'anniversaire de la Liberté recouvrée par les Français. [...] Lord Stanhope certifia que cette pierre avait été réellement tirée de l'antre affreux où le despotisme faisait gémir en France ses malheureuses victimes." Transcription of issue from Holmes, "*Moniteur de la Louisiane* in 1798," 236.
36. Hanger's article is cited by Carolyn Cossé Bell in *Revolution, Romanticism, and the Afro-Creole Protest Tradition,* 25.
37. Hanger found documentation of this trial in the Louisiana State Museum Historical Center, New Orleans, Spanish Judicial Records, October 7, 1791, and in AGI, Estado 14, no. 60, February 11, 1794.
38. Bell, *Revolution, Romanticism, and the Afro-Creole Protest Tradition,* 25. Bell's sources are Fortier, *History of Louisiana,* 2:152; and Grace King, *New Orleans, the Place and the People* (New York: Macmillan, 1896), 142–43.
39. Ms. Vol. 19,248. MSS.MICRO/5912, Papeles de la historia de Florida (sheet 209r–210v), Biblioteca Nacional, Madrid.
40. "Les mêmes scènes d'horreur parmi vous." Francisco Luis Héctor, baron de Carondelet, "Circulaire, adressée par le gouvernement à tous les habitans de la Louisiane," Tulane University, Kuntz Collection, Spanish Colonial Period, 1783–1795, box 4, doc. 55 (hereafter "Circulaire").

41. "Scélérats," "infâmes séducteurs répandus parmi vous." Carondelet, "Circulaire."
42. "Vous laisserez-vous éblouir par l'espoir trompeur d'une liberté, d'une égalité qui n'ont pu s'établir en France, ni dans ses Colonies? [. . .] La liberté de la presse, loi fondamentale de la Constitution, a été indignement violée, et ensanglantée impitoyablement par le massacre de ceux qui ont écrit contre les opérations des membres de la Convention." Carondelet, "Circulaire."
43. "Tout Français sans exception a été arraché sous peine de la vie à sa famille." Carondelet, "Circulaire."
44. The trend in gothic novels started in England in the eighteenth century, and these were translated into French and Spanish. They reached a height of popularity in France from the 1790s to the 1820s. See Prungnaud, "La traduction du roman gothique anglais en France."
45. "Fantôme de la liberté," "les meurtres, les incendies, la dévastation," "les torrents de sang qui coulent depuis quatre ans." Carondelet, "Circulaire."
46. "Théâtre de Massacres et d'horreurs." Carondelet, "Circulaire."
47. "Le pillage, la perte de vos propriétés; le massacre de vos familles; le renouvellement de toutes les calamités qui ont dévastées St. Domingue; voilà ce que vous préparent les Monstres échappés du Cap, et qui se rassemblent sur l'Ohio." Carondelet, "Circulaire."
48. Johnson, *Fear of French Negroes*, 24.
49. "Les Nègres eux-mêmes après avoir été ballotés alternativement par les partis contraires, victimes du fol espoir de la liberté dont on les avait bercés, et qui n'a été cimentée que par le massacre d'une grande partie des plus braves d'entre eux."
50. "D'un Souverain qui vous a comblé constamment de ses bienfaits depuis vingt-trois ans que vous vivez sous ses lois" "vif intérêt que je prends à votre félicité." Carondelet, "Circulaire."
51. In terms of the slave trade specifically, La Rochelle was second only to Nantes among the French cities, but British and Portuguese ports conducted three times the volume of slaving ships that French ports did. Forrest, *Death of the French Atlantic*, 25.
52. Vidal, *Caribbean New Orleans*, 482.
53. Forrest, *Death of the French Atlantic*, 27.
54. "La vénalité de l'ancien gouvernement," "les grands intérêts de la Nation sacrifiées à la Louisiane." Société de la Rochelle, "Appel à la Convention nationale pour reprendre la Louisiane aux Anglais," ANOM, C13B 1, reel 64.
55. "S'il fallait éveiller les ressentiments sur cette désastreuse cession, et, par des souvenirs douloureux animer les vengeances contre l'Espagne, nous devrions évoquer les mânes de six héros massacrés de sang-froid au sein du Mississippi pour avoir fait avec tous leurs concitoyens un acte de leur loyal attachement à une patrie qui les abandonnait; nous présenterions ces illustres victimes livrées par l'infâme visir Choiseul." Société de la Rochelle, "Appel à la Convention nationale."

56. "Trafiquer au boudoir d'une courtisane, comme au temps du despotisme, de l'honneur et des propriétés de la France." Société de la Rochelle, "Appel à la Convention nationale."
57. "On s'en sert encore quelquefois en Poësie, & dans le stile sublime." *Dictionnaire de l'Académie française*, 1694.
58. "Consolez-vous, ombres généreuses, de nous avoir précédé dans la lutte contre les tyrans! Bientôt le signe éclatant de leur destruction réjouira par son aspect ces bords encore couverts du crêpe funèbre que votre trépas leur a fait prendre!" Société de la Rochelle, "Appel à la Convention nationale."
59. "Ce fut un Irlandais nommé O'Reilly, qui vient à la Louisiane un an après l'expulsion d'Ulloa, exercer les vengeances espagnoles sur les malheureux habitants." Société de la Rochelle, "Appel à la Convention nationale."
60. "L'une des victimes, l'immortal Marquis, vieillard plus que sexagénaire, découvre sa poitrine couverte de cicatrices, et s'écria: votre lâche plomb pourra bien déchirer cette poitrine, qui a bravé pendant 40 ans les [balles] prussiennes et autrichiennes, mais il ne détruira pas la haine que j'ai vouée à votre infâme nation." Société de la Rochelle, "Appel à la Convention nationale."
61. The account from La Rochelle also contains a detail that we will see later, in the more elaborate 1802 account by the comte de Vergennes, about the refusal of locals to act as executioners, but the letter from La Rochelle simply states, "Les nègres refusés à l'exécution, on y employa les soldats espagnols" (The Blacks refused to exeute them, so Spanish soldiers were used instead), not mentioning the cut-off hand. Société de la Rochelle, "Appel à la Convention nationale."
62. "Ce sont des enfants toujours affectionnés qui doivent rentrer au sein d'une mère qui les a méconnus trop longtemps." Société de la Rochelle, "Appel à la Convention nationale."
63. "Législateurs, il appartient surtout aux habitants de cette cité, longtemps unis par des rapports commerciaux, et toujours par les liens du sang et de la fraternité avec les colons de la Louisiane, de se porter pour exécuteur testamentaire de ces magnanimes infortunés dont le dernier cri appelait encore leur patrie au milieu des supplices." Société de la Rochelle, "Appel à la Convention nationale."
64. "Tout y est français; les habitants, leurs mœurs, leur langage, le fer même qui sillonne leurs champs; ce sont nos amis, nos frères, nos enfants, dont les cœurs aspirent leur réadoption dans la grande famille républicaine à laquelle nulle puissance ne peut les enlever plus longtemps. Leurs titres? Législateurs, s'ils avaient pu être oubliés ou méconnus, ils les retrouveraient au fond du Mississippi, scellés de leur plus pur sang." Société de la Rochelle, "Appel à la Convention nationale."
65. Durand Echevarria, introduction to "General Collot's Plan," 513.
66. "Les habitants de la Louisiane vous offrent par mon organe leurs voeux. Ils gémissent sous le joug du despotisme: ils sont français et veulent faire partie de la République: ils voient avec horreur l'inquisition qui s'exerce sur eux: ils

gémissent en secret sur leur triste situation et demandent de les rendre libres." La Gautrais to "Citoyens Représentants," 2 Germinal, An III (March 22, 1795), Tulane University, Kuntz Collection, Spanish Colonial Period, 1783–1795, box 4, doc. 90.

67. "Tous les habitants sont français: ils désirent faire partie de la République, ils ne peuvent porter leur réclamation que chez les Français: c'est d'eux qu'ils doivent attendre leur liberté." Capitaine La Gautrais, Tulane University, Kuntz Collection, Spanish Colonial Period, 1783–1795, box 4, doc.t 91.

68. "Le temps est favorable et le moment est précieux. Profitons-en, et portons la liberté parmi ce peuple, victime du despotisme. Poursuivons nos ennemis jusqu'au delà de l'océan. Vous possèderez cet avantage en établissant la liberté, par là vous ferez connaître la République à ce peuple malheureux, et le ferez sortir de l'esclavage où il est réduit depuis vingt-cinq ans." La Gautrais, Tulane University, Kuntz Collection, Spanish Colonial Period, 1783–1795, box 4, doc. 91.

69. "Quelles sont les dispositions du peuple dans les états du sud relativement au gouvernement fédéral, et à la France? Sont-ils réellement républicains, veulent-ils être libres, indépendants?" Echeverria, "General Collot's Plan," 517.

70. Echeverria, "General Collot's Plan," 518. Echeverria provides the text of this section only in English translation.

71. The reports from Carondelet's point of view can be found in the Archivo Histórico Nacional, Madrid, Papeles de Estado, legajo 3900.

72. David Narrett provides a summary of the trip in *Adventurism and Empire*, 234–37.

73. "Extrait d'un Mémoire sur la nécessité, pour la République française, d'avoir la Louisiane, vu sous les différents rapports politiques, commerciaux et maritimes," General Collot to Citizen Adet, Ministre plénipotentaire, "pour être présenté aux Ministres des Rélations extérieures et de la Marine" (to be presented to the foreign minister and the minister of the marine), 15 Germinal, An IV (April 4, 1796), Tulane University, Kuntz Collection, Spanish Colonial Period, box 5, doc. 7. The original is in ANOM, C13B 1, fol. 489.

74. "La perte que la France a faite dans la cession de la Louisiane [...] l'injustice qu'elle a commise en abandonnant ses propres enfants." Collot, "Extrait d'un Mémoire," 1.

75. "Si les rois avaient le droit de céder la Louisiane?" "Je demanderai à la Convention si elle *m'entend par une voix qui lui crie du fond* de ses vastes forêts: 'eh quoi!' 'vous avez *abandonné des enfants sortis de votre sein* qui, malgré leur juste désespoir, n'ont cessé d'ensemencer et de cultiver leurs terres, dans l'espoir d'être un jour revendiqués par vous, qui, après avoir fertilisé la terre de leur sueur, l'ont encore arrosé de leur sang pour vous la conserver, et qui se glorifiant de votre nom, ont cherché par des actes de bonté et de bienfaisance à l'illustrer parmi les nations les plus sauvages, restées vos amis fidèles par leurs soins?'" Collot, "Extrait d'un Mémoire," 8.

76. "Après l'avoir fertilisé de mes sueurs, ne l'ai-je pas arrosé de mon sang pour te le conserver?" Raynal, *Histoire des deux Indes,* vol. 4, bk. 16, p. 119.
77. "Des hommes, qui ont toujours eu en horreur le joug sous lequel ils vivent; qui ont fait tous leurs efforts pour le secouer et que leur faiblesse seule a pu contraindre à porter des fers. Brûlants d'amour pour la liberté, pour leur patrie, malgré son ingratitude et son insensibilité, oubliant nos droits, oubliant vos devoirs, vous n'avez pas daigné réclamer des enfants en brisant des liens qu'ils détestent, et leur accorder la seule consolation à laquelle ils aient jamais aspiré, de vivre sous vos lois." Collot, "Extrait d'un Mémoire," 8–9.
78. "Lors de la tyrannie un gouvernement perfide nous a vendus contre les droits des gens à des étrangers oppresseurs, intolérants et superstitieux." Collot, "Extrait d'un Mémoire," 8.
79. "Malheureusement la France sous l'ancien régime trompée par des ignorants ou des avaricieux, opprimée par des visirs présomptueux, a méconnu tous ses avantages, et l'Espagne sa faiblesse." Collot, "Extrait d'un Mémoire," 7–8.
80. "Si Mr. de Choiseul, ou le ministère alors, eût mieux connu la Louisiane; que des hommes éclairés eussent été chargés de l'administrer; qu'ils eussent mis leur gloire à en faire connaître toute l'importance à la France, cette colonie autrefois méconnue et méprisée serait aujourd'hui un grand dédommagement de la perte momentanée que la République vient de faire de ses îles." Collot, "Extrait d'un Mémoire," 6.
81. "Vraies raisons d'état," "la calomnie s'appelait histoire et la persécution républicanisme." Collot, *Voyage dans l'Amérique septentrionale,* 2:309.
82. "Durante estas diversiones se cantan canciones revolucionarias y susceptibles de inducir a los vasallos más leales a la rebelión." Carondelet, letter of December 1, 1796, Archivo Histórico Nacional, Madrid, Papeles de Estado, legajo 3900.
83. "Quand nous serons Republicains ... bis

    Nous punirons tous les coquins ... bis
    Cochon de lait le premier sera guillotiné
    Dançons la Carmagnolle, vivent les sons, vivent les sons,
    Dançons la Carmagnolle, vive la ronde, vivent les sons, de nos chansons

    1er
    Le Contador aura sa part ... bis
    On le pendra sur le rempart ... bis
    L'Auditeur en sera, le public en rira
    Dançons la Carmagnolle ...

    2^{e}
    Le gras Hevia maitre larron ... bis
    suivons de pres son bon patron ... bis

On l'accrochera, au vent il dansera
Dançons la Carmagnolle: vive le son de nos chansons

3ᵉ
Notre Intendant ne craindra rien ... bis
Si il est toujours homme de bien ... bis
Nous n'oublierons jamais
ses généreux bienfaits
Dançons la Carmagnolle: vive le son de nos chansons

4ᵉ
Le grand Mestaignier pret la main
Ainsi que l'amiral Cuen, cuen
D'applaudir le projet du fameux cochon de lait
Dançons la Carmagnolle: vive le son de nos chansons

5ᵉ
Le dessein du cochon de lait
fut divulgué par Asseret
Mais son coup a manqué graces a Mr. Brognier
Dançons la Carmagnolle: vive le son de nos chansons

6ᵉ
On me pendera par Pontalba
On le fouettera par la [suite?]
Et nous le garderons pour en faire un espion
Dançons la Carmagnolle: vive le son de nos chansons"

AGI, Papeles de Cuba, legajo 1447.

84. "*Ronde de table,* ou simplement *Ronde,* une chanson à refrain, où chacun chante tour à tour." *Dictionnnaire de l'Académie Française,* 5th ed., 1798, https://www.dictionnaire-academie.fr/.

85. "Veinte mil negros a quienes la primera conspiracion a inspirado el deseo de la libertad y el pensamiento de adquirirla por le muerte de los blancos, la inquietud natural, el fanatismo de estos para la Nueva Constitucion francesa, la inclinacion que los hombres conservan generalmente para su patria primitiva, la pobreza, o el desarreglo de la fortuna de muchos que esperan encontrar en una insurrection los medios de encubrir su mala fe, todo conspira en la Luisiana Baja a una revolucion." AGI, Papeles de Cuba, legajo 153-1 (153A), No. 140 Reservada, p. 274. Accessed from the Library of Congress, Washington, DC, Manuscript Division.

86. "La cancion patriotica tiene esparcida con arte la provincia cuya copia remití a V.S. [... el] peligro que corria la colonia como que muchos se estaban armando en sus habitaciones, otros tratando [de] apoderarse de mi y del auditor,

otro de asesinarme durante alguna confusion excitada [. . .] y en [arboles] la bandera tricolor." Carondelet, New Orleans, letter of July 30, 1795, AGI, Papeles de Cuba, legajo 153–1. Copies from the Library of Congress, Washington, DC, Manuscript Division.

87. "Informacion juridica contra varios habitantes principales sospechados de ser los autores o de haber dejado cantar en sus casas la cancion patriotica." AGI, Papeles de Cuba, legajo 153–1.
88. See Sollors, *Neither Black Nor White Yet Both,* 118.
89. "Disant qu'on avait très bien fait de tuer le roi, parce que c'était un coquin, et un homme comme tous les autres." AGI, Papeles de Cuba, legajo 153–1.
90. "Quand le cas viendrait, ils prendraient bien les armes, mais après, ils les tourneraient contre les Espagnols, à qui dans la nuit leur couperaient la tête." AGI, Papeles de Cuba, legajo 153–1.
91. "Je promets partout désintéressement et pureté, appui dans le bien et répression dans le mal. J'espère beaucoup de ces colons, parce que c'est une bonne race d'hommes." Laussat, *Mémoires sur ma vie,* 32.
92. "Tous les Louisianais ont le cœur français." Laussat, *Mémoires sur ma vie,* 30.
93. "Il était temps que le gouvernement français se montrât et annonçât ici ses droits et ses intentions." Laussat, *Mémoires sur ma vie,* 31.
94. "Votre séparation de la France marque une des époques les plus honteuses de ses Fastes, sous un gouvernement déjà faible et corrompu, après une guerre ignominieuse et à la suite d'une paix flétrissante.

   A côté d'un abandon lâche et dénaturé, vous offrîtes le contraste d'un amour, d'une fidélité et d'un courage héroïques.

   Tous les cœurs français attendris, et n'en ont jamais perdu la mémoire: ils s'écrièrent alors, avec orgueil, et ils n'ont depuis cessé de répéter que *leur sang coulait dans vos veines."*
   Laussat, *Proclamation.*
95. "Ont reporté sur vous leurs regards," "ils voulaient que votre rétrocession signalât leur première Paix." Laussat, *Proclamation.*
96. "Il fallait qu'un Homme parut." Laussat, *Proclamation.*
97. "Cet Homme, il préside aujourd'hui à nos Destinées, et, dès ce moment, LOUISIANAIS, il vous répond des vôtres." Laussat, *Proclamation.*
98. "Resserrer chaque jour les nœuds qu'une même origine, les mêmes mœurs, les mêmes inclinations établissent entre cette Colonie et la Mère Patrie." Laussat, *Proclamation.* This image of France is an androgynous one, since the etymology of *patrie* refers to a father.
99. "Vous vous applaudirez donc sous tous les rapports d'être redevenus Français: vous sentirez de jour en jour, davantage, le prix de ce beau titre, objet aujourd'hui d'envie sur tout le Globe." Laussat, *Proclamation.*
100. "Une proclamation, où je faisais quelque allusion aux atrocités d'O'Reilly contre les Français, quand il prit possession de la colonie pour l'Espagne, a

déplu au gouverneur Salcedo; mais elle encourage le dévouement national des colons. Les ennemis du nom Français, soit crainte ou jalousie, cherchaient à aigrir les esprits, à les inquiéter et même à les irriter." Laussat, *Mémoires sur ma vie*, 30.

101. "Nous savons néanmoins, LOUISIANAIS, et nous ne voulons pas le dissimuler, que, durant trente ans, l'Espagne, par la douceur d'un gouvernement réparateur et généreux, s'est efforcée de vous faire oublier la faute sanglante d'un Agent indigne de cette noble Nation. Elle est l'amie étroite et fidèle de la nôtre: ce n'est pas nous qui vous inspirerons de la payer d'ingratitude." Laussat, *Proclamation*.

102. "On ne fit donc point éclater ces marques de contentement qu'aurait produit en d'autres temps le retour des Français." Barbé-Marbois, *Histoire de la Louisiane*, 226.

103. "Fait pour transporter de joie et de contentement tous les cœurs sensibles, et principalement tous les bons et vrais français." Berquin-Duvallon, *Vue de la colonie espagnole*, 217.

104. "Point de réjouissances, ni de fêtes publiques ou particulières, consacrées à célébrer cet heureux événement, malgré qu'on soit dans le temps des bals et des spectacles (le carnaval)." Berquin-Duvallon, *Vue de la colonie espagnole*, 218.

105. "Les Créoles du lieu sont, pour la plupart, sans énergie morale." Berquin-Duvallon, *Vue de la colonie espagnole*, 216.

106. "Quelle peut être la mesure de leur prétendu patriotisme, et de l'attachement qu'ils affectent pour la France, leur ancienne patrie?" Berquin-Duvallon, *Vue de la colonie espagnole*, 216.

107. "Ne les a-t-on pas vus, il y a quelques années, après s'être agités machinalement [...] et s'être enfin donné des fêtes où, devant leurs esclaves, les imbéciles chantaient, à tue-tête et avec une imprudence inconcevable, les hymnes français où sont célébrés les droits de l'homme?" Berquin-Duvallon, *Vue de la colonie espagnole*, 216–17.

108. "Vain étalage et bruyant fracas," "rentrer dans leurs coquilles et se ranger sous la férule du gouvernement espagnol, comme un troupeau de moutons sous la houlette du berger." Berquin-Duvallon, *Vue de la colonie espagnole*, 217.

109. "On me dira peut-être: 'Mais ces mêmes habitants ont plusieurs fois demandé à être réunis sous leur ancien gouvernement, à redevenir français. Qui plus est, depuis l'époque de la révolution, il a paru, en leur nom collectif et pour ce même objet, une pétition rédigée et signée par un membre de la Société des amis de la Constitution, Des Odouarts-Fantin, agissant pour les colons.' Cela est vrai. Mais, que l'on se rapporte, en esprit, aux dates de ces diverses demandes, et même à celle de cette pétition, faite en 1790, et qu'au surplus on examine attentivement l'objet principal, le point essentiel de toutes ces demandes." Berquin-Duvallon, *Vue de la colonie espagnole*, 219–20. I was unable to trace the document signed by this person, Des Odouarts-Fantin.

110. "On verra [. . .] que les réclamations des Louisianais, à cet égard, ont eu, pour base et pour motifs directs, non pas, à proprement parler, leur attachement inné à la France, mais bien leur crainte du régime prohibitif des colonies espagnoles." Berquin-Duvallon, *Vue de la colonie espagnole,* 221.
111. "La France perd une colonie à qui les plus belles destinées sont promises. En attendant son émancipation naturelle, par laps de temps, nous y pouvions jeter le germe d'une immense population française. [. . .] Une nouvelle France s'y fût formée. [. . .] Tout s'évanouit; il ne me reste que le regret d'une année d'oisiveté, d'une inutile transmigration de famille vers un nouveau monde, de beaucoup de dépenses et de tracas et de dérangement sans nul fruit." Laussat, *Mémoires sur ma vie,* 93–94 (August 18, 1803).

Conclusion

1. These two creators, also responsible for *The Wire,* were not New Orleanians, but they hired consultants, writers, and actors from the city, such as journalist Lolis Eric Elie.
2. Davis, "Reasons of Misrule."
3. See Roach, *Cities of the Dead;* and Roach, "Mardi Gras Indians and Others."

Bibliography

Manuscript Collections

Archives Nationales d'Outre-Mer, Aix-en-Provence, France. COL C13A and C13B. Also available in microfilm in the Historic New Orleans Collection, New Orleans. Translated in *Mississippi Provincial Archives: French Dominion, 1701–1729*, vol. 2, edited and translated by Dunbar Rowland and Albert Godfrey Sanders (Jackson: Press of the Mississippi Department of Archives and History, 1929).
Archivo General de las Indias, Seville.
Archivo Histórico Nacional, Madrid. Papeles de Estado.
Biblioteca Nacional, Madrid. Papeles de la historia de Florida.
Bibliothèque de l'Arsenal, Paris. Archives de la Bastille.
Historic New Orleans Collection, New Orleans.
Library of Congress, Washington, DC.
Tulane University, New Orleans. Kuntz Collection.

Primary Sources

Balleroy, marquise de. *Les correspondants de la marquise de Balleroy*. 2 vols. Paris: Hachette, 1883.
Baudry de Lozières, Louis-Narcisse. *Voyage à la Louisiane, et sur le continent de l'Amérique septentrionale, fait dans les années 1794 à 1798*. Paris: Dentu, An XI/1802.
Bernardin de Saint-Pierre, Henri. *Voyage à l'Île de France*. In *Œuvres choisies*, 176–248. Paris: Firmin-Didot, 1928.
Berquin-Duvallon, Pierre-Louis. *Vue de la colonie espagnole du Mississipi, ou des provinces de Louisiane et Floride Occidentale; en l'annee 1802, par un observateur résident sur les lieux*. Paris: À l'imprimerie expéditive, 1803.
Bonrepos, chevalier de [pseud.]. *Description du Mississipi*. Paris: B. Gyrin, 1720.
Bossu, [Jean-Bernard]. *Nouveaux voyages dans l'Amérique septentrionale*. Amsterdam: Chez Changuion, 1777.
Buvat, Jean. *Journal de la Régence (1715–1723)*. 2 vols. Paris: Plon, 1865.
Champigny, [Jean Bochart de]. *État présent de la Louisiane, avec toutes les particularités de cette province d'Amérique, pour servir de Suite à l'Histoire des Etablissemens des Européens dans les Deux Indes*. La Haye: Frederic Staatman, 1776. Translated by Benjamin F. French as *Memoir on the Present State of Louisiana*, in *Historical Collections of Louisiana*, edited by French, 5 vols. (New York: Wiley & Putnam, 1846–53), 5:127–291.

Charlevoix, Pierre-François-Xavier de, SJ. *Histoire et description générale de la Nouvelle France.* 6 vols. Paris: Giffart, 1744. Translated by John Gilmary Shea as *History and General Description of New France,* 6 vols. (Chicago: Loyola UP, 1962).

———. *Journal d'un voyage fait par ordre du roy dans l'Amérique septentrionale.* Edited by Pierre Berthiaume. 2 vols. Montreal: Presses Universitaires de Montréal, 1994. Translated by Micah True as *The Jesuit Pierre-François-Xavier de Charlevoix's (1682–1761) Journal of a Voyage in North America* (Leiden: Brill, 2019).

Collot, Victor. *Voyage dans l'Amérique septentrionale.* 2 vols. Paris: Chez Arthus Bertrand, 1826.

Dangeau, marquis de. *Journal.* 19 vols. Paris: Firmin Didot, 1854–60.

Dictionnaire de l'Académie française. 2 vols. Paris: Coignard, 1694.

Dictionnaire de l'Académie française. 4th ed. 2 vols. Paris: Brunet, 1762.

Dictionnaire de l'Académie française. 5th ed. 2 vols. Paris: Smits, 1798.

Diderot, Denis, and Jean le Rond d'Alembert, eds. *Encyclopédie, ou dictionnaire raisonné des sciences, des arts et des métiers, etc.* 28 vols. Paris: Briasson et al., 1751–72. University of Chicago: ARTFL Encyclopédie Project (Autumn 2017), edited by Robert Morrissey and Glenn Roe. http://encyclopedie.uchicago.edu/.

Dubos, Jean-Baptiste. *Réflexions critiques sur la poésie et sur la peinture.* 3 vols. Paris: Mariette, 1740.

Duclos, Charles. *Mémoires secrets sur le règne de Louis XIV, la Régence et le règne de Louis XV.* Paris: Firmin Didot, 1846.

Dumont de Montigny, Jean-François-Benjamin. *The Memoir of Lieutenant Dumont, 1715–1747: A Sojourner in the French Atlantic.* Translated by Gordon M. Sayre. Edited by Gordon M. Sayre and Carla Zecher. Chapel Hill: U of North Carolina P, for the Omohundro Institute of Early American History and Culture, Williamsburg, VA, 2012.

A Full and Impartial Account of the Company of Mississipi, otherwise call'd the French East-India Company. Projected and settled by Mr. Law. London: R. Francklin, 1720. https://www.wdl.org/en/item/15531/view/1/1/.

[Genêt, Edmond Charles]. *Les Français libres à leurs frères de la Louisiane.* [Philadelphia], 1793. Thomas Jefferson Papers Series 1. General Correspondence. Library of Congress.

Hachard, Marie-Madeleine. *Relation du voyage des dames religieuses ursulines de Rouen à la Nouvelle-Orléans.* Rouen: Le Prevost, 1728.

[Lacroix, Paul]. *Mémoires du cardinal Dubois sur la ville, la cour et les salons de Paris sous la Régence.* Paris: Barba, 1833.

Lahontan, Baron de. *Œuvres complètes.* Edited by Réal Ouellet and Alain Beaulieu. 2 vols. Montreal: Presses de l'Université de Montréal, 1990.

Laussat, Pierre-Clément de. *Mémoires sur ma vie, à mon fils.* Pau: Vignancour, 1831.

———. *Proclamation.* New Orleans, 5 Germinal, An XI (Mar. 26, 1803).

Le Page du Pratz, Antoine-Simon. *Histoire de la Louisiane.* 3 vols. Paris: De Bure, Veuve Delaguette et Lambert, 1758.

Lesage, Alain-René. *Arlequin roi des Ogres ou Les Bottes de sept lieues*. In *Le Théâtre de la Foire ou Opéra-Comique*, edited by Dominique Lurcel. Paris: Gallimard, 2014.

Lettre du R.P. **** de la congregation de l'oratoire, a monsieur Le Page du Pratz, sur quelques nouveaux points d'astronomie. Paris: Veuve Robineau, 1760.

Lettres édifiantes et curieuses écrites des missions étrangères par quelques missionnaires de la Compagnie de Jésus. 34 vols. Paris: Chez Nicolas Le Clerc, 1702–76.

Locke, John. *Two Treatises of Government and A Letter Concerning Toleration*. New Haven, CT: Yale UP, 2003.

Marais, Mathieu. *Journal et mémoires sur la Régence et le règne de Louis XV, 1715–1737*. 4 vols. Paris: Firmin-Didot, 1863–68.

Mémoire des habitans et négocians, de la Louysiane sur l'événement du 29 octobre 1768. New Orleans: D. Braud, 1768. http://infoweb.newsbank.com/iw-search /we/Evans/?p_product=EAIX&p_theme=eai&p_nbid=I61H49NBM TQwNjgyMjkoMS44NTMyNDY6MToxMzoxMzcuNTQuMjkuMTc4&p _action=doc&p_queryname=1&p_docref=v2:0F2B1FCB879B099B@EAIX -0F2F8298543B0FD8@41839-1036BC8F74D88C98@0.

Montesquieu, Charles-Louis de Secondat, baron de. *Lettres persanes*. Vol. 1 of *Œuvres complètes*, edited by Jean Ehrard, Pierre Rétat, and Catherine Volpilhac-Auger. 22 vols. to date. Oxford, Naples, and Rome: Voltaire Foundation, Istituto italiano per gli studi filosofici, and Istituto della Enciclopedia italiana, 1998–.

———. *Œuvres complètes*. Edited by Roger Caillois. 2 vols. Paris: Gallimard/ Bibliothèque de la Pléiade, 1949–51.

———. *Persian Letters*. Translated by C. J. Betts. Harmondsworth: Penguin, 1973.

Narbonne, Pierre. *Journal des règnes de Louis XIV et Louis XV, de l'année 1701 à l'année 1744*. Paris: Durand, 1866.

Le Nouveau Mercure. 1717–21. English translations from Waggoner, *Le Plus Beau Païs du Monde*.

Poèmes satiriques du XVIIIe siècle. http://satires18.univ-st-etienne.fr/pr%C3 %A9sentation.

Prévost, Antoine François. *Histoire du chevalier des Grieux et de Manon Lescaut*. In *Œuvres de Prévost*, edited by Pierre Berthiaume and Jean Sgard, vol. 1. 8 vols. Grenoble: Presses Universitaires de Grenoble, 1978.

Quintilian. *Institutio Oratoria*. Edited by Harold Edgeworth Butler. 4 vols. Cambridge, MA: Harvard UP, 1920–22.

Raynal, Guillaume-Thomas. *Histoire des deux Indes*. 10 vols. Geneva: Pellet, 1780.

Recueil Clairambault-Maurepas: Chansonnier historique du XVIIIe siècle. 10 vols. Paris: A. Quantin, 1880–84.

Relation de la Louisiane, ou Mississipi, écrite à une dame, par un officier de Marine. In vol. 5 of *Recueil de voyages au nord*. 10 vols. Amsterdam: Chez Jean-Frédéric Bernard, 1715–38.

Saint-Simon, Louis de Rouvroy, duc de. *Mémoires*. Edited by Arthur de Boislisle, Jean de Boislisle, and Léon Lecestre. 43 vols. Paris: Hachette, 1879–1928.

Serrano y Sanz, Manuel, ed. *Documentos históricos de la Florida y la Luisiana, siglos XVI al XVIII*. Madrid: V. Suárez, 1912.

[Vallette de Laudun]. *Journal d'un voyage à la Louisiane, fait en 1720, par M***, Capitaine de Vaisseau du Roi*. La Haye: Chez Muster, fils et Fournier, 1768.

Vergennes, Charles Gravier, comte de. *Mémoire historique et politique sur la Louisiane*. Paris: Chez Le Petit jeune, An X (1802).

Waggoner, May Rush Gwin, ed. *Le Plus Beau Païs du Monde: Completing the Picture of Proprietary Louisiana, 1699–1722*. Translated by Michael Berkvam. Lafayette, LA: Center for Louisiana Studies, 2005.

Secondary Sources

Allain, Mathé. "Le passé louisianais, création et recréation: La Révolution de 1768 vue par trois dramaturges." *Francophonies d'Amérique* 1 (1991), 145–51. https://www.erudit.org/fr/revues/fa/1991-n1-fa1807140/1004271ar/.

Anderson, Benedict. *Imagined Communities: Reflections on the Origin and Spread of Nationalism*. Rev. ed. London: Verso, 2006.

Aravamudan, Srinivas. *Tropicopolitans: Colonialism and Agency, 1688–1804*. Durham, NC: Duke UP, 1999.

Armitage, David, and Sanjay Subrahmanyam, eds. *The Age of Revolutions in Global Context, c. 1760–1840*. London: Palgrave Macmillan, 2010.

Baker, Keith M. "Public Opinion as Political Invention." In *Inventing the French Revolution: Essays on French Political Culture in the Eighteenth Century*, 167–200. Cambridge: Cambridge UP, 2019.

Banks, Kenneth J. *Chasing Empire across the Sea: Communications and the State in the French Atlantic, 1713–1763*. Montreal: McGill-Queen's UP, 2002.

Barbé-Marbois, François. *Histoire de la Louisiane*. Paris: Firmin Didot, 1829.

Barthes, Roland. *Sur Racine*. Paris: Seuil, 1998.

Beer, William. "History of Libraries in Louisiana." *Louisiana School Review* 14 (Sept. 1906), 127–28.

Bell, Carolyn Cossé. *Revolution, Romanticism, and the Afro-Creole Protest Tradition in Louisiana, 1718–1868*. Baton Rouge: Louisiana State UP, 1997.

Berthiaume, Pierre. "Louisiana, or the Shadow Cast by French Colonial Myth." *Dalhousie French Studies* 58 (2002), 10–25.

Bigelow, Allison. "Gendered Language and the Science of Colonial Silk." *Early American Literature* 49:2 (2014), 271–325.

Boimare, A. L. "La Floride et l'ancienne Louisiane: Notes bibliographiques et raisonnées," *Louisiana Historical Quarterly* 1:2 (Sept. 14, 1917), 9–78.

Brasseaux, Carl. *Denis-Nicolas Foucault and the New Orleans Rebellion of 1768*. Ruston, LA: McGinty, 1987.

———. *The Founding of New Acadia: The Beginnings of Acadian Life in Louisiana, 1765–1803*. Baton Rouge: Louisiana State UP, 1987.

Brazeau, Brian. *Writing a New France, 1604–1632: Empire and Early Modern French Identity*. Farnham, UK: Ashgate, 2009.
Campbell, Peter R. "The Politics of Patriotism in France (1770–1788)." *French History* 24:4 (2010), 550–75.
Campbell, Wesley J. "The Origin of Citizen Genet's Projected Attack on Spanish Louisiana: A Case Study in Girondin Politics." *French Historical Studies* 33:4 (2010), 515–44. https://doi.org/10.1215/00161071-2010-009.
Cañizares-Esguerra, Jorge. *How to Write the History of the New World: Histories, Epistemologies, and Identities in the Eighteenth-Century Atlantic World*. Stanford, CA: Stanford UP, 2001.
Carpenter, John. *Histoire de la littérature française sur la Louisiane de 1673 jusqu'à 1766*. Paris: Nizet, 1966.
Caughey, John Walton. *Bernardo de Gálvez in Louisiana, 1776–1783*. Berkeley: U of California P, 1934.
Chaix d'Est-Ange, Gustave. *Dictionnaire des familles françaises anciennes ou notables à la fin du XIXe siècle*. 20 vols. Évreux: C. Hérissey, 1903–29.
Chandler, R. E. "Ulloa's Account of the 1768 Revolt." *Louisiana History: The Journal of the Louisiana Historical Association* 27:4 (Autumn 1986), 407–37.
Chartier, Roger. *Lectures et lecteurs dans la France d'Ancien Régime*. Paris: Seuil, 1987.
Chaussinand-Nogaret, Guy. *Le cardinal Dubois, 1656–1723*. Paris: Perrin, 2000.
Clark, Emily. *Masterless Mistresses: The New Orleans Ursulines and the Development of a New World Society, 1727–1834*. Chapel Hill: U of North Carolina P, for the Omohundro Institute of Early American History and Culture, Williamsburg, VA, 2007.
Coronado, Raúl. *A World Not to Come: A History of Latino Writing and Print Culture*. Cambridge, MA: Harvard UP, 2013.
Cosandey, Fanny, and Robert Descimon. *L'absolutisme en France: Histoire et historiographie*. Paris: Seuil, 2002.
Crest, Aurélie du. *Modèle familial et pouvoir monarchique (XVIe–XVIIIe siècles)*. Aix-en-Provence: Presses Universitaires d'Aix-Marseille, 2002.
Darnton, Robert. *Poetry and the Police*. Cambridge, MA: Belknap Press of Harvard UP, 2012.
Dart, Henry P. "The Adventures of Denis Braud, the First Printer of Louisiana, 1674–1773." *Louisiana Historical Quarterly* 14:3 (July 1931), 349–65.
Davis, Natalie Zemon. "The Reasons of Misrule: Youth Groups and Charivaris in Sixteenth-Century France." *Past & Present* 50 (Feb. 1971), 41–75.
Dawdy, Shannon Lee. *Building the Devil's Empire: French Colonial New Orleans*. Chicago: U of Chicago P, 2008.
———. "Enlightenment from the Ground: Le Page Du Pratz's *Histoire de la Louisiane*." *French Colonial History* 3 (2003), 17–34.
DeJean, Joan. *The Queen's Embroiderer: A True Story of Paris, Lovers, Swindlers, and the First Stock Market Crisis*. New York: Bloomsbury, 2018.

Delon, Michel. "L'appel au lecteur dans l'*Histoire des deux Indes*." In *L'Histoire des deux Indes en Europe et en Amérique au XVIIIe siècle,* edited by Hans-Jürgen Lüsebrink and Manfred Tietz, 53–58. Studies on Voltaire and the Eighteenth Century, 286. Oxford: Voltaire Foundation, 1991.

Delporte, Christian. *Une histoire de la séduction politique.* Paris: Flammarion, 2011.

Denis, Delphine. *Le Parnasse galant: Institution d'une catégorie littéraire au XVIIe siècle.* Paris: Champion, 2001.

Duchet, Michèle. *Anthropologie et histoire au siècle des Lumières.* Paris: Albin Michel, 1971.

Duranton, Henri. "Les Philippiques." In Reynaud and Thomas, *Le régent entre fable et histoire,* 88–108.

DuVal, Kathleen. *Independence Lost: Lives on the Edge of the American Revolution.* New York: Random House, 2015.

Echevarria, Durand. "General Collot's Plan for a Reconnaissance of the Ohio and Mississippi Valleys, 1796." *William and Mary Quarterly* 9:4 (Oct. 1952), 512–20.

Edelstein, Dan. *The Terror of Natural Right.* Chicago: U of Chicago P, 2009.

Edelstein, Dan, Robert Morrissey, and Glenn Roe. "To Quote or not to Quote: Citation Strategies in the *Encyclopédie*." *Journal of the History of Ideas* 74:2 (2013), 213–36.

Esmein-Sarrazin, C. "'Parler roman': Imaginaire de la langue et traits de style romanesques au XVIIe siècle." *Revue d'histoire littéraire de la France* 109:1 (2009), 85–99. doi:10.3917/rhlf.091.0085.

Falaky, Fayçal. *Social Contract, Masochist Contract: Aesthetics of Freedom and Submission in Rousseau.* Albany: SUNY P, 2014.

Farge, Arlette. *Subversive Words: Public Opinion in Eighteenth-Century France.* Translated by Rosemary Morris. University Park: Pennsylvania State UP, 1995. Originally published as *Dire et mal dire: L'opinion publique au XVIIIe siècle* (Paris: Seuil, 1992).

Farge, Arlette, and Jacques Revel. *The Vanishing Children of Paris: Rumor and Politics before the French Revolution.* Translated by Claudia Miéville. Cambridge, MA: Harvard UP, 1991. Originally published as *Logiques de la foule: L'affaire des enlèvements d'enfants, Paris 1750* (Paris: Hachette, 1988).

Faure, Edgar. *La banqueroute de Law, 17 juillet 1720.* Paris: Gallimard, 1977.

Ferret, Olivier. "Philippe d'Orléans dans les pièces manuscrites du temps de la Régence." In Reynaud and Thomas, *Le régent entre fable et histoire,* 63–87.

Festa, Lynn. *Sentimental Figures of Empire in Eighteenth-Century Britain and France.* Baltimore: Johns Hopkins UP, 2006.

Forrest, Alan. *The Death of the French Atlantic: Trade, War, and Slavery in the Age of Revolution.* Oxford: Oxford UP, 2020.

Fortier, Alcée. *A History of Louisiana.* 4 vols. New York: Goupil & Co. of Paris, Manzi, Joyant & Co., successors, 1904.

Foucault, Michel. "The Discourse of Language." In *The Archaeology of Knowledge and the Discourse of Language,* translated by A. M. Sheridan Smith, 215–39. New York: Pantheon Books, 1972. Originally published as *L'ordre du discours* (Paris: Gallimard, 1971).
———. "What Is an Author?" In *Language, Counter-Memory, Practice: Selected Essays and Interviews,* translated and edited by Donald F. Bouchard, 113–38. Ithaca, NY: Cornell UP, 1997. Originally published as "Qu'est-ce qu'un auteur?," in *Dits et écrits,* 4 vols. (Paris: Gallimard, 1994), 1:789–821.
Gayarré, Charles. *History of Louisiana.* 4 vols. New Orleans: Armand Hawkins, 1885.
Geggus, David. "The Caribbean in the Age of Revolution." In Armitage and Subrahmanyam, *Age of Revolutions in Global Context,* 83–100.
Giraud, Marcel. *Histoire de la Louisiane française.* 4 vols. Paris: PUF, 1953–74.
Goetzmann, William N., Catherine Labio, K. Geert Rouwenhorst, and Timothy G. Young, eds. *The Great Mirror of Folly: Finance, Culture, the Crash of 1720.* New Haven, CT: Yale UP, 2013.
Goodman, Dena. *The Republic of Letters: A Cultural History of the French Enlightenment.* Ithaca, NY: Cornell UP, 1994.
Guillorel, Éva. "Complaintes de tradition orale en Bretagne sous l'Ancien Régime: Apports d'une démarche pluridisciplinaire." *Cahiers d'ethnomusicologie* 22 (2009), 35–48.
Habermas, Jürgen. *The Structural Transformation of the Public Sphere: An Inquiry into a Category of Bourgeois Society.* Translated by Thomas Burger. Cambridge, MA: MIT Press, 1991.
Habib, Claude. *Galanterie française.* Paris: Gallimard, 2006.
Hanger, Kimberly. "Conflicting Loyalties: The French Revolution and Free People of Color in Spanish New Orleans." *Louisiana History* 34 (Winter 1993), 5–33.
Harrol, Corinne. "The Passion of 'Oroonoko': Passive Obedience, the Royal Slave, and Aphra Behn's Baroque Realism." *ELH* 79:2 (2012), 447–75.
Hazard, Paul. *La crise de la conscience européenne, 1680–1715.* 1935. Reprint, Paris: Livre de Poche, 1994.
Holmes, Jack D. L. "The *Moniteur de la Louisiane* in 1798." *Louisiana History* 2:2 (Spring 1961), 230–53.
Hunt, Lynn. *The Family Romance of the French Revolution.* Berkeley: U of California P, 1992.
———. "The French Revolution in Global Context." In Armitage and Subrahmanyam, *Age of Revolutions in Global Context,* 20–36.
Hutchinson, Ross. *Locke in France, 1688–1734.* Oxford: Voltaire Foundation, 1991.
James, C. L. R. *Black Jacobins: Toussaint Louverture and the San Domingo Revolution.* Rev. ed. New York: Vintage Books, 1963.
Jameson, Fredric. *The Political Unconscious: Narrative as a Socially Symbolic Act.* Ithaca, NY: Cornell UP, 1981.

Johnson, Sara E. *The Fear of French Negroes: Transcolonial Collaboration in the Revolutionary Americas.* Berkeley: U of California P, 2012.

Kaiser, Thomas E. "Money, Despotism, and Public Opinion in Early Eighteenth-Century France: John Law and the Debate on Royal Credit." *Journal of Modern History* 63:1 (Mar. 1991).

Kapferer, Jean-Noël. *Rumors: Uses, Interpretations, and Images.* Translated by Bruce Fink. New Brunswick, NJ: Transaction, 1990. Originally published as *Rumeurs: Le plus vieux média du monde* (Paris: Seuil, 1987).

Kaplan, Steven L. *The Bakers of Paris and the Bread Question, 1700–1775.* Durham, NC: Duke UP, 1996.

Kaul, Suvir. *Poems of Nation, Anthems of Empire.* Charlottesville: UP of Virginia, 2000.

Kenny, Neil. *The Uses of Curiosity in Early Modern France and Germany.* Oxford: Oxford UP, 2004.

Klooster, Wim. *Revolutions in the Atlantic World: A Comparative History.* New York: New York UP, 2009.

Labio, Catherine. "Staging Folly in the Dutch Republic, France, and England." In Goetzmann et al., *Great Mirror of Folly*, 142–57.

Lamb, Jonathan. *Preserving the Self in the South Seas, 1680–1840.* Chicago: U of Chicago P, 2001.

Leemans, Inger. "Verse Weavers and Paper Traders: Financial Speculation in Dutch Theater." In Goetzmann et al., *Great Mirror of Folly*, 175–90.

Letts, Janet T. "Responsive Readers of the *Mercure Galant*, 1680–1710." *Cahiers du Dix-septieme: An Interdisciplinary Journal* 5:2 (Fall 1991), 211–28.

Leumas, Emilie. "Ties That Bind: The Family, Social, and Business Associations of the Insurrectionists of 1768." *Louisiana History: The Journal of the Louisiana Historical Association* 47:2 (Spring 2006), 183–202.

Liebersohn, Harry. *Aristocratic Encounters: European Travelers and North American Indians.* Cambridge: Cambridge UP, 1998.

Liljegren, Ernest. "Jacobinism in Spanish Louisiana." *Louisiana Historical Quarterly* 22:1 (June 1939), 47–97.

Mapp, Paul. *The Elusive West and the Contest for Empire (1713–1763).* Chapel Hill: U of North Carolina P for the Omohundro Institute of Early American History and Culture, Williamsburg, VA, 2013.

Maza, Sarah C. "Le tribunal de la nation: Les mémoires judiciaires et l'opinion publique à la fin de l'Ancien Régime." *Annales. Économies, sociétés, civilisations* 42:1 (1987), 73–90.

Maziane, Leila. "Les captifs européens en terre marocaine aux XVIIe et XVIIIe siècles." *Cahiers de la Méditerranée* 65 (2002). http://cdlm.revues.org/45.

McMurtrie, Douglas C. *The Pioneer Printer of New Orleans.* Chicago: Eyncourt Press, 1930.

Mehta, Jayur Madhusudan. "Spanish Conquistadores, French Explorers, and Natchez Great Suns in Southwestern Mississippi, 1542–1729." *Native South* 6 (2013), 33–69.
Miller, Christopher L. *The French Atlantic Triangle: Literature and Culture of the Slave Trade.* Durham, NC: Duke UP, 2008.
Mills, Gary B. "The Chauvin Brothers: Early Colonists of Louisiana," *Louisiana History: The Journal of the Louisiana Historical Association* 15:2 (Spring 1974), 117–31.
Moore, Frank Frankfort. *The Life of Oliver Goldsmith.* New York: E. P. Dutton, 1911.
Moore, John P. *Revolt in Louisiana.* Baton Rouge: Louisiana State UP, 1976.
Morin, Edgar. *La rumeur d'Orléans.* Paris: Seuil, 1969.
Murphy, Antoin. *John Law: Economic Theorist and Policymaker.* Oxford: Oxford UP, 1997.
Narrett, David. *Adventurism and Empire: The Struggle for Mastery in the Louisiana-Florida Borderlands, 1762–1803.* Chapel Hill: U of North Carolina P, 2015.
Orain, Arnaud. *La politique du merveilleux: Une autre histoire du Système de Law.* Paris: Fayard, 2018.
———. "Le *Journal œconomique,* le cercle de Gournay et le pouvoir monarchique: Quelques preuves matérielles d'un lien organique." *Dix-huitième siècle* 45 (Jan. 2013), 565–83.
Ozouf, Mona. "Le concept d'opinion publique au XVIIIe siècle." *Sociologie de la communication* 1:1 (1997), 349–65. https://www.persee.fr/doc/reso_0043_7302_1997_mon_1_1_3847.
Padrón, Ricardo. *The Indies of the Setting Sun: How Early Modern Spain Mapped the Far East as the Transpacific West.* Chicago: U of Chicago P, 2020.
Petitfils, Jean-Christian. *Le régent.* Paris: Fayard, 1986.
Poovey, Mary. *Genres of the Credit Economy.* Chicago: U of Chicago P, 2008.
Prior, James. *Life of Oliver Goldsmith, M.B.* 2 vols. London: John Murray, 1837.
Prungnaud, Joëlle. "La traduction du roman gothique anglais en France au tournant du XVIIIe siècle." *TTR: Traduction, terminologie, rédaction* 7:1 (1994), 11–46.
Quétel, Claude. *De par le Roy: Essai sur les lettres de cachet.* Toulouse: Privat, 1981.
Quintero Saravia, Gonzalo M. *Bernardo de Gálvez: Spanish Hero of the American Revolution.* Chapel Hill: U of North Carolina P, 2018.
Rabalais, Nathan. *Finding Cajun: Let the Search Begin.* Baton Rouge: Louisiana Public Broadcasting, 2019. 59 min.
Reddy, William M. *The Navigation of Feeling: A Framework for the History of Emotions.* Cambridge: Cambridge UP, 2001.
Rey, Jean-Michel. *Le temps du crédit.* Paris: Desclée de Brouwer, 2002.
Reynaud, Denis, et Chantal Thomas, eds. *Le régent entre fable et histoire.* Paris, CNRS, 2003.
Richter, Melvin. "The Concept of Despotism and l'abus des mots." *Contributions to the History of Concepts* 3:1 (2007), 5–22.

Riffaterre, Michael. "Prosopopeia." *Yale French Studies* 69 (1985), 107–23. https://www.jstor.org/stable/2929928.

Ritter, Luke. "The American Revolution on the Periphery of Empires: Don Bernardo de Gálvez & the Spanish-American Alliance, 1763–1783." *Journal of Early American History* 7 (2017), 177–201.

Roach, Joseph. *Cities of the Dead: Circum-Atlantic Performance*. New York: Columbia UP, 1996.

———. "Mardi Gras Indians and Others: Genealogies of American Performance." *Theatre Journal* 44:4 (Dec. 1992), 461–83.

Rodríguez Casado, Vicente, ed. *Primeros años de dominación española en la Luisiana*. Madrid: Instituto Gonzalo Fernández de Oviedo, 1942.

Sayre, Gordon. "How to Succeed in Exploration without Really Discovering Anything: Four French Travelers in Colonial Louisiana, 1714–63." *Atlantic Studies* 10:1 (2013), 51–68.

———. *Les Sauvages Américains: Representations of Native Americans in French and English Colonial Literature*. Chapel Hill: U of North Carolina P, 1997.

———. "A Newly Discovered Manuscript Map by Antoine-Simon Le Page du Pratz." *French Colonial History* 11 (2010), 23–45.

Sgard, Jean. *Dictionnaire des journaux, 1600–1789*. http://dictionnaire-journaux.gazettes18e.fr/journal/0919-le-mercure-galant/.

———. *Vie de Prévost (1697–1763)*. Quebec: Presses de l'Université de Laval, 2006.

Sollors, Werner. *Neither Black Nor White Yet Both: Thematic Explorations of Interracial Literature*. New York: Oxford UP, 1997.

Spang, Rebecca. "The Ghost of Law: Speculating on Money, Memory and Mississippi in the French Constituent Assembly." *Historical Reflections* 31:1 (2005), 3–25.

Tinker, Edward Larocque. *Louisiana's Earliest Poet: Julien Poydras and the Paeans to Galvez*. New York: New York Public Library, 1933.

Tregle, Joseph, Jr. "Creoles and Americans." In *Creole New Orleans: Race and Americanization*, edited by Arnold R. Hirsch and Joseph Logsdon, 131–85. Baton Rouge: Louisiana State UP, 1992.

Tsien, Jennifer. *The Bad Taste of Others: Judging Literary Value in Eighteenth-Century France*. Philadelphia: U of Pennsylvania P, 2011.

———. "Louisiana as a Figment of the Imagination: Raynal's Reflections on the French American Colony." In *Raynal's "Histoire des deux Indes": Colonial History, Global Exchange and Social Networks in the Age of Enlightenment*, edited by Cecil Courtney and Jenny Mander, 247–57. Oxford University Studies in the Enlightenment. Oxford: Voltaire Foundation, 2015.

———. "Quoniam le rôtisseur et les prisonniers du Mississippi." In *Gagnons sans savoir comment: Représentations du Système de Law du XVIIIe à nos jours*, edited by Florence Magnot-Ogilvy, 207–20. Rennes: Presses Universitaires de Rennes, 2017.

Turner, Frederick J. "The Origin of Genêt's Projected Attack on Louisiana and the Floridas." *American Historical Review* 3:4 (July 1898), 650–71.
Usner, Daniel H., Jr. *American Indians in the Lower Mississippi Valley: Social and Economic Histories.* Lincoln: U of Nebraska P, 1998.
Viala, Alain. *La France galante: Essai historique sur une catégorie culturelle, de ses origines jusqu'à la Révolution.* Paris: Presses Universitaires de France, 2008.
Vidal, Cécile. *Caribbean New Orleans: Empire, Race, and the Making of a Slave Society.* Chapel Hill: U of North Carolina P, for the Omohundro Institute of Early American History and Culture, Williamsburg, VA, 2019.
———. "Francité et situation coloniale: Nation, empire et race en Louisiane française (1699–1769)." *Annales* 5 (2009), 1019–50.
Villiers du Terrage, Marc. *Les dernières années de la Louisiane française.* Paris: Guilmoto, 1904.
Vincent-Buffault, Anne. *Histoire des larmes, XVIIIe–XIXe siècles.* Paris: Rivages, 1986. Translated by Teresa Bridgeman as *The History of Tears: Sensibility and Sentimentality in France* (London: Palgrave Macmillan, 1991).
Wahnich, Sophie. *Les émotions, la Révolution française et le présent: Exercices pratiques de conscience historique.* Paris: CNRS, 2009.
Weber, David J. *Bárbaros: Spaniards and Their Savages in the Age of Enlightenment.* New Haven, CT: Yale UP, 2005.
Whitaker, Arthur P. "Antonio de Ulloa." *Hispanic American Historical Review* 15:2 (May 1935), 155–94.
White, Sophie. *Wild Frenchmen and Frenchified Indians: Material Culture and Race in Colonial Louisiana.* Philadelphia: U of Pennsylvania P, 2012.
White, Sophie, and Trevor Burnard, eds. *Hearing Enslaved Voices: African and Indian Slave Testimony in British and French America, 1700–1848.* New York: Routledge, 2020.

Index

absolutism, 8–9, 18, 45, 49, 51, 66, 79, 83–84, 94–99, 110–19, 123, 179n134, 192n33. *See also* monarchy
Acadians, 1, 2, 5, 16, 18, 88, 101–2, 105–7, 167nn1–2, 190n5
Acosta, Joseph Melchior de, 101–2, 109
Adet, Pierre-Auguste, 148–49
American Revolution, 6–7, 86, 109, 126, 134, 135–38, 148
Anderson, Benedict, 108
animal metaphors, 105, 111, 118, 133, 139
animals of North America, 29, 34, 67; alligators, 34; beavers, 37; cats, 69–70, 78; fish, 37, 59, 67–69; oysters, 69–70, 78; snakes, 34, 70
arcana imperii. See secrecy
Asia: European travelers to, 64; route to, 4, 33, 57–58, 172n50. *See also* Choisy, abbé de; despotism: "Oriental"; Western Sea
astronomy, 22, 69–72. *See also* heliocentrism
Aubry, Charles-Philippe, 88, 93, 101, 122

Barbé-Marbois, marquis de (François), 16, 60, 142, 159
Bastille prison, 7, 11, 45–46, 62, 142–43
Baudry de Lozières, Louis-Narcisse, 89, 131–34
Berquin-Duvallon, Pierre-Louis, 131–33, 159–61
biblical references, 54; Joshua, 72–73; the Promised Land, 26–27, 30; "a voice cries out in the desert" (Book of Isaiah), 115–16, 141, 149–50
Bienville, Jean-Baptiste Le Moyne de, 4, 34, 92
billets d'état. See paper money
Black residents, 18, 85, 91, 103, 104–8, 144–45, 149, 153, 154–55, 163, 168n17, 168n20, 211n61; scholarship about, 2, 10, 14–16, 169n28. *See also* free people of color; Haiti; slavery
Bodin, Jean, 94
Bonrepos, chevalier de, 35–40, 41
Bossu, Jean-Bernard, 129–33, 147

Bossuet, Jacques-Bénigne, 31, 94
Boswell, James, 108
Bourbon dynasty. *See under individual kings*
Braud, Denis. *See* printing press

Cajuns. *See* Acadians
Canada, 4, 5, 58–60, 61, 86–87, 101–2, 105, 113, 163, 168n18. *See also* Acadians; Lahontan, baron de; Native Americans: Iroquois
Caresse, Pierre, 102, 134, 191n28
Caribbean islands, 2, 86–87, 117, 148, 169n29. *See also* Haiti; Spanish colonies: Cuba
Carlos III (king of Spain), 9, 89, 95, 136
Carlos IV (king of Spain), 9, 136
Carnival, 75–76, 164, 178n120. *See also* Mardi Gras
Carondelet, baron de (Francisco Luis Héctor), 19, 143–45, 149, 151–56
Catholicism, 5, 9, 12, 30, 31, 34, 64, 73–77, 79, 85, 95, 105, 124, 156, 158; clergy, 5, 7, 11, 85, 114–15; Jesuits, 30, 58–60, 64, 76, 80–83; Ursulines, 13–14, 26, 176n101, 191n15; vestments, desecration of, 74–76. *See also* monarchy: divine right of kings
censorship in France, 9, 12, 18, 28, 36, 40, 43, 54, 57–65, 71, 73–74, 85, 127–28, 138, 155, 175n91, 198n1. See also *privilège*
Champigny, chevalier de (Jean Bochart), 89, 110, 119–29, 130, 133, 135, 139, 144
Charlevoix, Pierre-François-Xavier, 10–11, 12, 13, 17, 58–60, 65, 66, 79, 85
Chateaubriand, vicomte de (François-René), 54–55, 63, 121, 171n32
Chauvin brothers, 91–92, 123
Chickasaws. *See under* Native Americans
child metaphors, 94, 96–97, 116–19, 139, 147, 149–50, 158, 163, 193nn51–52, 208n17
China. *See* Asia
Chitimachas. *See under* Native Americans
Chocktaws. *See under* Native Americans
Choiseul, duc de (Étienne-François), 10, 14, 89, 104, 112, 115–16, 132, 133, 146, 150–51

231

232   Index

Choisy, abbé de (François-Timoléon), 40–41, 59, 176n92
Clark, George Rogers, 138
Collot, Victor, 148–51
comic style, 45, 48–49, 50, 64, 67–68, 74–76, 78, 151–53, 156, 164–65, 178n120
commerce, 10, 18, 22, 33, 36, 58, 65–67, 89–90, 99–100, 102–3, 106–7, 145, 147–49, 158–60, 169n27. *See also* mercantilism; physiocracy
Compagnie d'Occident. *See* Mississippi Company
Convention. *See under* French Revolution
corn, 102–3, 196n90
Creeks. *See under* Native Americans
Creoles, 1, 2, 16, 87–88, 91–93, 105–8, 110, 131, 137, 159–60, 167n1, 167n4, 168n20, 193n52
Cuba. *See under* Spanish colonies
curiosity, 10, 21, 31–33, 63, 124

D'Abbadie, Jean-Jacques, 95
Dawdy, Shannon Lee, 16, 21–22, 41, 64
deism, 74, 124
de La Salle, René-Robert Cavelier, 4, 38–39
Denmark, 58, 120
despotism, 9, 19, 48, 56, 79–85, 87, 105, 115, 139; distinction from tyranny, 209n30; "enlightened," 136, 138–43, 146, 148, 150; "Oriental," 80–82, 146, 150
Diderot, Denis, 13, 71, 110, 113, 115, 116, 118, 147
Directoire. *See under* French Revolution
disinformation, 101, 195n76
droit des gens, 114, 118, 129, 150
Dubois, cardinal (Guillaume), 47, 178n119
Dubos, Jean-Baptiste, 104
Dumont de Montigny, Jean-François-Benjamin, 60–61, 181n16

Encyclopédie, 13, 71, 80, 81–82, 115, 141, 186n78
England. *See* Great Britain
Enlightenment, 7–8, 13, 17–18, 57, 58, 60, 63–85, 86, 109, 110–11, 115, 121, 124–26, 129, 137–38, 139, 141, 150, 157. *See also* deism; despotism: "enlightened"; Diderot, Denis; *Encyclopédie;* Locke, John; Montesquieu, baron de; Raynal, abbé; Rousseau, Jean-Jacques; Spanish Enlightenment; Voltaire

family metaphors, 103, 112, 116–17, 119, 126, 140, 144, 146–47, 158, 159–60, 179n132, 192n31, 194n63. *See also* child metaphors; fraternal metaphors; maternal metaphors; Pacte de Famille; paternal metaphors
Farge, Arlette, 11–13, 15, 55, 90, 155
faux-saulniers, 50, 117n113
fiction: distinction from fact, 26, 30, 32–33, 40–41, 47, 58, 62–64, 76, 90, 112, 120–22. *See also* novels and novelistic tropes; women readers
fish. *See under* animals of North America
flags, 1, 88, 154
Florida, 98. *See also under* Spanish colonies
Foucault, Denis-Nicolas, 87, 101–3
Foucault, Michel, 12, 63
Franklin, Benjamin, 120–21
fraternal metaphors, 6, 140, 145, 147–48, 157, 163, 179n132
free people of color, 14, 19, 106, 143, 144–45, 154–55
French and Indian War. *See* Seven Years' War
French colonies. *See* Canada; Caribbean islands; Nouvelle France
French Revolution, 6–8, 13, 19, 28, 52, 86, 98, 109, 124, 130, 132, 134, 136, 138, 142–48, 151–58, 160, 165; Bastille Day commemoration, 142–43; Convention, 138–39, 143–44, 145–51; Directoire, 148–49, 157; historiography of, 6–7, 92; oratory, 111–14, 138–39; Terror, 7–8, 198n5. *See also* songs

galanterie, 13, 21–23, 28–31, 34–35, 36–42, 46, 47, 52–54, 123; definition of, 22
Gálvez, Bernardo de, 5–6, 137–38
Gayarré, Charles, 16, 89
Genêt, Edmond-Charles, 19, 138–45, 149, 207nn8–9
German settlers, 18, 27, 88, 101–3, 105, 168n18
gold and silver, 4, 10, 23–27, 32–33, 37, 41–44, 50, 53, 57, 59–60, 66, 85, 197n111
Goldsmith, Oliver, 120, 123
gothic literature, 144, 210n44
Great Britain, 22, 26, 51, 54, 58, 86, 91, 93, 96, 98, 105, 109, 110, 120–21, 137–38, 142, 151, 190n5, 197n104, 210n44, 210n51
Guadeloupe. *See* Caribbean islands
Gulf of Mexico, 3–4, 41, 58, 61, 113–14, 144

habeas corpus, 51
Habermas, Jürgen, 11, 168n22
Hachard, Marie-Madeleine, 13–14, 26, 176n101
Haiti, 60, 69, 86, 109, 134, 157, 159; immigration to Louisiana, 6, 131, 142, 198n118; Revolution, 6, 7, 13, 19, 86, 136, 142–45
heliocentrism, 63–74, 185n70
Hurons. *See under* Native Americans

Iberville, Pierre Le Moyne de, 92, 114
Île Dauphine, 61
Illinois tribe. *See under* Native Americans
Incas. *See under* Native Americans
Indigenous people. *See* Native Americans
Iroquois. *See under* Native Americans

James, C. L. R., 7
Japan. *See* Asia
Jaucourt, chevalier de (Louis). See *Encyclopédie*
Jefferson, Thomas, 6, 168n19
Jesuits. *See* Catholicism: Jesuits; Charlevoix, Pierre-François-Xavier; Marquette, Jacques, and Louis Jolliet

Katrina, Hurricane, 156, 163–64
Kentucky territory, 141

La Frénière, Nicolas Chauvin de, 5, 18, 87, 89, 91–109, 111, 118, 122–23, 127, 130–34, 136, 140, 191n28
La Hontan. *See* Lahontan, baron de
Lahontan, baron de, 18, 58, 63–64, 76, 79, 85
Lamothe-Cadillac, Antoine Laumet de, 61–62, 92
La Rochelle, 145–48, 210n51
Latin America. *See* Spanish colonies
Laussat, Pierre Clément de, 89, 157–61
Law, John, 4–5, 7–8, 17, 21, 23–28, 36, 40–42, 44–45, 47, 50, 54–56, 60–61, 114. *See also* Mississippi Bubble; Royal Bank
legal argumentation, 13, 91, 94, 112, 149–50
legal documents, 14, 16, 111–12, 154–55
Le Maire, François, 57–58
Le Page du Pratz, Antoine-Simon, 12, 14, 17–18, 57, 63–85, 90, 107, 167n9, 172n46
Lesage, Alain-René, 50

lettres de cachet, 9, 12, 46–47, 51–52, 112, 179n132, 179n134
literacy, 13–14, 91–92, 108, 127–28, 169n26
Locke, John, 71, 97, 106, 115, 139, 193nn50–51, 208n17
Louis XIV (king of France), 4, 9, 11, 23, 52, 54, 66, 82, 83, 85, 131–32, 141, 168n23, 180n6
Louis XV (king of France), 4–5, 9, 23, 66, 88–89, 93–100, 110, 127, 132, 141, 146, 151
Louis XVI (king of France), 133–34, 141
Louisiana Purchase, 3, 6, 17–19, 134–35, 142, 151, 161

magistrates, 93–94, 96–97
Manon Lescaut (Prévost), 13, 17, 45, 52–55, 110
Mardi Gras, 41, 156, 159, 164
Marquette, Jacques, and Louis Jolliet, 4
Marquis, Pierre, 105, 127, 130, 132–34, 147
maternal metaphors, 116, 147, 149–50, 157–58
mercantilism, 98–99
Mer de l'Ouest. *See* Western Sea
Mexico. *See under* Spanish colonies
Miamis. *See under* Native Americans
Milhet, Jean, 87, 131, 134
Ministère de la Marine, 57, 61, 145, 146, 149, 177n113, 181n9
Miró, Esteban, 143
Mississippi, 3, 4, 5, 8–9, 17, 27, 29, 33, 36, 38, 43, 44, 46, 48–51, 58, 60, 62, 64, 65–66, 80, 85, 86, 113–14, 146–47; access to river, 140–41, 148; name, 167nn8–9
Mississippi Bubble, 1, 4–5, 17, 22–28, 40–42, 55–56, 79, 170n10, 179n128
Mississippi Company, 4, 7–8, 9, 17, 23–24, 27–29, 36, 39, 42–43, 50, 61–62, 79, 177n113
Missouris. *See under* Native Americans
monarchy, 3, 6–12, 18–19, 22, 39, 44, 45, 49, 51–52, 55–56, 58, 66, 79–85, 86, 94–100, 110–19; divine right of kings, 8, 82, 114–15, 123, 126, 132, 134–35, 136, 138, 140–41, 145–46, 150, 155–57. *See also under individual kings;* absolutism; despotism; *lettres de cachet;* Orléans, duc d', Philippe; paternal metaphors; social contract; tyranny
Moniteur de la Louisiane, Le, 142

Montesquieu, baron de (Charles-Louis de Secondat), 10, 13, 18, 80–82, 91, 125–26, 141, 146, 193n50, 203n73
Morocco, 106

Nagin, Ray, 156, 163
Napoleon, 2, 3, 6, 17, 23, 55, 89, 121, 130–32, 134, 145, 157–61, 181n14
Natchez. *See under* Native Americans
Native Americans: Chickasaws, 4, 15, 38, 42; Chitimachas, 173n55; Choctaws, 76; Creeks, 151; Hurons, 41, 63–64, 76, 79; Illinois, 18, 41, 81; Incas, 106, 107; Iroquois, 4, 39, 41, 61; Miamis, 38; Missouris, 74–76; Natchez, 5, 14, 17–18, 37, 63, 72–84, 107, 141–42, 181n18; Ojibwes, 167n9; Osages, 151; Tunicas, 4
natural law, 3, 91, 106, 111, 118, 198n5
New Orleans, 6, 11, 13–17, 26, 39, 41–42, 63, 86–87, 92, 104, 137, 142–43, 156, 157–61, 163–65; construction of, 4, 9; in fiction, 53, 123–26. *See also* Revolt of 1768
Nouveau Mercure, Le, 17, 21–22, 27–35, 40, 62, 107
Nouvelle France, 4, 10, 13, 58–60, 79, 119
novels and novelistic tropes, 13, 17, 18, 23, 26, 27, 29–30, 35, 37, 40–41, 47, 52–55, 68, 110, 113, 120–23, 133, 137, 140, 143–44, 147, 159, 168n17, 192n31, 206n105, 210n44. *See also* Chateaubriand, vicomte de; Diderot, Denis; *Manon Lescaut;* Montesquieu, baron de; *1001 Nights;* Rousseau, Jean-Jacques; Scudéry, Madeleine de; Voltaire
Noyan, Jean-Baptiste de, 104, 134

Ojibwes. *See under* Native Americans
1001 Nights, 32–33, 172n47
oral communication, 6–7, 12, 15, 31, 33, 44, 62, 101, 127, 131, 143, 151, 167nn1–2, 169n28; *bruits*, 55, 143, 177n109, 181n8; crying out, 93–94, 100, 102–3, 112, 115–17, 119, 125, 127, 147, 149–50; groans, 142–43, 148; murmurs, 100, 127; oratory, 13, 31, 78, 83, 90, 93, 110–12, 114–18, 123, 127–35, 139, 143, 145–47, 156–61; rumors, 5, 8, 11–13, 17, 33, 39, 44–52, 55, 59, 69, 127–28, 133–34, 143, 151, 154–55, 156, 159, 163, 177n106; voices, 12, 14–15, 100–101, 117–18, 122, 127, 148, 149–50, 160, 163. *See also* biblical references: "a voice cries out in the desert" (Book of Isaiah); Farge, Arlette; songs
O'Reilly, Alejandro, 89, 92, 93, 100–101, 108, 123, 127–29, 133–34, 136–37, 147, 158, 160
"Oriental" despotism. *See under* despotism
Orléans, duc d', Philippe (Regent of France), 4–5, 9, 11–12, 17, 21–25, 28, 36, 39–40, 45–52, 53–56, 62, 85, 98, 109, 141, 168n23, 170n8, 170n10
Osages. *See under* Native Americans

Pacte de Famille, 89, 95, 200n24
paper money, 4–5, 24–27, 42–44, 59–60, 102
parlements, 11, 51, 97, 109, 168n23, 194n56
paternal metaphors, 4, 9, 18, 51–52, 94–99, 102–3, 116, 140, 145–47, 150, 160, 167n9, 179n132, 192n31, 192n33, 193nn50–52, 215n98
patriotism, 65, 72, 75, 79, 89–91, 106–7, 125–26, 135, 143, 152–54, 159–60, 194n56
periodicals, 17, 28, 46, 60, 88, 98. *See also Moniteur de la Louisiana, Le; Nouveau Mercure, Le*
Peru. *See under* Spanish colonies
peuple, 11–12, 71, 90, 94
physiocracy, 64–65, 66, 183n37
Pointe Coupée, 145, 151, 153
Pompadour, marquise de (Jeanne-Antoinette Poisson), 10, 14, 146
Pontchartrain, comte de. *See* Ministère de la Marine
Poydras, Julien, 137
précieux style, 34, 173n57
Prévost, Antoine François. *See Manon Lescaut*
printing press, 18, 88, 92–93, 108
privilège (permission to publish), 28, 64–65, 175n91
prosopopeia, 117, 149
prostitutes, 5, 42, 50–51, 54
Protestants, 72, 83, 85, 113, 145
provincial revolts, 96, 118; Brittany, 109; Corsica, 108
public opinion, 11–12, 21–23, 44, 111, 168n22

Quintilian, 117
Quoniam case, 45–52, 54, 55–56, 118

race, 14, 154, 167n1. *See also* Black residents; Native Americans; White residents

Raynal, abbé (Guillaume-Thomas), 8, 63, 64–66, 72, 83–85, 109, 110, 113–19, 121, 129, 135, 139, 149–50, 163
Regent of France. *See* Orléans, duc d', Philippe
Revolt of 1768, 5, 8, 10, 18, 86–109, 110–13, 119, 123–35, 136, 139–40, 144–47, 165
Roach, Joseph, 15, 164
Rousseau, Jean-Jacques, 8–9, 64, 91, 96, 108, 110–11, 115, 123, 125, 193n48
Royal Bank, 24, 27
rumors. *See under* oral communication

Saint-Domingue. *See* Haiti
Saint-Simon, duc de (Louis de Rouvroy), 50
Sayre, Gordon, 16–17, 33
science. *See* animals of North America; astronomy; heliocentrism
Scudéry, Madeleine de, 23, 36, 47
secrecy, 6, 41, 46, 52, 60, 87, 95, 98, 114, 116, 151. See also *lettres de cachet*
sensibilité, 13, 19, 37, 94, 107, 110–12, 113, 116, 118, 122, 127–35, 140, 142, 144–45, 148–50, 156–57, 159–60, 163
Seven Years' War, 2, 5, 10, 18, 86, 95, 108
Siam. *See* Asia
silk production, 33, 38, 61, 172n49
slavery, 6, 7, 10, 117–18, 132, 168n17, 206n105; enslaved Africans, 14, 85, 91, 104, 142, 154–55, 160, 169n28; enslaved Native Americans, 34; as a metaphor, 10, 18, 97, 105–7, 115–16, 139, 148–49, 197n104; slave revolts, 13, 19, 144–45, 153; slave trade, 2, 145, 210n51
social contract, 9, 51, 91, 115, 125
songs, 11, 12, 13, 15, 17, 19, 40, 42–52, 63, 86, 109, 118, 151–57, 197n104; *Ça ira*, 142, 143, 156; *La Carmagnole*, 152–53; *La Marseillaise*, 143, 156
South America. *See* Spanish colonies
South Sea Bubble, 26
Spanish colonies, 2, 3, 155, 160; Cuba, 2, 88, 104, 130, 143; Florida, 2, 113; Guatemala, 99; Mexico, 59, 98, 105, 137; Peru, 37, 59, 87, 105, 190n3; Texas, 4, 137; Venezuela, 7

Spanish Enlightenment, 136, 137. *See also* Gálvez, Bernardo de; Ulloa, Antonio de: as scientist
sublime style, 122, 133, 146
Superior Council of New Orleans, 62, 87–88, 90, 92–94, 97–105, 131
Swiss residents, 18, 105, 127, 147, 168n8, 183n34

Terror, the. *See under* French Revolution
theater, 28, 75, 143, 198n1; *comédie larmoyante*, 116, 147; comedy, 22, 35, 50; melodrama, 112, 118, 128, 130, 151, 159; tragedy, 53–55, 94, 110, 118–19, 122–23, 127–35, 146–47, 151, 161, 180n40, 206n105
tragedy. *See under* theater
Treaty of Aranjuez (1801), 6
Treaty of Fontainebleau (1762). *See* Seven Years' War
Treaty of Paris (1763). *See* Seven Years' War
Treaty of San Ildefonso (1800), 6, 157
Tunicas. *See under* Native Americans
tyranny, 10, 66, 85, 99, 102, 107, 126–27, 132–33, 141, 146, 150. *See also* despotism

Ulloa, Antonio de, 87–88, 99–106, 112, 122–25, 132, 137, 147; as scientist, 190n3
utopia, 123–26, 203n73

Vallette de Laudun, 36, 40–42, 53, 63, 113
Vergennes, comte de (Charles Gravier), 133–34
Villeré, Joseph de, 88, 101–2, 134
Voltaire, 8, 64, 74, 125, 172n47

Washington, George, 6, 135, 138, 142, 145
Western Sea, 4, 71–72, 167n7
wheat, 61, 103
White residents, 15, 18–19, 91, 103, 104, 105–8, 143, 144, 153–54
wine, 104
women readers, 13, 16–17, 21–23, 27–28, 29–42, 169n26, 172n47; duchesse des Lesdiguières, 59–60, 180n6

Writing the Early Americas

Forms of Relation: Composing Kinship in Colonial Spanish America
  Matthew Goldmark

Before American History: Nationalist Mythmaking and Indigenous Dispossession
  Christen Mucher

The Sun of Jesús del Monte: A Cuban Antislavery Novel
  Translated and edited by David Luis-Brown

Letters from Filadelfia: Early Latino Literature and the Trans-American Elite
  Rodrigo Lazo

Sifilografía: A History of the Writerly Pox in the Eighteenth-Century Hispanic World
  Juan Carlos González Espitia

Creole Drama: Theatre and Society in Antebellum New Orleans
  Juliane Braun

The Alchemy of Conquest: Science, Religion, and the Secrets of the New World
  Ralph Bauer

www.ingramcontent.com/pod-product-compliance
Lightning Source LLC
Chambersburg PA
CBHW030619230426
43661CB00053B/2070